D0746832

Technology, Education—Connections
The TEC Series

Series Editor: Marcia C. Linn
Advisory Board: Robert Bjork, Chris Dede,
Carol Lee, Jim Minstrell, Jonathan Osborne, Mitch Resnick

THE LEARNING EDGE

WHAT TECHNOLOGY CAN DO
TO EDUCATE ALL CHILDREN

Alan Bain
Mark E. Weston

foreword by
John Hattie

Teachers College
Columbia University
New York and London

Published by Teachers College Press, 1234 Amsterdam Avenue, New York, NY 10027

Library of Congress Cataloging-in-Publication Data

Bain, Alan, 1957–
   The learning edge : what technology can do to educate all children / Alan Bain, Mark E. Weston ; foreword by John Hattie.
      p. cm.
   Includes bibliographical references and index.
   ISBN 978-0-8077-5271-5 (pbk. : alk. paper) — ISBN 978-0-8077-5272-2 (hardcover : alk. paper)
      1. Educational technology. 2. Education—Effect of technological innovations on. I. Weston, Mark E. II. Title.
   LB1028.3.B357 2012
   371.33—dc23

2011037738

ISBN 978-0-8077-5271-5 (paperback)
ISBN 978-0-8077-5272-2 (hardcover)

Printed on acid-free paper
Manufactured in the United States of America

19 18 17 16 15 14 13 12   8 7 6 5 4 3 2 1

To our parents

Contents

Foreword

If Alexander Graham Bell returned, Rip van Winkle style, in the 1990s he would have immediately recognized his invention, the telephone. He would have remembered the ring, the use of the word he invented—*hello*—and would have been able to use phones. But if he returned today he would hardly recognize his invention: Mobile phones, computers, and cameras have been combined; they are handheld; and the integration means they are ubiquitous—in and out of schools. Most students have a mobile phone, play video games, and on average spend as much time—if not more—playing games and playing on the Internet as they spend in the classroom. Teachers are also among high users of computers in their work and daily life. The authors ask why, then, are technologies not prevalent in the ways we teach and learn (other than using word processors, making PowerPoint, and searching for resources for worksheets)?

This book deals with this conundrum and not only provides some excellent answers to the question, but, just as important, provides excellent case studies of technology in action in teaching and learning. Bain and Weston show that when teachers "perceive" technologies as part of their teaching and part of students' learning, there can be greater gains to both surface and deep understanding. They particularly argue that teachers need to be more disciplined in using research-based findings to integrate what is "everyday" for the students (when it comes to access to and use of technologies) into their daily teaching.

Among Bain and Weston's most important claims is that the typical "theory into action" models that teachers often have about technologies are misleading and these need to be attended to before technology will be used in classrooms as part of learning. In writing my book *Visible Learning* (Hattie, 2009), I came to realize that teacher mind frames are the most important enhancer and barrier to students' learning. How and what they think makes the difference—not the methods, conditions, resources, or test scores! Achievement is enhanced *if* teachers believe they are change agents, that all students can learn, and that they are the major agent for encouraging students to feel confident and take on challenges, providing safety nets for error, and communicating the hierarchies of knowledge. Bain and Weston begin by identifying faulty mind frames—such as the notions that access to technology will make the learning occur, that teaching changes magically when they introduce technologies, or that technology leads to achievement gains.

In contrast, they highlight the challenge involved in the way one teacher can maximize the learning and achievement of every student and how the use of technologies can help, particularly to maximize learning for *all* students in the class. The move from the current model to this new model where *all* students are progressing involves changes to differentiated curricula, moving to deeper as well as surface knowing, using collaborative methods among peers, and making feedback immediate, rich, and specific. There is much more richness in this text to work through these ideas.

Most important, the authors include many case studies at all levels—classroom, school, district, professional associations, policy, and the computer industry. Their messages of co-evolution, dispersed control, and scalability are well illustrated at each level, and the major message is not to do "more" but how to do things "differently." The stories are compelling reading, and they led to a "Why not do it here?" sense for me as the reader. Bain and Weston use practical methods that they have developed, been involved in, and researched over many years: the A to B Toolkit, Performance Arrays, and Co-development Tools. A major advantage of these methods is that they reduce the cognitive load for teachers (in contrast to most of the current uses of technologies, which increase this load), they allow teachers to see learning through the eyes of students, and they enable students to become their own teachers—creating a truly shared partnership in learning melded by the use of technologies.

Bain and Weston's bottom line is that students can access learning and teaching on a 1:1 basis, provided that teachers make a major change in their thinking about teaching, use edge-technologies, and become more collaborative. The way to reach this desired situation is by determining the optimal set of problems to be solved (which are often quite different from the usual demands for more of this or that) so that all stakeholders not only contribute but also gain in-time, worthwhile information for making immediate and high-power decisions about teaching and learning. Scaling up requires teachers and students to envelope these new ways of thinking about using technologies in learning, as this then avoids the blockages and major system changes to which schooling is most resistant.

Technology will not force its way into classrooms; for decades, teachers and schools have shown remarkable kickback (e.g., to radio, television, and movies). Computers are present in schools and it is rare for parents not to want to run cake stalls and so on to raise the money to provide even more. This book asks the hard question: How do we change the mind frames we have about technology in teaching and learning, how do we make less of more, shortening the cognitive distance between stakeholders, building their capacity for 1:X, and creating an edge?

This book is a worthy follow-up to the exciting work that Larry Cuban has been contributing. He has asked, "Why do teachers *not* use the available technologies?" One of the major answers is because the available technologies do not fit into the ways our teachers teach, and the ways they have been teaching for the past

200 years! This book is a true successor to Cuban's work. It goes much further and offers a way to start an understanding of teachers' current thinking to show ways to influence them to achieve a commonly claimed attribute—to effectively teach more students in a differentiated and successful manner.

I work in teacher education, and the absence of technologies is ever-present—except as a medium for instruction (e.g., distance courses, searching the Web, accessing libraries). Perhaps it is no wonder that new teachers barely change their ways of thinking about teaching and technologies. Teacher educators often aim to re-create classrooms as they best knew them, and once again, there is a resistance in the system to anything new or different. This resistance is not necessarily in the willingness or proficiency to see the power of the technologies; it is often resistance to seeing how to use the technologies within the currently understood ways of teaching. Bain and Weston offer a direction and a set of solutions. Not only do they show that there needs to be a difference in thinking about teaching and learning, but also they show the efficiencies, engagement, and edges that can be gained. They provide real-life examples of the effects of these differences that are not only engaging but exciting. Despite all this, I have a hunch that little will change in the next decade because the dominant mind frame of teaching is still teachers talking, teachers controlling the flow of lessons, and teachers continually asking for more time and resources with fewer students in front of them—unless the students revolt!

This book provides a way forward between these two extremes.

—John Hattie

Preface

To date, the field of education has been largely impervious to efforts that would try to change the way it serves the learning of all children. Reformers have struggled to develop models that exert sustainable and scalable change in the ways teachers teach and students learn. Surprisingly, largely unaddressed is an integrated approach to the systemic reform of districts, associations, policymaking, and corporations necessary to sustain and scale reforms within individual schools.

Unlike other fields, Information and Communications Technology (ICT)—an umbrella term for computing related devices (e.g., cell phones, personal computers, and servers), software applications (e.g., word processing and video editing), the Internet and World Wide Web, and the services associated with all—has played a largely insignificant role in addressing the challenge of change and progression of the field of education. In this book, we ask why—after 3 decades, investments of trillions of dollars, thousands of studies and reports, and immeasurable efforts by educators, policymakers, and manufacturers—are students and teachers so unaffected by ICT? At the same time, why is it impossible to think about transforming education without ICT? Moreover, what specifically can be done to change these circumstances?

In answering these questions, we contend that by failing to make disciplined, practical use of the research-based knowledge of the field, education has failed to capture the potential of ICT for bringing about sustainable, scalable, and systemic change. The casualties of this failure are the majority of students who do not fit comfortably or succeed within the current model of schooling. We contend that technology had nothing to do with the creation of this problem, yet has everything to do with finding a successful resolution. Articulating a resolution is the purpose of the book.

In the chapters that follow, we show what can be done with ICT to stimulate transformational change from the classroom to the corporation and all levels of the educational system in between. The case we make is one informed by our direct experience in school reform, policy development, and in the corporations that serve education. During the past 3 decades, we have led major site-based school and systemic ICT reforms, conducted extensive applied research on the topic, designed state and national ICT policy initiatives, consulted with leading educational associations, and provided strategic guidance to global technology companies. Of particular significance is an 18-year project that was the first comprehensive school reform associated with a 1:1 computer installation. The project is a common denominator of our respective work and a a subject of much research that we use to substantiate claims made in the book. We bring our direct experience at all levels of the education system, and use our research to address the question why education has failed technology.

Each chapter focuses on one level (e.g., classroom, school, district, association, and so on) of a multi-level educational system, and helps answer the book's central question, using case examples and characters from our own experience and research. We use a theory of self-organizing systems to thread key ideas throughout the chapters. Collectively, the chapters form a real-world narrative replete with scenarios and characters about how certain assumptions and realities emerge at each level of the educational system, what their effects are, and how specific shifts in practice can resolve challenges at each level and contribute to system-wide transformation.

As you read the book, we ask you to keep four caveats in mind. First, one of the key ideas we echo throughout pertains to the role that research plays in building bodies and cultures of professional practice in major disciplines such as medicine, engineering, and law. We intentionally use the plural of bodies and cultures here because we readily acknowledge that research in the field of education is contested. Our approach is not to privilege or promote one best way. Instead, our basic concern is the failure of the field of education to build any rigorous models of research-based practice for the conduct of education in schools at scale. We are not wedded to a particular philosophy, model, or pedagogical point of view. Rather, our approach is about rigorously walking the walk from theory to research to practice with any well-considered educational model or design.

Second, when describing student achievement, we reference standardized tests. Please know that we heartily acknowledge the limitations of such tests for determining student growth and guiding practice. Our reference to such tests, in part, reflects the predominant use of such measures in large-scale studies.

Third, we emphasize that there is a difference between running a controlled study, program evaluation, or action research project and sustained and scalable systemic change in classrooms, schools, and districts. Studies, programs, and projects are too often conflated with systemic change, thus engendering a myth of sustained research-informed practice that does not exist at scale.

Finally, we give much attention to the power of self-similarity—stakeholders employing common practices at various levels of the educational system—that comes from those stakeholders systemically sharing a commitment to research-based practice. Our support for this idea does not mean we believe all teachers should be doing the same thing. Quite the opposite—we contend that all professional fields, including education, require a foundation of research-informed practice if they are to capture the genius of the individuals who engage with them.

Acknowledgments

Our work benefits from the scholarly efforts of many theorists and researchers. We are especially grateful for the influence asserted on us by the following and their works: Benjamin Bloom (1976), *Human Characteristics and School Learning;* Milton Friedman (1962), *Capitalism and Freedom*; Murray Gell-Mann (1994), *The Quark and the Jaguar: Adventures in the Simple and the Complex*; John Hattie (2009), *Visible Learning: A Synthesis of Over 800 Meta-analyses Relating to Achievement*; Stuart Kauffman (1995), *At Home in the Universe: The Search for Laws of Self-Organization and Complexity;* Thomas Kuhn (1996), *The Structure of Scientific Revolutions;* and Ilya Prigogine (1984), *Order Out of Chaos: Man's New Dialogue with Nature.*

THE LEARNING EDGE

CHAPTER 1

Education and Technology

A person hears only what they understand.
—Johann Wolfgang von Goethe

Why has education failed technology? Why aren't all children being educated to levels of learning that exceed their aptitudes? Moreover, why is this not happening at scale? Overall, the field of education has failed to meet these challenges by inadequately capturing the benefits of Information and Communications Technology (ICT). A series of faulty assumptions and simplified realities has hijacked ICT practices, policies, and product development. These contentions are supported by research, dismantles the foundation on which ICT in education currently rests. We use an A to B paradigm shift metaphor (Weston & Brooks, 2008) to reconceptualize the role of ICT. In it, A is the current educational paradigm and B is an alternate one in which ICT shifts from ancillary and supplementary to indispensable in resolving the essential classroom and school challenge—*genuine learning for all students*. Shifts of thought, theory, and action from the A paradigm to the B alternative frame the new role for ICT. *E*dge is the name we give technology that plays this new role by extending, connecting, and developing the capacities of all educational stakeholders in pursuit of genuine learning for all students. The first letter of *edge* is italicized to denote the educational focus of the technology. In this book, we present a framework for helping stakeholders take up the challenge, attain scale, and sustain their efforts.

THE PROBLEM OF ICT USE IN EDUCATION

To date, the most stunning feature of the narrative about ICT in education is the minimal overall impact that ICT has exerted on the way teachers teach and students learn (Herrington & Kervin, 2007; Jaillet, 2004). Students and teachers, armed with ICT, were expected by technology advocates to progress along a trajectory of aspiration for profound change in instruction and learning to a genuine widespread transformation of educational practice (Johnstone, 2003, 2006). That trajectory was supposed to lead to dramatic improvements in teaching and learning for all students at scale. What actually happened is a different story, one with many unanswered questions (Lei & Zhao, 2006) and an incomplete (Moje, 2009), often methodologically problematic (Barrow & Rouse, 2005; Heck, 2004), and frequently self-serving literature (Cuban, 2001). How did this happen?

Twenty-five years ago, personal computers (Moreau, 1984) and the Internet (Berners-Lee & Fischetti, 1999) emerged as a distinct advantage for many countries (McChesney, Wood & Foster, 1998), their economies (Bruk, 1961), businesses (Cortada, 2004), and citizenry (Turner, 2006). The unprecedented successes of ICT in those quarters fostered a wide-eyed belief that ICT could improve the way almost everything was done (Cetron & Davies, 1997). A resulting and broadly held view was that since ICT helped transform factories, homes, offices, and stores, it could also help transform schools and classrooms (DiSessa, 2000; Pflaum, 2004). Not surprisingly, the one common element of all recommendations for improving education worldwide during this period was to expand access to ICT (Glennan & Melmad, 1996; Johnson & Maddux, 2003; Shaw, 1998).

Around 1985, the typical classroom did not have a computer (NCES, 2008), Internet access (Becker, 1999), or a teacher who wanted either (Fisher, Dwyer & Yocam, 1996). In the succeeding decade, an unprecedented infusion of ICT in schools and classrooms occurred (Rathbun & West, 2003). For instance, in the United States, one computer for every 125 students was the norm in 1985; 10 years later, the norm was one computer for every nine students. In 2008, the ratio was one computer per three students (NCES, 2008). Similar infusions and drastic changes in ratios have occurred throughout the world (Law, Pelgrum, & Plomp, 2008).

Three circumstances drove the increase in access to ICT in education. One of these was persistent doubt about the efficacy of current educational approaches for educating all students (Clinchy, 1996; Dixon, 1994; Finn, 1991; Lieberman, 1993). In the United States, *A Nation at Risk* epitomized the doubtful-about-education sentiment when it reported, "The educational foundations of our society are presently being eroded by a rising tide of mediocrity that threatens our very future as a Nation and a people" (NCEE, 1983, p. 1). Reports from Australia (Dawkins, 1988), New Zealand (Picot, 1988), and the United Kingdom (Department of Education and Science, 1985) voiced similar sentiments. Fueled by such doubts—yet without any clarity or agreement about how best to resolve those doubts—public support for improving schools skyrocketed (Public Agenda, 1995, 1999, 2003).

A second circumstance that drove increased access to ICT was a perceived need to prepare students for the inevitability of workplaces where ICT skills would be essential for knowledge-economy workers (Marshall & Tucker, 1992). An American report gave voice to this point, saying, "No nation has produced a highly qualified technical workforce without first providing its workers with a strong general education" (CSAW, 1990, p. 3). Reports from other countries made the same point (Dahlman & Aubert, 2001; Kinsella & McBrierty, 1998; Miller, 1996; Sheehan, 1995; Winslow & Bramer, 1994).

Finally, increased access to ICT resulted from the ever-escalating arrival of new technologies: personal computers (Raum, 2008), software applications (Campuzano, Dynarski, Agodini, and Rall, 2009), the Internet (Tuomi, 2002), computer games (Barab, Gresalfi, & Arici, 2009), interactive white boards (Leask & Pachler, 2005), smart phones (Kolb, 2008), and so on. Slick ad campaigns promoted the latest iteration of each technology (King, 1995), along with focus-group-tested messages (Till & Heckler, 2009) and cool imagery (Wedel & Pieters, 2008). For many consumers, the promise of the next "new thing" (Lewis, 2000) and the difference it was expected to make in the lives of its users was seductive (Nusselder, 2009). Students who had the new technological gadgets at home often did not have them at school, leading one report to say, "Today's education system faces irrelevance unless we bridge the gap between how students live and how they learn" (Partnership for 21st Century Skills, 2002, p. 4).

The dominant discourse of the day held that (a) children with access to ICT would learn to use ICT in masterful ways, (b) such access and mastery would change the way children learned other things, and (c) this would serve as a lever for changing education (Negroponte, 1995; Papert, 1993a, 1993b; Tapscott, 1998; Thornburg, 1995). The discourse birthed an agenda for improving education, one that conflated *access* to ICT with *effect* on learning in an unsubstantiated cause-effect relationship.

That agenda claimed that the way to improve education was to increase the amount of access that students and teachers had to ICT (CEO Forum, 1997). Students and teachers having greater access to ICT became a deeply entrenched concept in the educational zeitgeist (Johnson & Maddux, 2003). The responsibilities of ICT professionals often subsumed those of building administrators, curriculum leaders, and classroom instructors (Hall, 2008). The prime metric of success became the amount of access to ICT, as reflected in the number of network ports, network bandwidth, software licenses, and the all-important computer-to-user ratio (Rathbun & West, 2003). Student-to-computer ratios became proxies for educational quality (CEO Forum, 1997). The mantra of technology advocates became how many, how much, and how often (Didsbury, 2003). The battle cry of the true believers became "If only I had the next new thing" (Lewis, 2000).

The combination of persistent circumstances driving the access to ICT agenda and a professional literature that was emerging in the field of education fueled a steady buzz about increasing technology in classrooms and schools. What the buzz sorely lacked, however, were experimental studies showing the broad-based effects of increased access to ICT on teaching and student learning at scale and the sources of those effects. Hoping such effects would be forthcoming, technology advocates moved their access agenda forward without evidence.

In the absence of rigorous research findings, the advent of 1:1 computing initiatives tested the belief that access to ICT would yield instructional, learning, and achievement effects (Lei, Conway, & Zhao, 2008). The 1:1 initiatives—often high-profile, policy-driven, and well-funded—represented a logical extension of the access argument that, for nearly 2 decades, had asserted that ICT would deliver on its promise of educational effects when student-to-computer ratios reached low levels (MacMillan, 2006). The actual attainment of low ratios in the form of 1:1 computing initiatives constituted an endgame for the access to ICT agenda. Problem Example 1.1 describes the advent of the State of Maine Learning Technology Initiative (MLTI) providing every grade 7 and 8 student and teacher with a laptop computer.

Problem Example 1.1: Maine Steps Up

In 2000, due to an unanticipated revenue spike, the state of Maine, despite an economic downturn, had a $70 million surplus to spend (Nemitz, 2000). Angus King, the state's popular second-term governor, seized the opportunity and proposed a program "to ensure a basic level of access to technology, the Internet and training and learning opportunities for all Maine public schools, students and teachers, at the middle and high school levels" (McCarthy & Breen, 2001, p. 39). King believed "giving kids computers will change their future and Maine's" by "putting Maine on the technological map," improving the state's competitiveness with a better technology-rich education system (King, 2000). King said, "There is no question that jobs in the future . . . all will involve computers and Internet literacy . . . and those individuals and societies that are the most competent and at ease with this technology will be the most successful" (King, 2000). King's vision was heavily influenced by the extensive interactions that he had had with Seymour Papert (Muir, 2005), founder of the Media Lab at MIT (www.media.mit.edu). Papert believed that if children were given access to computers, the way they learned would change and subsequently transform teaching, schooling, and society for the better (Curtis, 2003). King used Papert's notions to undergird MLTI (Williams, 2000). As King had hoped, by "being first," MLTI positioned Maine as a world leader for providing students and teachers with access to laptop computers (Curtis, 2003). Such leadership has garnered invitations for state officials to explain their program to a far-ranging audience, including the Organization for Economic Cooperation and Development and the governments of Australia, China, Ireland, and Scotland, among others (Waters, 2009).

MLTI exemplifies the access agenda and the three circumstances that drove it. Explicit in King's arguments for MLTI are doubts about the efficacy of prior efforts in the state and elsewhere to improve education. Equally explicit is an aspiration for the initiative to "transform Maine into the premier state for utilizing technology in kindergarten to grade 12 education in order to prepare students for a future economy that will rely heavily on technology and innovation" (McCarthy & Breen, 2001, p. vi). Further, the initiative coincided with the arrival of affordable laptop computers that provided users with wireless access to the Internet (Raum, 2008).

MLTI and other similar initiatives lacked components for assessing how the increased access to ICT they provided would pay educational dividends (Cuban, 2001). Penuel, Kirn, Michalchik, Lewis, Means, and Murphy (2001) conducted a review of the literature that found few studies of sufficient rigor and quality for determining the effects of 1:1 computing on student learning. Another review found only four studies that met their quasi- or experimental standards of rigor and that addressed achievement effects. Of those four, all studied single schools and three only addressed effects on technological literacy, not on academic learning or achievement (Peneul, 2006). Despite the lack of educational research and demonstration of effect at scale, a number of jurisdictions continued to pursue large-scale high access to ICT deployments (Bain & Weston, 2009).

With no clear picture of how to create genuine educational advantage, initiatives to increase access to ICT played out predictably (Weston & Bain, 2010). For example, an evaluation of MLTI reported that only 60% of participating teachers used their laptop computer weekly to (a) conduct research for lesson plans, (b) develop instructional materials, or (c) provide classroom instruction (Silvernail, 2007). In a study of the Texas Technology Immersion Pilot (TxTIP), a 1:1 initiative comparable to MLTI, Shapley, Sheehan, Sturges, Caranikas-Walker, Huntsberger, and Maloney (2009) reported "students' access to and use of laptops for learning within and outside of school continued to fall short of expectations in the fourth year" (p. 88). As for classes that regularly access computers, what does the data indicate? An evaluation of the 1:1 program at Quaker Valley School District (QVSD) in Leetsdale, Pennsylvania, reported that access and use varied significantly across subjects and grade levels (Kerr, Pane, & Barney, 2003). A study of the Denver School of Science and Technology (DSST) reported that only 38% of the 9th- and 10th-grade teachers and 58% of the 11th- and 12th-grade teachers even asked their students to access laptops daily for academic work in class or at home (Zucker & Hug, 2007).

A 4-year study of the 1:1 laptop program at the Henrico County Public Schools in Henrico, Virginia, found only three-quarters of the students who were eligible to receive a laptop from the school district opted to do so (Mann, 2008). Similarly, when MLTI, which had provided every 7th- and 8th-grader with a laptop computer for 8 years, allowed districts to use funds to provide laptop computers to students in grades 9 through 12, only half of the districts opted to do so (Ash, 2009).

These sorts of findings are the norm, not the exception, and they are not restricted to 1:1 computer initiatives. Studies of educational settings consistently indicate that even when access to ICT is high, the use of ICT is low (Cuban, Kirkpatrick, & Peck, 2001), the type of use varies markedly (Lathouwers, de Moor, &

Didden, 2009), and its effect on student achievement remains, at best, inconclusive (Barton & Coley, 2009; Wainer, Dwyer, Dutra, Covic, Magalhaes, Ferreira, et al., 2008). Moreover, if exceptional findings are claimed by researchers, the design and methodology of the studies do not possess the control over key variables to confidently attribute found positive effects to the ICT (Fouts, 2000).

These disconcerting findings stimulated research and practice on getting to scale with ICT (Dede, Honan, & Peters, 2005). However, at this time, and when viewed summatively, research and evaluation reports of 1:1 indicate quite clearly that at scale, the ever-increasing access to ICT does not co-vary with higher scores on standardized achievement tests at local, state, national, and international levels. Figure 1.1 presents student computer ratios and performance on key international tests from1984 through 2007, showing that there was no bump in student performance (Gonzalez, 2004; Martin, 2004; Martin, Mullis, & Chrostowski, 2004) to correspond with students and teachers having much greater access to ICT in their classrooms, schools, districts, and homes (NCES, 2008; OECD, 2008; UNESCO, 2008).

The lack of covariance between increased access to ICT and test scores should have raised pedagogical concerns about possible conceptual flaws in the access to ICT agenda. Technology advocates, however, did not take up the tough ques-

Figure 1.1. NAEP, PISA, TIMSS, and Computers Per Student

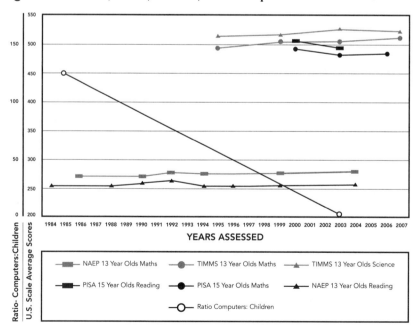

tions that the lack of covariance raised. In part, because the three circumstances—doubts about the prevailing education system, the need for technologically literate workers, and the continual arrival of new technology—that originally fueled the access to ICT agenda in education remained firmly in place. Worldwide, the annual expenditure for educational technology is now over $19 billion, of which $8.9 billion annually goes toward providing ICT in American classrooms (NCES, 2008; OECD, 2008; UNESCO, 2008).

In sum, the findings of limited use and weak outcomes run counter to the lofty aspirations of ICT having a transformative scalable effects on teaching, learning, and achievement. The ascent of 1:1 computing in Maine and elsewhere provide practical examples of what happens when access to ICT is conflated with effects on learning at scale. Clearly, giving every child and teacher a computer will not produce the expected transformational and wide-scale effects that supporters of the access agenda expected.

FAULTY ASSUMPTIONS ABOUT ICT AND SCHOOLS

Why has the access to ICT agenda failed to demonstrate attributable, scalable, and sustainable learning effects in education? The answer is embarrassingly simple. It involves five faulty assumptions that underlie the access to ICT agenda: (a) children with access to ICT learn to use ICT in masterful ways, then apply that masterful use to their other learning; (b) teachers spontaneously change their teaching practices when they gain access to ICT; (c) teaching teachers how to use ICT redresses poor learning results of students; (d) improved access to ICT improves the quality of ICT use; and (e) improved access and use increases student achievement. In the following section, we contest each assumption, using the available empirical and evaluative evidence.

Assumption 1: Children with access to ICT learn to use it in masterful ways, then apply that masterful use to their other learning. Despite rhetoric among ICT advocates about a digital generation (Tapscott, 1998) of students forever altered by technology, it is clear that children lead parallel lives in relation to their use of ICT. Although ICT use (e.g., Facebook, MySpace, Twitter, YouTube) has dramatically and often spontaneously changed the social lives of children, accounts of ICT use in schools show no comparable sweeping change in the ways students use ICT for education. Moreover, ICT mastery has not dramatically and spontaneously transferred from the broader home-use dimension of children's lives to the education dimension (Clotfelter, Ladd, & Vigdor, 2008). With some exceptions, most students simply use educational technology in ways that automate the traditional forms and function of schooling such as taking attendance, reporting grades, and managing course materials (Golon, 2008).

Assumption 2: Teachers spontaneously change their existing teaching practices when they gain access to ICT. Go visit any classroom or school. It is self-evident in a vast majority of them that ICT has failed to produce spontaneous changes in instructional practice. According to Cuban (2001), "Abundant availability of a 'hard' infrastructure (wiring, machines, software) and a growing 'soft' infrastructure (technical support and professional development) in schools in the late 1990s has not led, as expected, to frequent or extensive teacher use of technologies for tradition-altering classroom instruction" (p. 171). Further, there is little evidence that schools with large amounts of ICT are readily absorbing it into existing practice. For example, Shapley, Sheehan, Sturges, Caranikas-Walker, Huntsberger, and Maloney (2009) estimated that after year 4 of TxTIP "just a quarter of middle schools (6) achieved substantial immersion levels whereas the remaining schools (15) had minimal to partial immersion levels" (p. 80). There is no basis for the assumption that giving a teacher access to ICT will in and of itself change her or his instructional practice.

Assumption 3: Teaching teachers how to use ICT will redress poor learning results at scale. Few persons will argue against more and better preparation for teachers. Not surprisingly, throughout the 1990s, lack of professional development was often cited as cause for poor integration of ICT in classrooms and schools and lack of improved instruction, learning, and student achievement (NCREL, 2008). Cuban (2001) described the situation as "blame and train" (p. 130) because teachers were blamed for not delivering on the promise of ICT and were then "trained up" (p. 130) to alter outcomes. Circumstances relative to professional development have changed markedly—more on-line training, new professional associations—since the access agenda began, especially in relation to factors such as collaborative and collegial environments known to influence the quality of professional development (Darling-Hammond, Wei, Andree, Richardson, & Orphanos, 2009; Desimone, Porter, Garet, Yoon, & Birman, 2002; Guskey, 2003; Linn & Hsi, 2000). However the overall results pertaining to the effect from professional development (PD) at scale have not changed. For instance, a study by Ertmer (2005) reported that 85% of teachers believed they were prepared to use ICT in their teaching. Conversely, another study showed that teachers who were prepared to use ICT did not use it in transformative ways in their instruction (Becker, 2001). Yet another study showed that even when participating teachers believed they were adequately trained to use specific software applications, neither their training nor the software positively effected student performance on standardized tests (Dynarski, Agodini, Heaviside, Novak, Carey, Campuzano, et al., 2007; Campuzano, Dynarski, Agodini, & Rall, 2009). Equally, there is a body of research showing positive effects from some summer programs (Garet, Porter, Desimone, Birman, & Yoon, 2001) and targeted professional development activities on science learning (Varma, Husic & Linn, 2008). PD can make a difference.

However, what is missing in the expanding universe of PD activity is an impact on the field of education at scale. No matter how intuitively appealing, to assume it will do so is a simplified reality. Getting the field of education to scale with ICT-based innovation remains a complex challenge.

Assumption 4: Improved access to ICT improves the quality of ICT use. Cumulative work that includes evaluative and experimental studies of (a) specific 1:1 initiatives (Kerr, Pane, & Barney, 2003; Zucker & Hug, 2007), (b) multiple sites that are part of the same initiative (Becker, 1999, 2001; Shapley et al., 2009; Silvernail, 2007), and (c) singular sites studied multiple times (Dwyer, 2000) shows that this assumption is unsubstantiated. For instance, an evaluation of MLTI showed that 6 years into the initiative, only 45% of the teachers in the program strongly agreed that "having a laptop computer has helped me access more-up-to-date information" and 20% of the same teachers strongly agreed that they "can individualize curriculum to fit student needs with a laptop" (Silvernail, 2007). The facts are clear; more access to ICT does not improve the quality of ICT use.

Assumption 5: Improved ICT access and use increases student achievement. Attempts to establish the impact of ICT on achievement test scores of students have generally been inconclusive. Four examples illustrate this point. First, Wenglinsky (1998) found that student achievement was negatively related to frequency of use and positively related to type of use. He also found a positive relationship between using ICT to teach higher-order thinking skills and academic achievement, but noted that higher-order use rarely occurred in grade levels below middle school because the focus there is largely on computational skills. Second, a study of Israeli schools reported that computer-aided instruction did not translate into higher test scores (Angrist & Lavy, 2002). Third, an analysis of two programs that provided computers to students in the Netherlands found an overall negative point estimate for both and a high detriment to girls' achievement (Leuven, Lindahl, Oosterbeek, & Webbink, 2004). Last, Shapley et al. (2009) reported that "Technology Immersion had no statistically significant effect on TAKS [Texas Assessment of Knowledge and Skills] reading achievement for [8th graders] or [7th graders]—however, for [9th graders], there was a marginally significant and positive sustaining effect" (p. 85). Moreover, they found that "Technology Immersion had a statistically significant effect on TAKS mathematics achievement for [8th graders] and [7th graders]. For [9th graders], the sustaining effect of immersion on TAKS mathematics scores was positive but not by a statistically significant margin" (p. 85). Increasing access to and use of ICT has no effect on student achievement.

Problem Example 1.2 shows how the five faulty assumptions play out practically in co-author Alan's sons' use of ICT inside and outside his sons' classrooms.

Problem Example 1.2: Alan Reflects

To understand how education fails ICT, watch what your children do with it. Mine come home with an endless stream of homework tasks most often involving ICT use. At face value, the tasks appear to be of educational value—Internet research, desktop publishing, and creation of products—seemingly for good learning effect. However, when I watch what my 9-, 14-, and 16 year-old boys actually do for homework, the reality falls far short of the promise of the task. This has been the case for each boy in educational systems in Australia, Canada, and the United States. Their use pattern goes like this: They jump onto the computer; use Google to troll for information, text, graphics, and images; then they develop a spreadsheet and graph to present their newfound data. Next, they cut and paste, paraphrase (after reading and thinking—at least, one would hope), insert graphics, and set up layouts and borders, forming a document that appears to exude deep learning. The color printer chugs out a professional-appearing document that looks fantastic in terms of production value. With their homework tasks done, the boys then get back to their real technology work—PlayStation, Xbox, Facebook, Twitter, and instant messaging. The assignments are turned in and, for the most part, receive satisfactory grades.

I am quite certain that my kids would be thankful for the efficiency of it all if they knew something different. They do not—the Web, computers, color printers, and mobile phones have always been there for them. Unfortunately, this type of cut-and-paste project is merely a newer iteration of what many of us experienced in grammar school 40 years ago. Back then, instead of surfing the Net for text, graphics, and images, we trolled magazines, rummaged through library stacks, and scoured the family encyclopedia (if you had one). Instead of a computer and mouse, we completed homework tasks using crayons, scissors, Elmer's glue, and pieces of poster board. There is little reason to think that a digital version of this exercise yields more or better learning than its "analog" precursor.

The actual recurring events in the lives of Alan's boys reflect in simple, practical ways the faulty nature of the five assumptions and the flawed idea of children as newly minted digital natives. Children master the use of technology for learning in ways that reflect what they are asked to do. Hence, they will not spontaneously reinvent teaching or learning for the field. Similarly, teachers will not spontaneously transform their practice. In fact, they are much more likely to co-opt ICT for engaging in the teaching and assessment approaches that have been the norm for generations. Professional development in ICT is unlikely to alter this circumstance unless it directly addresses teaching and learning.

Access to more ICT is unlikely to make a learning difference if we continue to hold the same faulty assumptions. Applying ICT to do the same old work of schools and expecting different outcomes is unrealistic.

THE CHALLENGE OF MAKING ICT EFFECTIVE IN EDUCATION

Advocates who focus on the increasing access of student and leader to ICT do so at the expense of meeting the essential challenge that confronts every teacher in every school in every classroom in every country across the globe: *How can one teacher maximize the learning and achievement of each student in her or his class-room?* This fundamental challenge, not access to ICT, lies at the heart of contemporary educational efforts and probably has been part of educational efforts for as long as learning has occurred in groups.

Among educational reformers, maximizing the learning and achievement of all students, not just some, has been the focus of a concerted push to make teachers, classrooms, and schools more inclusive and responsive to individual differences (Berube, 1994). Beginning in the 1950s and extending to the present day, policymakers in the United States (Ravitch, 1983), Australia (Hyams & Bessant, 1972), Brazil (Reiter, 2009), Canada (Lawr & Gidney, 1973), India (Ghosh, 2007), the United Kingdom (Bunch & Valeo, 2009), and elsewhere have pushed for providing a quality education to *all* children (Mitchell, 2005).

Despite these worldwide efforts, doubts among business and education leaders persist about the capacity of schools to prepare students for entering the increasingly competitive and global marketplace (Hayes, 2004; Kearns & Doyle, 1989). Such doubts are supported by data showing that only two out of three students eligible to attend public school in the United States (Young & Hoffman, 2002) and in other developed countries (Miller, Sen, & Malley, 2007) complete their schooling within the prescribed timeframe (typically 12 years). Moreover, of the students who do finish their schooling on time, approximately one in 10 needs pullout help, another one in 10 requires special accommodations, and yet another one in 10 reports being "under challenged" (NCES, 2005, 2006, 2008, 2009; OECD, 2008). In the United States, the percentages for the categories are higher for students who are non-Caucasian and from lower socioeconomic backgrounds (Rothman, 2005). Moreover, in urban and rural areas and in underdeveloped countries, the percentages are closer to one in three students (UNESCO, 2007).

Benjamin Bloom (1976, 1977) showed that a single teacher working with one student could accomplish a 2–standard deviation improvement in learning, but when that teacher had a classroom full of students, learning gains were much lower (1984a, 1984b). His research indicated that if patterns of practice—including tutorial instruction, reinforcement, feedback, and time on task—were optimized, then a teacher with a classroom of students could attain results approaching those of one teacher working with just one student, making profound learning gains possible for all students (1988). By making this point, Bloom issued a de facto challenge to educators everywhere: Find methods of group instruction that are as effective as one-to-one tutoring (Bloom, 1984a, 1984b).

Finding methods for one teacher, who is charged with the design, delivery, and management of a learning experience, to educate a classroom of diverse students well—not increasing student and teacher access to ICT—should have been the primary focus of efforts to improve education via ICT all along. Instead, advocates for the access to ICT agenda caused the field of education to focus on student to computer ratios that conflated access and effect. To meet Bloom's challenge, the learning ratio is key: one teacher successfully responding to the learning needs of many students. The learning ratio and its attainment at a scale beyond a few classrooms is what we call *1:X*, a term that refers to the essential challenge that emerges when one teacher must meet the needs of many students.

Extensive research focuses on creating an optimal learning ratio for diverse learners (Cole, 2008). The research includes examinations of (a) how to manage groups of students (Larrivee, 2009), (b) effective pedagogies for inclusion (Mitakidou, 2009), (c) strategies for differentiating assessment (Blaz, 2008), and (d) techniques for making content more accessible (McGrath, 2007). Although the empirical findings derived from this literature are compelling, to date they have generated neither practical nor comprehensive models yielding robust, scalable, and sustainable effects on student learning of the type that Bloom showed possible.

MAKING SHIFTS IN THOUGHT TO IMPROVE EDUCATION

If ICT plays a profoundly different and more powerful role, the research can be reconciled in a workable, sustainable, and scalable model of inclusive practice. Moreover, the 1:X challenge can only be resolved when ICT is used to build and deliver the model because the tasks in today's schools are too complex for teachers who lack technological support. The role of ICT in the lives of teachers must be reconceptualized from something they access to something they use regularly with sophistication and ease to meet the individual learning needs of their students. If the role of ICT is effectively reconceptualized, teachers may readily (a) design and manage a differentiated curriculum, (b) make abstract concepts accessible to students, (c) communicate and collaborate with students and other stakeholders in pursuit of increased learning and improved instruction, and (d) make feedback immediate, rich, specific, and tied to adaptations in practice so ever-higher levels of learning are attainable.

ICT is integral to the way curriculum and pedagogy address differences among individual learners. It is also integral to solving the paramount educational problem of our time: educating all students to heights that have never been reached before in classrooms and schools and addressing the 1:X challenge. Foundational shifts in thought, theory, and action are required to realize the vision.

Shift one: 1:X requires a shift in thought about what is required for all students to learn. Such a shift in thought begins with (a) a deeply held shared understanding about teaching, learning, and student achievement; (b) the recognition and adoption of specific approaches for improving performance; and (c) a commitment to sustained use of the approaches at scale (Bain, 2007).

Research on the culture of schools clearly indicates that these conditions rarely occur at the school level and beyond (McLaughlin & Talbert, 2001; Sarason, 1996). Even though many researchers have demonstrated the possibility and promise of all sorts of educational innovations, reforms, and changes, none has shown a trajectory for taking the aspirations inherent in the possibilities and promises to routine practice at scale (e.g., the No Child Left Behind Act). Large-scale studies of improvement efforts in education show more inconsistency from teacher-to-teacher implementation within participating schools than between schools. They also show a more or less gradual washout of the efforts over time (Aladjem & Borman, 2005; Berends, Bodilly, & Natarj-Kirby, 2002). Further, the absence of a shared school-level perspective contributes to high levels of divisiveness, inconsistency, and instability within schools (Bain, 2007; Dimmock & Hattie, 1994).

Within the field of education, the lack of consensus about teaching and learning approaches for improving performance and a common commitment to overall improvement of performance is also a reason why no major effort to innovate, reform, or change education has produced a sustained effect on student achievement at scale. It is the elephant in the room that everyone sees but no one wants to acknowledge. A shift in thought involves recognizing and responding to the elephant in the room and agreeing to the aspiration of educating all students to high levels of learning.

Shift two: A different, more complete, and practical educational theory is required to shift thinking about inclusively and comprehensively framing the problem of 1:X and generating plausible and scalable solutions for that problem. History clearly shows that the current educational paradigm is incapable of producing significant and wide-scale improvements in student learning and achievement as measured by standardized tests. This is because the paradigm is the product of an age of linear reversible science and scientific method where change is viewed as a predictable and reversible phenomenon (Merry, 1995). In contrast, our approach, which is based on six principles (Bain, 2007), applies processes and practices derived from the theories of complex and self-organizing systems (Gell-Man, 1994; Kauffman, 1995; Merry, 1995; Morrison, 2000; Waldrop, 1992).We use the theories of complex and self-organizing systems to explain an educational approach capable of emergent bottom-up resolution of needs, drivers, and problem and that is capable of attaining 1:X at scale.

The first principle is that self-organizing systems possess simple rules (Seel, 2000) and commitments to specific practices that guide their activity and the system as a whole. In a self-organizing school, stakeholders make commitments to research-based practice. When they are shared, these commitments, for instance to cooperative learning, make it possible for a classroom, school, or district to have a common understanding of teaching and learning—a prerequisite for addressing the elephant in the room described in shift one and working toward the consensus that is so rare in education.

Second, those commitments to practice are embedded in the design of the educational system, making it possible for stakeholders to "walk the talk" of the system. For instance, a school that has committed to having high levels of collaboration among teachers and students might embed a collaborative meeting protocol in the day-to-day operation of the school. The teachers and students would then use the collaborative meeting protocol for all committee and team meetings. By doing so, the school's commitment to collaboration is made explicit through the use of the protocol. Processes and tools can then be developed to manage and provide feedback about the school's use of the collaborative protocol. All of the school's commitments to practices can be handled in similar fashion. By doing so, the schools commitments are embedded in its design and operation.

Third, embedded design contributes to "self-similarity" at different levels and among various stakeholders in the system (Waldrop, 1992). Self-similarity is the repetition of a shape, form or behavior at different levels in a complex system. For example, when students, teachers, and school leaders utilize the same approaches (e.g., collaborative meeting processes) at different levels in the design of the school, they build self-similar capabilities to have well-structured and productive meetings. As a result, groups that normally function in disconnected or isolated ways share the capacity to join together at different levels in the school and pool their collective intelligence.

Fourth, self-organizing systems also disperse control to stakeholders (Merry, 1995). Distributing leadership and responsibility from systems to schools and from schools leaders to teachers has long been a goal of educational systems despite the fact that mechanisms (e.g., policies, role descriptions, and standards) for doing so are rarely spelled out. Though genuine dispersed control, the opportunities, needs, and problems of a system are responded to by those stakeholders who are most likely to successfully resolve them. For instance, in a self-organizing school the teachers closest to underperforming students would have greater control dispersed to them for responding to and managing the underperformance. The many actions of the teachers would inform the rules, design, self-similarity, and control within the school. Similarly, in Chapter 2, we show that when teachers disperse control for teaching and learning to students, that students can mediate the learning experience of their peers within and beyond the classroom. When students are taught to teach, students lead learning in ways that build their learning capacity. As the students' capacity increases, all members of the system can be empowered.

Fifth, constant bottom-up feedback from stakeholders is the fuel of a self-organizing system. It is the way the system talks to itself (Pascale, Milleman, & Gioja, 2000), and adapts and changes according to the dynamic conditions in its broader environment; a classroom in a school, a school in a district, a district in a state, and so on. In a self-organizing school, feedback becomes something that happens all the time instead of only when grade reports are due, tenure decisions are pending, or when advocates wish to make an after-the-fact determination of the impact of ICT on achievement. ICT makes "all the time" feedback possible.

Sixth, the combined effect of simple rules or commitments, embedded design, self-similarity, dispersed control, and feedback is the evolution of a system schema, a conceptual thought framework for the way the system functions that guides the activity of its stakeholders (Gell-Mann, 1994). For the attainment of 1:X, teachers, schools, and systems need schema—a framework for organizing behavior and clustering structures of practices—for the professional conduct of their work. Schema engender shared understanding, the communication of professional practice, and coherent action. Like everything else in a self-organizing system, the schema is dynamic, subject to change based on the feedback of its agents.

Finally, attractors are forces or events that sustain the system or force the system to change. There are two types of attractors. A point attractor helps systems stay the same—the school days ends when the bell rings, buses run on a schedule. A strange attractor forces the systems to change the way they function (Gleick, 1987), such as changes in school enrollment or a school's budget. Strange attractors, prevent systems from finding an equilibrium point in the way they operate. Point attractors draw systems to an equilibrium condition (Pascale, Milleman, & Gioja, 2000). In this way, equilibrium is a negative feature, since changing operational conditions are inevitable. In short, staying the same in the face of change is a prelude to system failure (Prigogene & Stengers, 1984). We will describe the role of educational leaders at various levels of the system as attractors throughout the book, along with the other six tenets, illustrating their roles in making an education system self-organizing.

Shift three: A theory of paradigm change (Kuhn, 1996) is required for enabling the action necessary for getting from where we are in education to 1:X. In order for the field of education to have a common theory of enactment, each level of the overall educational system must make profound shifts in the thoughts, theories, and actions that are unique to the level (Weston & Brooks, 2008). The shifts, when viewed together, constitute a complete and distinct alternate paradigm that links ICT with proven pedagogy, welcomes the elephant to the room, and opens Pandora's box even wider. For this reason, realizing those shifts will require each level—and the system overall—to reconceptualize the role of ICT in each.

To illustrate the shifts in thought, theory, and action required of the various levels of the system for an alternate paradigm to take root, we present examples of fictional, but fact-based educational stakeholders doing normal work in various educational settings (e.g., classroom, association, business) and then present examples of the same characters doing their educational work in an alternate, theoretically derived way, using tools designed specifically for the alternate paradigm. We refer to the alternate paradigm as "B" and the current one as "A." We use the A-B device to breathe life into our theory of enactment. By doing so we show that the same setting, when the theory of enactment is applied and the paradigms shift (e.g., B replaces A), is viewed in an entirely different way with entirely different outcomes produced.

WHAT IS EDGE TECHNOLOGY AND HOW CAN IT HELP EDUCATION?

Type-A education is a product of the current educational paradigm. Decades of data show that application of its theory structure—beliefs, values, practices, tools—results in some, but not all, students being educated well. Type-B education derives from a different paradigm that has a different theory structure that focuses on achieving 1:X. In the former, technology plays a passive role; in the latter, an essential one.

By failing to embrace its own research and practice, Type-A education has failed itself. By not capturing the potential of ICT, Type-A education has failed all children. Failure is the norm for Type-A education. Conversely, the Type-B approach makes tighter connections among stakeholders; develops their capacities in ways that eluded Type-A efforts to innovate, reform, and change education; and makes educating all children possible at an unprecedented scale. The capacity for the Type-B approach to do these things is only possible with ICT.

In Type-B education, ICT is the systematic means for achieving, sustaining, and refining 1:X. It is also the best way to extend the capacities of stakeholders for pursuing both. As stakeholder capacities extend, existing capacities are instantiated, new ones are developed, and research-based transactions are embedded in tools (e.g., software and organizational processes) that serve stakeholders. A theoretically derived, ICT-driven effort *extends, connects,* and *develops* the capacities of the Type-B education system's agents—students, teachers, administrators, association staff, policymakers, and business leaders.

Extend. In cognitive science, the study of human-machine relationships seeks ways for humans and machines to cooperate on high-level tasks by externalizing human cognitive functions to devices (Facer & Sandford, 2009). The resulting tools complement rather than replace human abilities. Moreover, the tools often articulate sophisticated cognitive tasks that make it easier for humans to engage with the tasks those tools make possible (Roy, 2004).

There is no better example of a complex cognitive task than a teacher tackling the 1:X challenge by attempting to address the individual learning needs of many students in the same classroom. In a Type-A classroom, meeting the needs of many students is impossible because the set of tasks that the teacher must complete exceeds most teacher's cognitive capacities. However, in Type-B one, it is readily possible because ICT extends the teacher's capacities to design, deliver, and evaluate the work of education and address the educational needs of students differentially by shifting some of the teacher's load to the tools. The load shifting includes the way ICT can help a teacher manage classroom groups or a superintendent make a critical policy decision by interrogating the data that emerge from the teacher's classroom and others in the district. In each case, ICT extends the capability of the user and makes a challenging and sometimes inaccessible task more accessible.

Connect. In network theory, an *edge* is the connection between two agents on a network (Barabási, 2003). A network is ADD definition. Typically, in networks that do not work well, the distance between agents is long, structure is overly hierarchical, and communication flows poorly. Schools, when viewed as loosely coupled systems (Weick, 1976), have similar characteristics—information flows mostly top-down, structures are hierarchical, and communication about the key transactions of teaching and learning is centralized and transmissive. ICT, in the form of information sharing and feedback generating tools, helps flatten network structures, and makes the flow of information multidirectional. ICT by flattening structures and increasing information flow effectively shortens the cognitive distance between individual members (e.g., teachers and superintendents) who work at different levels in the same hierarchical network. Shortening the cognitive distance makes the network more effective and makes the overall system more responsive as the individual agents in the network communicate more effectively with each other.

Develop. If ICT makes sophisticated tasks more accessible by extending human cognition (Facer & Sandford, 2009), then ICT can also be a vehicle for helping stakeholders develop greater capacity for dealing with those tasks. For example, the challenge of teaching a class of students with widely varied abilities requires a teacher to have a highly sophisticated schema related to designing, delivering, and evaluating differentiated instruction that results in all students attaining high levels of learning. In practice, ICT, by requiring users to define and structure the tasks assigned to the technology, can articulate a common schema for meeting such challenges via tools that support teachers managing differentiated groups (e.g., leveling) of students, teaching and assessing at different levels, and dealing with the practical challenges associated with managing such classrooms. By using those same tools teachers learn about the schema for and practice of meeting the challenges of a Type-B classroom. Moreover, teachers' use of the tools can reconcile the pedagogical, curricular, and other forms of knowledge about learning, in ways that can help teach teachers and students build those capacities. Plus, since in Type-B mode teachers and students use the tools to address the 1:X challenge, teachers and students who are new to the schema and process can use the tools to readily develop their capacities for meeting the 1:X challenge as well. In this way the same tools that extend a capability in differentiated classrooms are used to teach those capabilities in a professional development program. Such tools can also blur the distinction between field-based knowledge about education and of the tradition use of ICT as a means to increase productivity. The tools by articulating cognitive structures not only extend the cognitive capability of users, but they also can help develop the capacity of users to act upon that structure. The following section introduces those tools.

THE TOOLS OF *E*DGE TECHNOLOGY

*E*dge technology contains three categories of tool sets (i.e., software applications). Each category can extend, connect, and develop sophisticated cognitive capacities of their users. The term edge refers to the connector between nodes in a network. In common language, an edge is an advantage. In Type-B education, thanks to edge technology, the advantage belongs to all stakeholders, not just some.

One category is the *A to B Toolkit*. It includes tools required for doing the work in Type-B classrooms, schools, districts, and so on. This category includes tools that help teachers design differentiated learning experiences, assist school leaders to make their schools more collaborative, and help superintendents engage parents with the districts' goals and processes. These tools help teachers to design differentiated learning experiences, assist school leaders to make their schools more collaborative, and superintendents to engage parents with the district's goals and processes.

The second category is comprised of *Arrays*. These tools manage, analyze, and data-mine information in ways that enable stakeholders to look into Type-B educational settings at many levels and identify challenges, needs, current strengths, and future prospects in less speculative and more informed ways. They include tools for looking into the quality of teaching and the performance of students. Arrays also help stakeholders generate and interrogate the kind of feedback required to make Type-B classrooms, schools, and districts dynamic and responsive to accurate, deep, and timely information about what is going on in those settings. They aid teachers to reflect upon and improve their practice and school leaders to identify and respond to the professional growth needs of teachers. *Co-development Tools* are the third category. These tools reflect the view that all educational endeavors exist within a broader context of policy, practice, and funding. Every Type-B classroom, school, or district functions within a broader and larger education system that may work in ways that can be supportive of or digress from the drivers, needs, and directions of a Type-B educational paradigm.

Co-Development Tools help them manage knowledge of the broader educational milieu and reconcile that knowledge with the needs and drivers of a B-type education. They reconcile policy statements, association briefings, and sources of discretionary funds, with data generated within schools and districts about their current practice and overall performance. They assist leaders to make connections between their needs and the state of play in the broader educational system at the state and national levels.

SCHEMA: A NEW SHARED VIEW
TO IMPROVE EDUCATION

Resolving the 1:X challenge by building a Type-B educational system requires integrating ICT with research-based practices for learning in group settings. This requires stakeholders of the Type-B system to have a shared schema to guide and support their work. That schema helps stakeholders integrate ICT and practice. Schema development involves stakeholders using our three step framework to consider education and ICT in a manner that brings 1:X to scale. The framework guides the decisions, practices, policies, products, and interests of all stakeholders in a Type-B effort. It consists of a three-phase process. In the first phase, stakeholders examine the assumptions or commitments underlying Type-B education. They consider the demands associated with Type-B education, the applicable research, and so forth. In the second phase, stakeholders turn their assumptions into processes and practices by mapping, building, and integrating solutions into the operation of their particular setting. The third phase involves stakeholders turning their plans into measurable actions. By working through these phases, stakeholders are better able to reconceptualize their view of education (e.g., the shift from Type-A to Type-B), design ICT applications that support their new view, and develop strategies for bringing their view to scale in schools. The phases, reflecting an open architecture metaphor for educational problem-solving, enable stakeholders to bring multiple perspectives and solutions to bear against the 1:X challenge. In doing so, stakeholders are better able to avoid the one-best-way approach that characterizes most innovation, reform, and change efforts in education (Bain, 2007).

New Assumptions

New approaches that stand in contrast to those that have dominated the ICT discourse require new assumptions. At a minimum, new assumptions must acknowledge a range of circumstances (e.g., different ability levels of students and teachers) that drive change, foster and support agreement about practices for resolving those circumstances, reflect research about such practices, show a pathway to measurable results, and reduce the cognitive load of stakeholders. To advance the ICT discourse, five assumptions that meet these criteria follow.

Assumption one: Since Type-B places additional and complex demands (e.g., utilizing sophisticated instructional strategies while accommodating individual differences among students) on stakeholders—demands that often vary across stakeholders—Type-B is only achievable with ICT. A case in point is the demand for teachers to create and differentiate curriculum. The task demands the extended cognitive capacity delivered by ICT. In the chapters that follow, we will show how ICT can be employed to differentiate curriculum and the learning experience of all children.

Assumption two: Research on teaching and learning must define the role of ICT. Remarkably, the application of ICT in education rarely intersects with the extensive research about learners, teachers, classrooms, and curriculum (Bain & Parkes, 2006). According to Shurville, Browne, and Whitaker (2008), such an intersection "involves facilitating learning and improving performance by creating, using, and managing appropriate technological processes." There is little evidence that intersections occur consistently in current educational settings. Our longitudinal research, however, shows that when theory and research are embedded in ICT tools, teachers teach more effectively (Bain & Parkes, 2006) and students learn more and achieve at higher levels (Bain, Huss, & Kwong, 2000).

Assumption three: Learning through ICT and learning about ICT is indistinguishable when ICT finds its proper place in addressing the 1:X challenge. Instead of saying to teachers, "today we are going to have professional development about differentiated instruction," the key research-based transactions of differentiated instruction will be embedded in the A to B Toolkit they use for creating, differentiating, and delivering curriculum. In the latter, the A to B Toolkit incorporates and represents the cumulative research and practice knowledge of the field. Teachers and students learn about differentiated teaching and learning by using tools developed specifically for educating all students. Learning how to use the A to B Toolkit and learning about differentiation are indistinguishable. So, every time a teacher or student uses a tool in the A to B Toolkit, her or his capacity to function in Type-B mode is improved and knowledge of 1:X advances (Bain, 2007).

Assumption four: In a 1:X classroom or school, access to ICT is a simple yet fundamental requirement for dispersing control and generating the feedback required to get things done. The tools also make it possible to generate the "all the time" feedback that makes self-organization possible. When embedded at the core of all teaching and learning activity, ICT serves both teachers and learners.

Assumption five: Improved education through ICT improves student achievement. Research shows that, in general, better, more responsive classroom teaching and learning do improve student achievement (Hattie, 2009). When ICT is placed in a powerful mediating context that leverages well-researched professional practice, then 1:X teaching and learning are possible. As 1:X teaching and learning becomes more prevalent, achievement improves. The key is capturing ICT for education instead of vice versa. When education captures ICT at scale, then achievement of all students improves.

The five assumptions foster and support practices that can position ICT meaningfully as a vehicle for creating self-organizing capacity in schools. The practices that stakeholders embrace because they are research-based put the classrooms and school on a trajectory toward measurable results. Embedding the practices in the design of the school and the ICT tools that support the design reduces the cognitive load of stakeholders and establishes roles, responsibilities, and expectations.

New Design

The second phase of the framework for schema development consists of designing and building ICT applications, policies, decision-making processes, and so forth. The history of innovation, reform, and change in education indicates that this phase is mission critical. History also suggests that the big ideas inherent in the aforementioned assumptions, such as creating and differentiating a curriculum or connecting ICT and educational research, rarely translate into sustainable and scalable action in education (Fullan, 2007). The approach outlined below and depicted in Figure 1.2 helps stakeholders cross this critical hurdle by turning their assumptions into measurable instructional practices that are consistent across classrooms, schools, and systems. The phase has three components for stakeholders to complete: (a) solution mapping, (b) component building, and (c) design integrating (Bain & Swan, manuscript under review).

Solution mapping involves understanding—in educational terms—the research and professional knowledge about solving the 1:X challenge, one teacher meeting the learning needs of many students. It requires stakeholders to make specific pedagogical and curricular commitments that form a pathway to specific research proven practices. Such commitments might include the dif-

Figure 1.2. Three-Step Framework

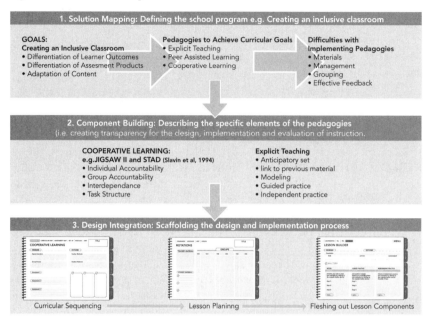

ferentiation of content by providing students in the same classroom with materials at varied ability levels, ongoing feedback between teachers and students that is tied to standards and rubrics and intended to contribute to continuous improvement of teacher and student, or specific instructional strategies such as cooperative learning and explicit teaching. The mapping component of Figure 1.2 depicts the relationships between commitments to 1:X practices in a classroom—connected in a cascading order—and the many roles that the teacher plays in acting on those commitments. These commitments are echoed in mapping at the level of a school or district, the policymaking of a legislature, or the product development of a technology company. Mapping 1:X in this way references all aspects of the design to tested educational research and to the practices to which the stakeholders are committed.

Component building involves using educational research to support, define, and articulate the commitments and roles of stakeholders. During this step stakeholders identify the most effective versions or forms of their commitments. Then they use those versions or forms to guide the designing of specific agendas, applications, materials, policies, processes, and tools that support 1:X. Drilling, identifying, and incorporating the features of practice that drive better teaching and learning leads to embedding of those features in the way ICT serves

1:X at many levels. For example, if a teacher is expected to design cooperative learning lessons or processes for managing different groups in a classroom, then what research-supported features (e.g., task structure, self-reporting) should the ICT application include? How should governmental policies reflect those features? What might associations or advocacy groups do to support those policies

During design integration, stakeholders translate the pedagogical and curricular commitments articulated in the design component into specific ICT-related products or actions. Tasks are assigned to a person or group. For instance, an assignment might include building a piece of software, drafting a policy, or designing a decision-making protocol. Part of the assignment involves integrating research, practice, and ICT as articulated in the mapping and solution-building components. This step permits the elements of research-based 1:X practice, such as mutual interdependence or individual accountability to be deeply embedded at all levels of the system (Bain & Swan, manuscript under review).

A PLAN OF ACTION TO GET WHERE WE NEED TO GO

The third phase is to build a detailed plan of action for stakeholders to follow to get their 1:X design to scale. This involves conducting a situational analysis of what must occur (e.g., new roles for ICT) to gain widespread acceptance within a school or system for 1:X. Stakeholders analyze their circumstances to determine who supports what commitment to practice and will influence whether an application of 1:X can take hold in their classrooms, school, district, or system. Designing research-based, thoughtfully developed policies, products, and processes for ICT to address the 1:X challenge is a necessary but insufficient condition for building meaningful roles for ICT in schools that are both sustainable and scalable. That is why in this phase we ask and answer questions about the context of interest and the challenges and opportunities that exist therein in order to build a realistic picture of the factors that make it affect whether a 1:X innovation with ICT will succeed.

For example, do teacher role descriptions, evaluation processes, and reward structures align with what teachers must do in 1:X? If not, then, what needs to change? Does the organizational structure of the school sustain 1:X? Does existing policy support 1:X at scale?

We then identify the sources and the forms of feedback (Annett, 1969) that will inform the three phases of the framework, including the way assumptions are modified, and the design process is refined in order to ensure the overall sustainability and responsiveness of the trajectory (Lippitt, 1965). Feedback creates the conditions whereby the framework talks to itself (Foot, 1977), generating the information required to alter any and all of its components in response to changing needs and conditions at any level—classroom, school, or system.

The chapters that follow show how the shema development framework—assumptions, design process, and trajectory building—is applied to meeting the 1:X challenge in classrooms, schools, and districts systems. After which a chapter is devoted to advocacy and support of 1:X by professional associations, development of public policy for 1:X, and development 1:X tools by ICT companies. Each chapter contains research-based examples, tools, strategies, and actions that reflect our assumptions, fulfill our design processes, and enable our by strategy for building trajectory for meeting the 1:X challenge.

SUMMARY

- Genuine learning for all students is the essential challenge facing the field of education. Meeting that challenge at widespread scale is 1:X.
- The idea that increased access to ICT will guarantee increased educational outcomes has created an agenda that has prevented the field of education from focusing on 1:X challenge.
- Meeting the 1:X challenge requires new methods that will allow one teacher to educate a classroom of diverse students to high levels of learning.
- Meeting the challenge involves profound shifts of thought, theory, and action that can help us move from the Type-A paradigm that educates some children to a Type-B paradigm that educates all.
- Type-B can only happen with and through ICT tools that extend, connect, and develop the capacities of all educational stakeholders.
- In such a partnership, the contexts in which ICT will be deployed must be referenced.

CHAPTER 2

The Classroom

Every addition to true knowledge is an addition to human power.
—Horace Mann

Edge technology makes educating all students to high levels of learning possible by extending, connecting, and building teacher and student capacities for teaching and learning. We (a) use examples to describe the challenge of 1:X, (b) discuss the three shifts in teaching and learning necessary for meeting that challenge, (c) describe the centrality of edge technology in making the shifts happen, and (d) introduce a technologically enabled model that defines the Type-B approach to education.

DEFINING THE PROBLEM OF ICT USE IN CLASSROOMS

When Benjamin Bloom challenged the field to find methods for group instruction that were as effective as one-to-one tutoring, he asserted the possibility that one teacher, by mastering effective practice, could be as successful in a classroom setting as a tutor working with just one student (Bloom, 1976). The 2-Sigma Effect is the name Bloom gave to all students learning to high levels in a classroom (Bloom, 1984a). For Bloom, better teaching and the primacy of better teachers was the way to achieve the effect.

Despite Bloom's work and thousands of studies demonstrating the impact of specific approaches to teaching and learning, it has proven difficult to attain 2-Sigma at a wide scale (Fraser, Walberg, Welch, & Hattie, 1987; Hattie, 2009; Marzano, 1998). Research-proven teaching practices, such as cooperative and mastery teaching, are like pieces of an unsolved puzzle that are yet to be snapped into a complete, sustainable, and scalable model of classroom practice. After a century of attempts to put the pieces in place, the puzzle remains unresolved (Ravitch, 2010; Tyack & Cuban, 1995).

Because the field has failed to find an alternative, the Type-A model of education—in which teachers teach, students respond, and a school's schedule dictates when learning happens in classrooms—has remained in effect. This approach places an immense load on teachers, fails to challenge students, limits learning to classrooms, and makes 1:X unattainable. Moreover, it limits ICT to the role of automating existing practice. In the examples that follow, we present a Type-B approach that serves as an alternative to the Type-A orthodoxy. In Type-B approach, edge technology plays a critical role. It connects teachers and students, builds the capacity of each in the teaching and learning process, and extends the places where learning happens, in and beyond classrooms and schools.

INTRODUCING THE TYPE-B CLASSROOM

The Type-B approach connects the research-based puzzle pieces in ways that make 1:X attainable for classroom teachers. Attaining 1:X is a complex undertaking. At a minimum, a teacher must demonstrate three capacities. One is knowledge about the content that needs to be taught and multiple, research-based approaches for teaching it (Jones, 2003). Another is the capability to adapt content and curriculum, differentiate instruction, manage resources, and provide feedback at different levels for both heterogeneous and homogeneous work groups (Tomlinson, 2001), including adapting the reading level of an assigned reading, building concept maps and organizers to scaffold student learning tasks, and managing different groups doing different things in the classroom setting. A third capacity involves being able to reconcile knowledge and pedagogy in a workable model of classroom practice (Shulman, 1986) to facilitate the adaptation of resources, differentiate of the learning experience, and manage that differentiated classroom on a daily basis.

What does a Type-B classroom look like in practice? We can find the answer to this question in the classroom where Bruce teaches the physics course every student must pass in order to graduate from the school. Classroom Example 2.1 describes a scene from it.

Classroom Example 2.1: Bruce Facilitates the Big Jump

There is a measure of excitement as students—after completing a 5-week learning module on projectile motion—make final preparations for their benchmark project. The project involves using a model racing car and track to simulate a jump across a canyon (i.e., stairwell in the school). Students must apply Newton's laws to get their cars safely to the other side. Each group, after testing the elements in its plan, gets just one chance to put the elements together in a video sequence of its jump.

Interrupting the students, Bruce draws their attention to an interactive whiteboard on which a matrix shows the activity of three different groups. When he hits the group's icon (on the left side of the display), the layout fills in with the materials and tasks associated with the activity for each group.

One group plans to use motion detection software and a simple ramp for its jump. The students in the group do not have the math background to design their canyon crossing from scratch. The software makes it possible for them to gather the data required. Another group determines the frictional force of its car and uses trigonometry in the plan for its jump. The group uses a ramp with a steep exit lip and builds its math formula from scratch. The third group uses motion detection software and a steeper ramp. Each student will write a report framed by the scientific principles underpinning the jump. Each report will vary according to the approach used.

Bruce reminds students that at the conclusion of the project, each must share the data generated with members of their respective group and each must use the data to write a report. When Bruce finishes reviewing the implementation plans, students resume working in their groups. He moves from group to group, periodically stopping to observe or interact with the students. In one instance, he asks the members of a group to explain the elevation of their track and provide an explanation for the approach.

(*Authors' note*: The Big Jump project was developed by Bruce Gorrill at Brewster Academy.)

Let us sort through the beehive of activity in Bruce's classroom using the four things required to resolve the 1:X challenge. First, Bruce uses a research-based cooperative learning approach that reconciles "content and pedagogy" (Shulman, 1986). He applies the principles of interdependence and individual accountability (Slavin, 1991) to structure the task and the groups. To do so Bruce makes sure that the big jump task is comprised of specific parts that are assigned to individual students. To complete the task students need to work together interdependently by sharing what they know about each part. Bruce ensures individual accountability by requiring that every student complete the assessment task individually. The design of the lessons indicates that Bruce understands how to translate research-based principles from theory to practice and the influence of that translation on each student's prior achievement and learning history.

Second, Bruce adapts the curriculum and materials for all students—regardless of their science and mathematics backgrounds. He adapts the assessment items to ensure that each student masters the curriculum principles at various levels. The way those principles are derived (e.g., motion detector software) and the sophistication of the students' understanding varies based upon their background and the specific nature of the differentiated learning experience.

Third, Bruce differentiates his teaching for multiple of student achievement. This is evidenced in the way he facilitates the cooperative process and the way all students understand what they have to do. For example, he spends time directly teaching those students who do not have a strong math background while also checking the calculations and game-plan of those who do.

Fourth, in Bruce's classroom, edge technology in the form of curriculum planning tools is prominent in the learning process. It extends his capacity to design, conduct, and evaluate his differentiated classroom by (a) gathering and recording data, (b) sharing content, (c) making key pedagogical transactions happen, and (d) designing and developing student presentations. Bruce's extended capacity makes it possible for him to design, manage, and evaluate genuinely differentiated instruction. It is much more than mere procedural support. It provides a way for Bruce to conceptualize and then take up the 1:X challenge by connecting content, pedagogy, management, assessment, and technological resources.

Bruce began teaching in a Type-A model. His approach changed when his school changed to Type-B. The difference between his Type-A and Type-B experiences is profound. Understanding the difference requires further examination.

TYPE-A: THE CLASSROOMS WE KNOW DON'T WORK

For most teachers, facilitating a module of cooperative learning like the one Bruce does is a challenge. Facilitating a series of modules is overwhelming. Managing a classroom curriculum of such modules is inconceivable. Bruce finds a Type-B classroom preferable to a Type-A one. Understanding his preference requires understanding what his classroom life was like before he switched to a Type-B structure.

Bruce briefly taught a general physics course at the school. It was an elective that students enrolled in via self-selection. A text drove his curriculum and lesson plans. He delivered his lessons mainly through lecture, punctuated by periodic PowerPoint™ presentations and whole- group discussions. Sometimes he used simulation software to demonstrate key concepts. Other times, despite having limited understanding of how to structure group tasks and assess students independently about their learning, he had students work on experiments in groups (Slavin, 1991). Classroom Example 2.2 presents an excerpt from a conversation between Bruce and Paul, a student in Bruce's physics class.

Classroom Example 2.2: Paul Reacts

"I just don't get it," says Paul. "I need to know advanced math to work this out!" Bruce looks at Paul's work, then says, "What's the problem? This formula is correct—you are doing fine." Paul says, "No! Jodie built the formula for our group. We each copied it down. I have no idea what she did. I know this stuff is on the test." Bruce is worried about the frustration and stress in Paul's indirect plea for help. He says, "Paul, have you done the end-of-chapter questions?" Paul says, "Yes. I can retell what it says in the chapter, but I still don't get what it means."

Bruce offers Paul a place in the extra-help session that he holds after school on Thursdays. Paul agrees to show up, having heard that students who attend the help session get to retake the unit test. He also knows that his problem extends well beyond some misunderstandings with the practical experiment. He needs the physics credit to get into a college engineering program, but he does not have the prerequisite math and science skills required to be successful in Bruce's class.

During the help session, Bruce goes over the end-of-chapter questions and reteaches some of the key concepts of the projectile motion unit. He also helps problem-solve students' issues. Paul realizes that attempting to learn the same material in the same way it was previously taught, only this time in a smaller group of students, is not going to solve his problem. He decides to go along, then take his chances on the retest. Maybe if he memorizes the formulae and the other things he does not understand, he will pass the test the second time around.

For Classroom Example 2.2, let us unpack the same four things we looked at in the previous example. First, Bruce uses a non-research-based lecture approach to teach every student the same way. Second, physics is an elective, text-driven course. Bruce has only one level of curriculum, and he assesses the performance of every student at the same level. Third, despite clear differences in student understanding and background, the in-class learning experiences for students is undifferentiated. Bruce tries to address the differences in student need with extra-help sessions and test retakes. He hopes that students will attend the help sessions during which he unpacks his class lectures at a slower pace. Because the curriculum, content, and Bruce's teaching do not adapt to the needs of students, the depth and validity of student learning from the help sessions and test retakes is minimal. Fourth, ICT is not prominent in the learning process. Bruce mostly uses ICT to do what he had done before. His teaching and curriculum remain unchanged. He uses PowerPoint™ to present content and simulations to demonstrate concepts. There is a clear mismatch between what Bruce knows and can do—his construction of practice—and his students' needs. Despite being dedicated, concerned, and hardworking, Bruce cannot address the 1:X challenge with what he has. His Type-A schema for practice does not include the basic research-based principles for practices such as cooperative learning. He doe not know about mutual interdependence and individual accountability and how to build those features into his lessons.

Bruce's classroom is a contrast in curriculum, pedagogy, assessment, and ICT. The latter scenario reflects a model of teaching and learning in which some students learn some things. The former reflects a model where all student learn at high levels of mastery. Classroom Example 2.3 presents Bruce's reflections on his experiences teaching in both Type-A and Type-B classrooms.

Classroom Example 2.3: Bruce Reflects

A few years ago, I could not imagine the combination of teaching, learning, and technology that was about to unfold at our school. Today, none of my students could possibly imagine just how different my class is from the way I taught physics just a few years back. Back then, everyone would come in, sit, and wait for me, as teacher, to do my job. They saw themselves as consumers of what I told them they needed to know. What's more, what I told them they needed to know was for me alone to determine.

Despite my best efforts, I inevitably had to make "one-size-fits-all decisions" about the content and level to aim at. Any attempt to individualize would soon devolve to the simpler state of one syllabus, teaching modality, because to do otherwise required a degree of organization and preparation that was not possible for me to organize. I did not have the time, the tools, or the expertise.

Now, the multileveled aspect of the curriculum and assessment, including my differentiated materials, assessment and classroom practice, allow me to meet each student where they are in both skills in doing science and in their ability to handle the content. The content informs the approach I use to differentiate the learning experience and vice versa. At the end of the module, each student produces a report focused on the same scientific principles. Their accounts of those principles and how they came to understand them vary according to the learning experience I differentiated for them.

The differentiation would not be possible without the use of information technology. First, there is the obvious procedural help it provides. For example, Group 1 students use spreadsheets with pre-established formulas. Groups 2 and 3 create their own. Graphing is no longer the task that takes up all of their time. Data become real and can be quickly gathered. Using motion detection software that provides students with data on their jump and spreadsheets, I can help students who do not have the math background to undertake such a sophisticated experiment.

Most important, I could not develop this overall curriculum and classroom game plan without the software. I use it to create the different levels, build lesson plans and the assessment products, and manage the class. It provides obvious practical support for the way I design and manage the learning experience, although it does much more. It provides a new map for my teaching that brings the content, the methods, the implementation, and evaluation together as a whole. It makes connections. The way I use it reflects the way I think about teaching and learning (Gorrill, 1999).

The juxtaposition of the Type-A and Type-B approaches is clear for Bruce. It is also uncontested in the world of research, especially for areas of evidence-based differentiated instruction (Gregory & Chapman, 2002; Mastropieri & Scruggs, 2009; Tomlinson, 2001). Unfortunately, for most teachers, the juxtaposition is not clear. Hence, Type-B practices are not present in their classrooms. Why is this case?

Over a 10-year period, thousands of teachers and administrators visited the school in which Bruce teaches. Hundreds of visitors observed Bruce in his classroom. Some even witnessed the big jump module. Bruce kept records of the questions they asked him. He found that their questions exposed the difficulty most visitors experienced when trying to understand Type-B. Classroom Example 2.4 presents a sampling of the questions visitors asked Bruce.

Classroom Example 2.4: Questions Visitors Asked

- Where do the differentiated curriculum materials come from? Who develops them?
- How is the curriculum organized?
- How do you manage a classroom where different groups of students are doing different things?
- When and where do teachers learn how to do this?
- How much more time will this take? For recordkeeping? Paperwork?
- How do you assess students who are doing different things at different levels?
- How does this type of teaching relate to high-stakes tests and everyone taking the same test?

The questions reveal a practice gap, as seen through the eyes of practicing educators, between an approach for educating some students and an approach for educating them all. These questions are a predictable reaction to something new and different. In this case, the teaching and learning departs substantially from their prior experience.

For decades, teachers have been bombarded with policies, professional development sessions, and rhetoric about inclusion and differentiation. All point to the possibility of what was observed in Bruce's class. Yet the puzzle pieces required to do what was witnessed there—meeting the 1:X challenge—were not resolved in a workable model of classroom practice that was scalable. So the questions they asked of Bruce reflect their desire to understand why and how his classroom worked.

Notably absent from the list are questions about *why* Bruce choses to teach in Type-B mode. This is because the questioners know that the 1:X challenge is valid. Every day in their classrooms and schools, they experience the consequences of the unresolved puzzle in their inability to address the differences in students' learning backgrounds and needs. They also know that taking on 1:X with a superficial and incomplete solution would open a Pandora's box of educational issues—things most teachers are not prepared or willing to handle.

What visitors do not know is that the behaviors they *see* in Bruce's classroom reflectes the *unseen* work he does prior to their visits. For instance, before the visitors arrive, he develops and acquires differentiated content, masters multiple teaching practices, and designs a process of assessing students. In fact, his work prior to class is greater than his work during class. So, when visitors triangulate what they see with what they know, things do not compute. For this reason, they ask questions about developing materials, managing classrooms, training teachers, and assessing students. The things that happens in Bruce's Type-B classroom are beyond their experience, capability, and knowledge.

SHIFTS CLASSROOMS MUST MAKE TO SUCCEED

Understanding how Bruce finds facilitating a more complex Type-B classroom less demanding than teaching in a Type-A classroom is to understand three foundational shifts that he and his colleagues made when their school changed from the Type-A to Type-B approach. One shift consists of bringing down the cognitive load associated with classroom teaching and learning. This involves teachers making less of more by adopting a more realistic and practical classroom approach for addressing the needs of all students. A second shift consists of reconceptualizing the "student role" in classrooms and the school. This is the difference between students waiting to consume Bruce's instruction and their making instruction happen through the dispersed control for learning. A third shift involve extending learning beyond the classroom to new locations so learning will happen more often and in more places. In the following account each shift is unpacked and the role of edge technology described.

Shift one: Bringing down the load. In Type-A classrooms, teaching involves multitasking; delivering content, managing processes and students, providing feedback, and organizing the use of space, technology, and time. This places a large cognitive load on teachers (Feldon, 2007; Sweller, 1988). Mix in the stress of knowing that no matter how well teachers prepare and plan only some students will learn at a mastery level, and the cognitive load becomes overwhelming. Bruce faces this challenge in his Type-A classroom; his construction of practice could not meet the demands he experiences. Paul demonstrates this challenge. His frustration is a symptom of Bruce's overload and inability to meet his needs.

Teachers deal with cognitive load by developing schema (Anderson, Spiro, & Montague, 1977), mental frameworks that they use to construct their practice. Schemas help teachers deal with the regularities and novel stimuli like interruptions and those unpredictable classroom behavior management challenges that arise in their teaching. For instance, underpinning Bruce's Type-B teaching is a research-based schema for differentiated teaching and learning. Day-to-day, he uses it to address the 1:X challenge. His comfort and confidence with the complexity of the Big Jump module comes from knowing that it can meet his students' needs.

For his Type-A teaching, Bruce has invented a schema to handle the challenges he faces. It includes extra-help sessions, unpacking lectures, and test retakes. It is much simpler than the one that now underpins his teaching, but does not include cooperative learning, differentiation, or 1:X. His simpler schema of one lesson plan, one teaching approach, and extra-help causes cognitive overload because it cannot address the challenges his students faces. This makes the Type-A approach more demanding for him.

It is not unusual in the Type-A approach for a teacher, like Bruce, to have his own schema. Ethnographic studies of schools (Goodlad, 1984; Lortie, 1975; McLaughlin & Talbert, 2001) show that most teachers autonomously construct their practice in ways that are largely uninformed by research in the field (Bain, 2007). Not surprisingly, they cannot meet the 1:X challenge.

A major reason why efforts to innovate, reform, and change classrooms has fail at scale is because those efforts push teachers to or beyond the limits of their individual schemas. The resulting cognitive overload diminishes their capacity to invoke complex responses (e.g., the differentiation of the learning experience) to classroom problems and increases the likelihood that they will rely on older and simpler knowledge (e.g., extra help and test retakes) to guide their teaching (Feldon, 2007). The overload contributes to high levels of stress and burnout among teachers.

Teachers involved in large-scale improvement efforts know this to be the case. Post-hoc analysis consistently identifies teacher overload as a point of breakdown (Berends, Bodilly, & Nataraj-Kirby, 2002; Franceschini, 2002; Schmoker, 2004). The questions asked (and not asked) of Bruce reveal that the questioners are aware of the cognitive demands associated with the changes made at his school. Their Type-A schemas cannot reconcile the demands that they speculate such changes must entail.

Before Bruce's school changed to Type-B, a potentially crippling case of cognitive overload occurs when Rupert is asked to lead a school-level working group charged with differentiating the curriculum. He is a promising head teacher at the school. He has a background in research-based pedagogy and a commitment to differentiation. Classroom Example 2.5 summarizes Rupert's comments to work-group members.

Classroom Example 2.5: Rupert Expresses Concern

This is an impossible task. I get what we are trying to do here and I believe in it. I just can't make it happen. When it comes down to a detailed linking of the big themes and standards of the curriculum at three different levels to the assessment of products and lesson designs, well, no one can do that. It is too much to think about all at once. I have dozens of word-processing files and piles of paper with half-finished unit designs. They seem to flow. But when I check them against the big ideas, none makes sense. Similarly, the half-written differentiated lessons go nowhere. For a month, I have spent every spare lesson, as well as time at home, and have nothing to show for my efforts. I have bits and pieces, but nothing that sticks together. There are three beginning teachers in my history department. There is no way they can do this, either.

Rupert's concerns are the same ones broadly reflected in the literature about inclusion. For instance, when asked about including students with diverse learning needs in regular classrooms, generalist teachers express concern about their capacity, level of professional development, and work overload (Avramidis & Norwich, 2002; Leatherman & Niemeyer, 2005; Scruggs & Mastropieri, 1996; Tait & Purdie, 2000). Like the visitors to Bruce's classroom, they lack a schema for differentiated practice. Taking up the 1:X challenge is beyond their capacity.

Rupert's reaction mirrors the frustration expressed by student Paul in Bruce's Type-A classroom. Paul reverts to an older and simpler approach by memorizing formulae and content from the textbook. Confronted with an equally daunting task, Rupert reverts to his autonomously constructed practice instead of the one he is charged with creating. Rupert, like Paul, lacks the prerequisite knowledge, time, and tools needed to master the challenge. Even if Rupert perseveres and somehow produces a module of differentiated curriculum, it will be neither generalizable to his less-experienced peers nor sustainable.

Facing such realities, it would be no surprise that Rupert and his work group push back on the task given them, and in so doing, label themselves as "resistors to change" (Berends, Bodilly, & Natarj-Kirby, 2002; Franceschini, 2002; Schmoker, 2004). For them, the task is unrealistic because it represents a clear case of cognitive overload. The Type-B approach to education, by providing new schemas for practice, reduces the load on teachers, thus making 1:X an attainable goal for all.

Shift two: Reconceptualizing the role of students. The field of education's preoccupation with teacher primacy in the way learning happens in classrooms is a big reason why teachers experience cognitive overload. A singular focus on teachers overlooks students—the X in the 1:X ratio—and the role students can play in their learning. It typecasts them as consumers of curriculum, instruction, and schooling. The result is a lose-lose situation where students become disaffected by the passivity of their school experience and teachers become overloaded by the relentless demands of being the 1 in the 1:X ratio.

This is no small problem. Worldwide, 30% of students report that they dislike school (NationMaster, 2010). Moreover, a survey of 134,000 American secondary school students found that two-thirds of them were bored with school (HSSSE, 2010). Such student disaffection stems from formulaic learning, meaningless homework, lack of opportunity for independent thought, and rote memorization (Willingham, 2009).

Madeline Elliot-Ingram put forth the idea of engaging students in their learning by teaching them about the teaching and learning process. She combined the advice from great teachers that "people learn by doing" with an admonition from great leaders to "delegate your duties" to construct a learning-by-teaching model (Elliot-Ingram, 1941). Subsequent research in the areas of self-management (Briesch & Chafouleas, 2009; Mooney, Ryan, Uhing, Reid, & Epstein, 2005), constructivist teaching (Pelech, 2010), cooperative learning (Slavin, 1991), and peer mediation (Fuchs, Fuchs, Mathes, & Simmons, 1997; Jenkins & Jenkins, 1985) supports her approach. The research makes clear that it is possible for students to assume the roles that are usually the sole responsibility of a teacher in the Type-A classroom.

Meet Eladio, a Spanish teacher at a Type-B school. He is unhappy with the way students in his class exchange information when working with their peers. Even when they do a good job of research and preparation, they make too many mistakes in their group work. Eladio solves the problem by sharing his knowledge of teaching with his students. By doing so, he shifts the classroom dynamic in their favor. Classroom Example 2.6 describes how the role changed for students.

Classroom Example 2.6: Eladio Disperses Control

The topic of the day is Spanish grammar concepts. Students are working in a combination of cooperative learning groups and peer tutoring pairs. In each group, one student is the student teacher. Each interaction follows the same pattern: The student-teacher models or demonstrates the concept and then leads a peer or group through a series of guided practice steps related to the conjugation of Spanish verbs. After each step, the student-teacher checks for understanding before moving on. The same thing occurs in every group and pair. The student-learners are attentive and engaged. Each one of these 10th-grade student-teachers knows how to deliver a complete mastery or explicit teaching lesson.

After about 25 minutes, the teacher stops the lesson and asks the students for their attention. He says, "I want some feedback on the teaching in your groups. What do you think of it?" The student learners begin to respond. One student says, "Pretty good—although the guided practice problem was harder than the example in the model." Another student says, "Great. I get it." Yet another says, "I need more independent practice problems" (Bain, 2007).

(*Authors' note*: The dispersed control approach was developed by Eladio Moreira at Brewster Academy.)

In Eladio's class, four student-teachers successfully deliver mastery-learning lessons to their peers. Such a feat is seldom accomplished by even the most competent teachers in the best Type-A classrooms (Antil, Jenkins, Wayne, & Vadasay, 1998). Moreover, when the student-teachers request feedback, the responses from their students indicates that they know as much about mastery learning as does Eladio (and student-teachers). This is possible because everyone shares an understanding of the pedagogy employed and has a professional language to use in discussing it.

The manner in which Eladio engages students goes further than Bruce's efforts, as described in the Big Jump example. Bruce and Eladio share a sophisticated Type-B schema for differentiated classroom practice. In Bruce's classroom, students participate in cooperative and mastery learning. In Eladio's class, the Type-B schema is even more sophisticated. Students actually used the approaches to teach others and to learn themselves. When Eladio shares control with his students, the other side of the 1:X ratio is activated. Learning no longer passes through the Type-A teaching process.

Eladio disperses control for learning and empowers his students with knowledge that, under traditional circumstances, is solely his domain. By sharing his Type-B schema with them, he no longer is singularly responsible for the activity of teaching. He can be confident about the quality of learning and teaching that occurs, even when he is not directly involved.

Shift three: Changing learning spaces and places. In Type-A education, teacher primacy drives where learning happens (e.g., classrooms) and the conditions (e.g., between the bells) under which it occurs. This Type-A way of doing things ignores a longstanding body of work that shows variability in the time it takes different students to learn the same things (Carroll, 1963; Gettinger, 1984). It also ignores the fact that focusing on the teacher (and where the teacher works) leads to centralized, high-pressure, one-size-fits-all classrooms where time to learn is a constant, not a variable. In them, homework is the safety valve for teachers. That is why, as students progress through Type-A schooling, homework becomes an increasingly important space and place for them to learn. Unfortunately, the spaces at home where such learning work is supposed to occur are too often problematic because they replicate the independent seatwork undertaken in classrooms. All too often students are faced with the challenge of completing homework tasks they do not fully understand in situations where they are unsupported.

Meet Phil, an American literature teacher at a Type-B school. Even though Phil teaches in a Type-B classroom, has a differentiated curriculum, and shares a schema with other teachers, he is challenged by the issues of time, mastery, cognitive style, and homework. Classroom Example 2.7 presents highlights from Phil's classroom.

Classroom Example 2.7: Phil Changes Direction

Students in Phil's class are engaged in a passionate discussion. Phil says, "Jane, please comment on John's critique of the poem." Jane says, "I'm unsure about the poem and John's critique." Moving on, Phil asks John the same question. Never lacking an opinion, John launches into a confident response that makes it clear he has not read the poem carefully nor has he completed the homework assigned for the previous night. Phil continues, ultimately finding a student who is able to provide a constructive response. When Phil reflects on his classroom exchanges, he is concerned about Jane's lack of preparedness to participate in class discussion and John's willingness to share how little he is doing. Jane's written work is outstanding, although Phil notices that she needs time to reflect and process before she will commit anything to a class discussion. He wants the class to benefit from Jane's insights and for Jane to get feedback from her peers. John is not getting it done in class or at home.

(Authors' note: The online discussion tool was developed by Phil Huss at Brewster Academy.)

The example shows that Jane's reflective cognitive style and her discomfort participating in group discussion makes it difficult for her to engage in class. She uses time away from school to reflect and construct her views. A self-starter, she excels with Type-A homework. It affords her the time she needs to develop her views in the safety of her own time and space. Despite her apparent success with homework, Jane misses the benefits of cooperative and collaborative learning and the cognitive elaboration that can only occur through an exchange of ideas with other students in a discussion format.

In contrast, for John, Phil's classroom is an excellent venue for his extroversion, while the extension of class time through homework fails him. It magnifies and exacerbates his problem with following through on his responsibilities in class (Polloway, Epstein, & Foley, 1992), especially without direct teacher management (Warrington & Younger, 1999).

Some teachers might respond to Jane and John by using an online student learning environment in which they can work. In it, Jane is safe and John has less distraction and more structure. Remarkable technologies are available for easily creating such environments. The technologies are visible in virtual schools, social networking sites, collaborative software, and next-generation tutoring systems (Deubel, 2009; Klopfer, Osterweil, Groff, & Haas, 2009).

Although online learning environments are heralded as a game-changing alternative (Christenson, Horn, & Johnson, 2008), research shows that they deliver results similar to those produced in typical Type-A classrooms (Smith, Clark, & Blomeyer, 2005). Prior ability, time management, confidence, self-esteem, and locus of control determine online success (Ferdig, Di Pietro, & Papanastasiou, 2005). These factors represent many of the same characteristics that are necessary for students to succeed in traditional homework environments. So, while Jane is more comfortable in an online learning environment, it is unclear how it would address her discomfort with large-group participation. Likewise, while John can be timed out from social situations through an online approach, doing so will not address his need to work more successfully with others. Questions about the suitability of online learning for Jane and John, surface significant issues about whether the cooperative, collaborative, and broader social dimensions of learning are satisfactorily addressed in online learning environments (Toch, 2010).

By way of contrast, research shows that students are more engaged by instructional methods that involve learning and working with peers and less engaged when they passively participate in their learning (HSSSE, 2010). Moreover, students can work successfully with peers outside of the classroom (O'Melia & Rosenberg, 1994). Studies of peer-assisted learning—including using students with special needs as tutors—suggest that students are capable of much higher levels of engagement in their learning (Greenwood, Maheady, & Delquardi, 2002). Such studies make clear that students of all abilities, when working with peers, can follow guides for implementing research-based practice.

Phil recognizes the need for a strategy that reconciles, rather than replaces, work undertaken in and out of the classroom and that specifically helps Jane and John. He is passionate about the Socratic method that he uses in his American literature class. Since it was the way he had been taught, he knows the method requires students to come to class prepared and willing to share in a large group. Also, he is aware of the research that shows the power of student cooperation (Greenwood, Maheady, & Delquardi, 2002; O'Melia & Rosenberg, 1994) and the ways it can address the difficulties that Jane and John experience.

In response, Phil develops an online discussion tool (Bain, Huss, & Kwong, 2000) that extends students' class discussions into their homework environment and sustains the quality interaction that has started in class (see Figure 2.8). With it, Jane can engage collaboratively in a way that accommodates her reflective style, and John can have disciplined and substantive engagement with his peers. Rather than creating an alternative to his Socratic classroom, Phil leverages the learning that occurs there beyond the time he spends with students.

HOW MAKING SHIFTS WORKS IN REAL CLASSROOMS

Bruce's module, Eladio's cooperative teaching, and Phil's online tool exemplify the self-organizing behaviors of individual teachers at the Type-B school. Their collective efforts afford insight into the way that self-similar schema and practice can reduce teachers' cognitive load. Also, their efforts show how the 1:X ratio is altered by (a) students assuming an expanded role, (b) extending classroom learning, and (c) not defining classrooms solely by physical location and predetermined schedules. The students' success in their new roles and learning places comes from the schema they share with their teachers. *Edge* technology makes the pedagogical intentions of the innovations possible. The *edge* technology that underpins the changes described above is unpacked below.

TOOLS THAT BRING EFFECTIVE ICT INTO CLASSROOMS

The tools described in this section are part of the A to B Toolkit. They exemplify how *edge* technology translates a schema from an abstract cognitive construct into a suite of practical tools for differentiating classroom practice. They disperse control for learning, elaborate and strengthen the connections between students and teachers, and deepen everyone's understanding of Type-B learning.

The A to B Toolkit contains several tools, one of which is the *Edge* Plan Book. At Bruce's school, there are teacher and student versions of the Plan Book. Each articulates the schema that everyone there shares. Embedded in them are the research-based practices to which the school is committed. Teachers use the Plan Book's components to frame curriculum and design lessons that they deliver in and beyond their classrooms. Students use their Plan Books to expand their roles and extend their learning. Figure 2.1 depicts the cover page of the Teacher Plan Book.

Bruce and Eladio use components of the Teacher Plan Book in their teaching. Figure 2.2 depicts the curriculum-framing component they use to connect content, units, lessons, and assessments to form a module. Bruce plans the Big Jump

Figure 2.1. Cover Page of the Teacher Plan Book

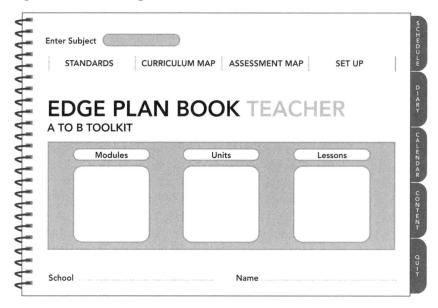

Figure 2.2. The Curriculum-Framing Component

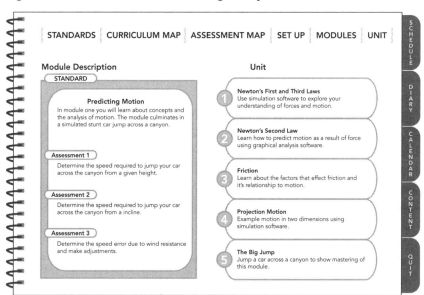

module with it. On the left side are elements of the module (e.g., differentiated assessment items). On the right side are the module's five units. By clicking on a unit name, Bruce can drill down to a detailed description of any of the units and get an overview of the lessons they include. In this way, the framing component manages the connections and considerations that comprise his practice. By doing so, it brings down the cognitive load he faces when doing 1:X work.

Eladio uses the lesson-planning component of the Teacher Plan Book (see Figure 2.3) to develop the cooperative teaching approach he uses to disperse control to students. He also uses the component to develop the outcomes that his students will master through their peer teaching. The lesson-planning component guides and prompts him through the development of the differentiated lessons that reflect his curricular goals. Figure 2.3 depicts the component.

The Teacher Plan Book includes a component for teachers in inclusive settings (e.g., students with differing abilities and capacities). It helpes them manage the group work of students. Figure 2.4 depicts the component. Eladio uses it to clarify the work his students do in the lesson sequence described earlier. With it, he keeps track of the time students spend in groups, identifies when and how he interact with them, and manages the materials they use.

Figure 2.3. Cooperative Learning

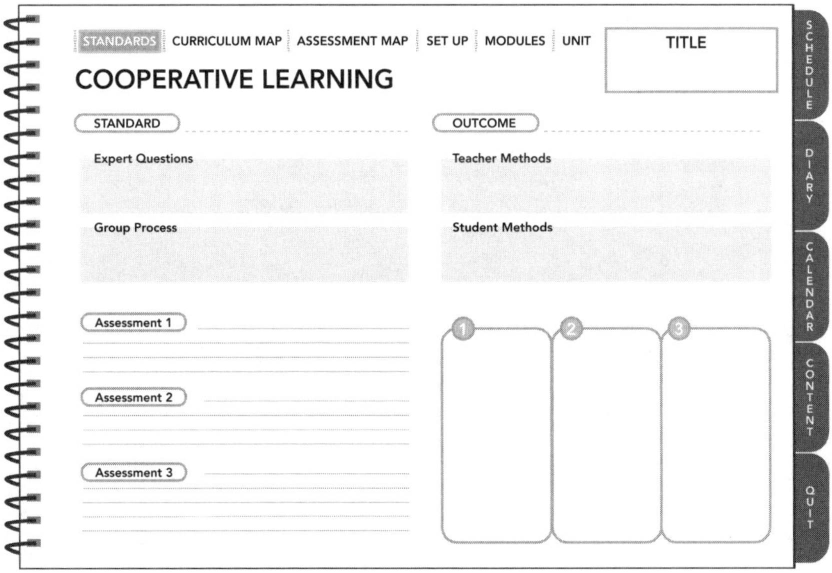

Figure 2.4. Rotations

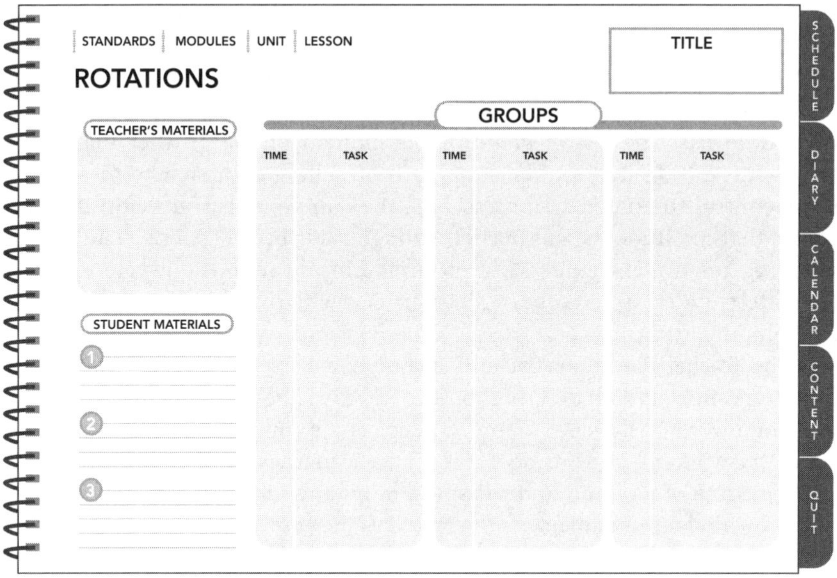

STANDARDS | MODULES | UNIT | LESSON   TITLE

ROTATIONS

TEACHER'S MATERIALS   GROUPS

TIME   TASK   TIME   TASK   TIME   TASK

STUDENT MATERIALS

①
②
③

SCHEDULE | DIARY | CALENDAR | CONTENT | QUIT

Figure 2.5. Lesson Builder

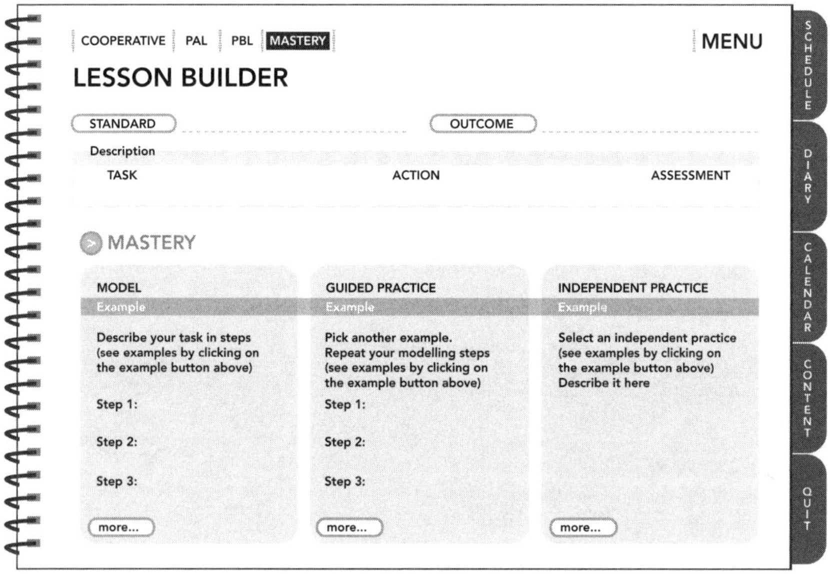

COOPERATIVE | PAL | PBL | **MASTERY**   MENU

LESSON BUILDER

STANDARD   OUTCOME

Description

TASK   ACTION   ASSESSMENT

◉ MASTERY

MODEL	GUIDED PRACTICE	INDEPENDENT PRACTICE
Example	Example	Example
Describe your task in steps (see examples by clicking on the example button above)	Pick another example. Repeat your modelling steps (see examples by clicking on the example button above)	Select an independent practice (see examples by clicking on the example button above) Describe it here
Step 1:	Step 1:	
Step 2:	Step 2:	
Step 3:	Step 3:	
more...	more...	more...

SCHEDULE | DIARY | CALENDAR | CONTENT | QUIT

Figure 2.5 depicts the lesson layout component of the Teacher Plan Book. It contains a curriculum standard, lesson outcome, and brief description of the lesson (e.g., task, action, assessment). A teacher, after developing a basic plan, can select an instructional approach to use. At the top of the layout are icons for four approaches: PBL (Problem-Based Learning), MT (Mastery Teaching), CL (Cooperative Learning), and PAL (Peer-Assisted Learning). Extensive research shows that each approach has powerful learning effects when used in classrooms (Hattie, 2009).

When a teacher clicks on one of the four icons, a builder is loaded that sets up the lesson for that particular approach and draws the content from the basic plan into the setup. After this, the teacher interacts with a series of prompts to transform a basic lesson into a research-based one. For example, a teacher who wants to use the mastery approach would click on the mastery icon. The lesson would then be formatted accordingly. The teacher would be shown how instructional tasks could be broken into steps—modeling, guided, and independent practice steps— features of which have been shown to exert significant effects on student learning.

Teachers using the lesson component can turn a basic lesson into a specific approach (e.g., cooperative learning). Doing so, they will learn about that practice. Every mouse click reiterates and reinforces their individual and collective knowledge of that practice, increases the likelihood that they and their colleagues will use it proficiently, and makes less of more in classrooms.

Bruce, Eladio, and Phil use their Plan Books to put their schema into practice. Their individual and collective capacity (e.g., knowledge and skills) for facilitating Type-B classrooms grows from its use. In this way, Plan Book use is analogous to well-constructed professional development. Key concepts and ideas are built into its design and created opportunities for Bruce, Eladio, and Phil to practice 1:X. Also, it creates an educational context for leveraging other technologies (e.g., Websites, simulations, and productivity tools). The A to B Toolkit and its Plan Book components are the answer to the questions the visitors asked Bruce. They constitute the unseen part of the classroom and serve as a vehicle for reducing Bruce and his colleagues' cognitive loads by providing cognitive tools to design, implement and evaluate differentiated classroom teaching and learning.

Research about the effect of the Teacher Plan Book was conducted over a 3-year period. It included 578 50-minute observations of high- and low-level users in classrooms (Bain & Parkes, 2006). The research found that teachers who had the Plan Book used evidence-based practices at high and unprecedented levels relative to the broader literature on secondary school reform and in comparison to low- or non-using peers. The effect size of .83 is based on a comparison of the overall scores of the high- and low-use groups. It indicates a profound influence on the actual practice of teachers (Bain, 2007). Additional research reveals that the Plan Book enabled less experienced teachers to function as successfully as their more experienced peers. Further, its high-level users were better at implementing the school's schema and design, more rapidly progressed in its career path, and received higher ratings from students (Bain, 2007). These findings echo Bruce's remarks about edge technology "making better teaching and learning possible."

The examples of Bruce and Eladio's use of the Plan Book makes it obvious that such cognitive tools serve teachers who are pursuing better student learning and 1:X well. Less obvious, but equally important, is the need for cognitive tools that serve students who play the teacher role in Type-B classrooms. Tools shared by teachers and students make sense. They enable both to partner in the process of teaching and learning, and by doing so, further reduce the cognitive load of both. Classroom Example 2.8 illustrates how this plays out for Jane.

Classroom Example 2.8: Jane Teaches Class

The topic of the day is *Romeo and Juliet.* Jane is responsible for teaching her group the first act of the play. Last night, Jane used the curriculum development tool of the Student Plan Book to develop the peer-teaching lesson she will deliver today. She did this by clicking on the resources icon that brought up a page where she can access and review a PowerPoint presentation. She inserted a link to a video sequence that she wanted to use to illustrate the way the characters of the play were developed by Shakespeare. Teacher Phil had approved the attachment and assigned Jane editing privileges. Jane rehearses the tutoring and tutee tasks that she plans to use. She also develops a question that she will ask students to discuss as homework. Students would go online in the evening after Jane teaches the lesson. There, Jane will engage in a real-time discussion of the scene using the question she developed. Jane will monitor the discussion as part of her teaching responsibility.

Jane's preparation for her teaching assignment is the embodiment of the adage that "the best way to learn is to teach." As Jane looks at the lesson plan, goes over the teaching steps, and reviews the homework question, she builds the deep knowledge required to "know" and "do" *Romeo and Juliet*. Moreover, as she learns about the play, she learned about learning. As she does, she gradually overcomes her shyness about class participation.

The Student Plan Book makes all the difference in that regard. Jane uses its components to access curriculum, attach resources, review curriculum goals (e.g., module expectations, lesson outcomes), and make specific transactions required for delivering the lesson. Jane gains the confidence needed to play a more active classroom role from the opportunity to review, plan, and prepare at home in a way that accommodated her reflective style. Phil enables her growth by dispersing control for learning to her via her Plan Book and by acting as a mentor, providing feedback about her teaching.

Figure 2.6 depicts the Student Lesson Planner that Jane uses. It shows her what to do to build her lesson and describes what tutors and tutees will do in it. She attaches digital resources to the lesson by clicking on the resources icon. The teacher input field is where Phil provides feedback to her and where she asks him questions that are automatically forwarded to him for a rapid response.

If asked, Jane will report that she is still more comfortable mediating her homework online than teaching in class. She has, however, come a long way as a teacher and is a better learner as a result. Similarly, John will report that he is more focused and involved in his learning; the responsibility he has to other students has served his learning style well. Figure 2.7 depicts linkages between the lessons in the Student Plan Book and student performance on the related assessment tasks.

John uses the feedback component of his Plan Book to get immediate feedback, thus staying focused on his lessons. Using the layout presented in Figure 2.7, John looks at his performance. Selecting a week and a subject, he views his performance on the assessment items for that period. The score list described in the field on the right of the layout identifies where he has been successful and unsuccessful. By clicking on the outcome associated with each score, he locates the part of the lesson where the outcome had been taught. He can also begin by looking at the lessons in the scrolling list view described in the field on the left side of the layout. Clicking on a lesson in the list view takes John to the full lesson plan. This

Figure 2.6. Student Lesson Planner

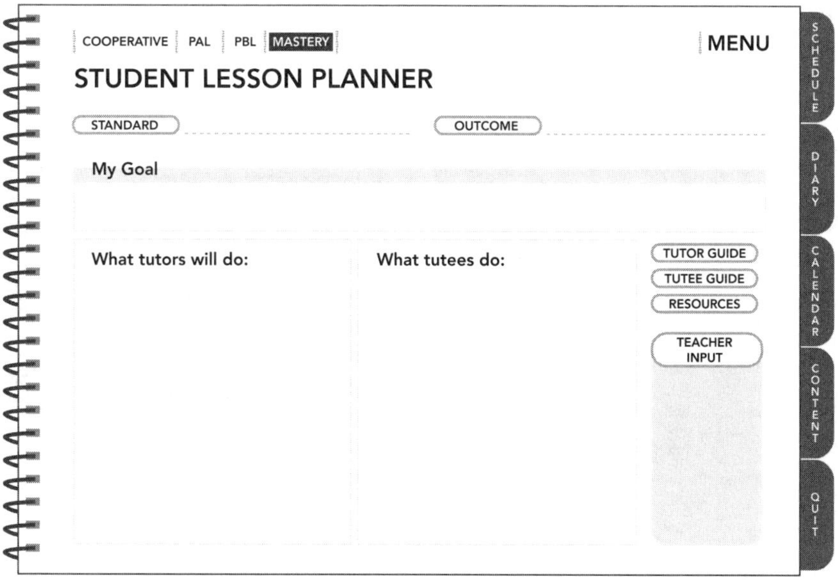

Figure 2.7. Student Plan Book and Student Performance

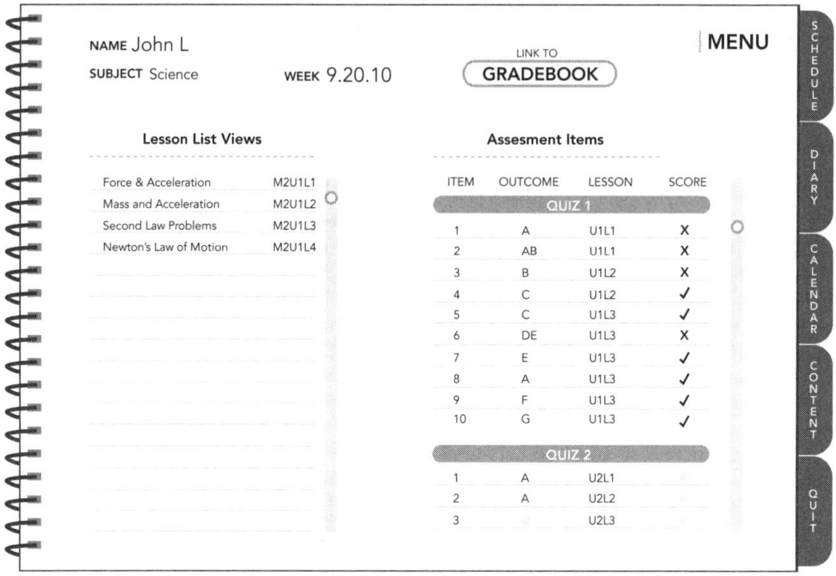

NAME John L		LINK TO	MENU
SUBJECT Science	WEEK 9.20.10	GRADEBOOK	

Lesson List Views

Force & Acceleration	M2U1L1
Mass and Acceleration	M2U1L2
Second Law Problems	M2U1L3
Newton's Law of Motion	M2U1L4

Assesment Items

ITEM	OUTCOME	LESSON	SCORE
QUIZ 1			
1	A	U1L1	X
2	AB	U1L1	X
3	B	U1L1	X
4	C	U1L2	✓
5	C	U1L3	✓
6	DE	U1L3	X
7	E	U1L3	✓
8	A	U1L3	✓
9	F	U1L3	✓
10	G	U1L3	✓
QUIZ 2			
1	A	U2L1	
2	A	U2L2	
3		U2L3	

Tabs: SCHEDULE, DIARY, CALENDAR, CONTENT, QUIT

Figure 2.8. Discussion Component for Collaborative Learning

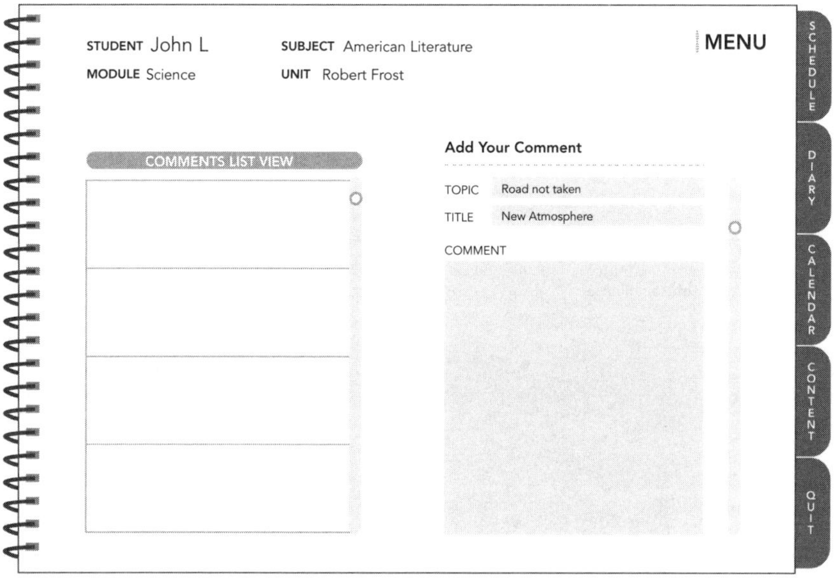

STUDENT John L	SUBJECT American Literature	MENU
MODULE Science	UNIT Robert Frost	

COMMENTS LIST VIEW

Add Your Comment

TOPIC   Road not taken

TITLE   New Atmosphere

COMMENT

Tabs: SCHEDULE, DIARY, CALENDAR, CONTENT, QUIT

reduces his frustration as he interrogates the feedback about his efforts on any lesson. More important, he quickly accesses the information he needs to relearn what he has misunderstood.

Providing students with new roles, skills, and tools is a key part of the Type-B classroom. It is how teachers share the load with student-teachers. The schema, which is embedded in each, serves as a platform for teaching that reflects their collaborative responsibility for learning.

Figure 2.8 depicts a discussion component developed by Phil that enables collaborative responsibility for learning. The discussion component promotes mastery teaching by extending the cooperative discussions held in class, thus replacing traditional homework. In this example, students are required to post their analyses of the literature discussed in class, then respond to the posts of other students using a cooperative learning scaffold that was embedded in the component's design. On some occasions, Phil monitors their exchanges in real time. Most often, students manage them.

Not surprisingly, Phil finds that students spend more time on work at home, participate more universally, comment more frequently about peers' work, and improves their mastery of key curricular concepts (Bain, Huss & Kwong, 2000). Most important, students create a learning network where their unique contributions and feedback make it possible for other students to learn successfully. In this way, the component breaks down the barriers between school and home. It creates a continuous learning experience that transcends the Type-A distinction of work done in both contexts by creating a seamless connection between home and school. It creates self-similar connections through which feedback can operate freely in service to students without direct teacher mediation. Again, as students teach their peers, they move to the left side of the 1:X ratio.

In the online discussion example, *edge* technology extends the use of well-researched classroom pedagogy. Its use is framed by cooperative learning practices shown to improve achievement and is subjected to research to determine its effect. Both are applied to the design of the component. "Actual" migrated to "virtual" as Type-B classroom teaching is extended into non-school contexts where "actual" has not previously been possible. The interaction of the three shifts and *edge* technology are exemplified in Classroom Example 2.9.

Classroom Example 2.9: Bruce Assigns the Graduation Project

Your task is to use the problem-based and cooperative learning components of your Student Plan Book to design an end-of-module project that captures the key content and skills in the Predicting Motion (i.e., Big Jump) module. You will work as teams to create an amusement park ride that tests the laws of projectile motion. You must incorporate the principles of cooperative and problem-based learning. Your module must be designed using your Plan Book, cover the key learning outcomes in the previous module, and include a practical demonstration of a model of the ride. Additionally, it must involve formal collaborative work conducted inside and outside of class that shows you using cooperative and mastery teaching and learning as part of your module's design.

There are four elements in this example. First, senior-level students are asked to design a curriculum module that disperses control for learning. In it, they are required to bring together what they know about the content and process of teaching and learning to create a Type-B learning experience for other students. Second, they demonstrate a working knowledge of subject content, pedagogy, management, evaluation, and edge technology tools. Third, they do work beyond the classroom—perhaps at home, a library, a coffee shop, skate park, or stadium—using a netbook, iPad, phone, laptop computer, and/or other device. Fourth, the edge tools make it possible for them to take Type-B learning wherever they go. The project is a logical extension of students being in a dispersed control environment—enabled by edge technology—where they shape and inform their own learning experiences rather than being in an environment in which their experiences are determined by others.

USING ICT TO TRANSFORM A TYPE-A CLASSROOM TO A TYPE-B CLASSROOM

The above examples show how edge technology helps develop and extend the capacities of students and shortens the cognitive distance between them and their learning. Specific tools help Bruce, Eladio, and Phil to extend the places where learning occurs and shorten the distance between them and their students. The A to B Toolkit that they use generates opportunities for making the cognitive connections that bring teachers and students together and extend their learning beyond classrooms and generate powerful emergent feedback that enables students and teachers to work together. These are the key and most critical features of edge technology.

One way to conceptualize the effects of edge technology and the shifts it enables is to consider how they influence the learning networks that occur in Type-A and Type-B classrooms. Figure 2.9 portrays how the networks are altered by edge technology.

The figure presents four configurations. In one, the Type-A network is hierarchical and centralized, reflecting the command and control structure of the Type-A classroom. Learning is predominantly teacher-mediated, with students working individually. This is the traditional homework scenario. In another, the

Figure 2.9. Type-A Transformed into Type-B Classrooms by Edge Technology

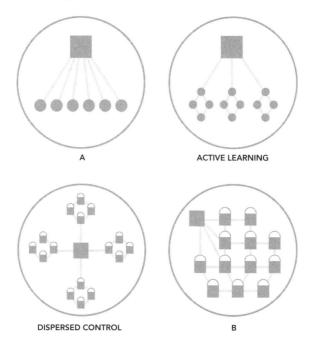

active learning network configuration retains the teacher-centric centralized structure. However, students work in cooperative and peer-assisted groups. They help each other learn with minimal teacher mediation. In the dispersed control and B scenarios the symbols show a blending of the roles of reacher and students. In the third, the dispersed control configuration reflects the "Jane as Spanish teacher scenario" previously described. In it, the teacher empowers students with the skills to teach. The teacher is positioned at the center, although the overall structure is "decentralized" (Baran, 2002). The fourth configuration is the Type-B learning paradigm. It depicts what happens when edge technology produces efficient feedback so students using their new teaching skills in emergent ways to self-organize their learning without teacher direction. The graduation project for Bruce's course epitomized this approach.

The expectation in the Type-B network is that the teacher is not disintermediated and that all learning is not self-organizing. Rather, students act collectively and cooperatively to build learning groups, complete curriculum tasks, or prepare forthcoming assessments. Removal of the boundary suggests that such learning can happen anywhere, but the result is not a product of technological determinism in the guise of "anytime anywhere" learning (Rockman, 1997); rather, it is about using technology to make cognitive connections and shorten the learning distance.

In the Type-A paradigm, the edge or connection between teacher and learners, as depicted in Figure 2.1, is long, tenuous, and classroom-centric, as seen in Bruce's Type-A experience. One-size-fits-all, homogenized teaching and curriculum forces him and his fellow teachers to operate from a cognitive distance under high cognitive load. Unable to break away from the group and respond to their undifferentiated learning circumstances, students rarely make the connections necessary for personal learning to happen. In the Type-A paradigm, ICT use does not shorten this distance. It just automates what already happens.

EXAMINING THE ASSUMPTIONS AND CHALLENGES OF TYPE-A AND TYPE-B CLASSROOMS

Let us now revisit the three-step schema-development framework presented in Chapter 1. It is used here as a lens for examining this chapter's key propositions.

New Assumptions

In contrast to the Type-A practices that are typically used in most classrooms, the Type-B approach has different drivers for change, commitments for resolving those drivers, and pathways to measurable results. Its assumptions about ICT are consistent with the five laid out in Chapter 1.

Assumption one: Since Type-B education places additional and complex demands on teachers and students, Type-B is only achievable via edge technology. Several examples of edge technology fostering Type-B learning and solution building for 1:X are presented in this chapter. The examples show Bruce, Eladio, and Phil using the tools for designing curriculum, planning lessons, and differentiating instruction to enact their more complex schemas for teaching and learning. The examples also show edge technology bringing users together, dispersing responsibility for the learning across them, and enabling and extending the places where learning happened.

Assumption two: Research on teaching and learning defines the role for edge technology. The reconceptualized roles and learning environments were defined by the research on teaching and learning and then embedded into tools. Research about the Plan Book components of the A to B Toolkit supports the idea that teachers and students learn more effectively through ICT than learning about or even with it (Bain, Huss, & Kwong, 2000).

Assumption three: Learning through edge technology and learning about edge technology are indistinguishable when ICT is in its proper place addressing the 1:X challenge in classrooms. In the examples, students learn more and teachers teach better when using edge technology (Bain & Parkes, 2006). Teachers used tools that include research-based characteristics of cooperative or mastery learning to build new capacity, which can be communicated to other teachers and to students, thus building the overall capacity of the community. Although ICT is critical to the vision described in this chapter, it is a means, not an end. Learning and teaching experiences are not determined by edge technology; rather, they result from research-based practices being leveraged into new roles through it.

Assumption four: In Type-B classrooms, access to edge technology is a simple yet fundamental requirement for dispersing control and generating the feedback needed for getting things done. Edge technology reaffirms that teachers and students are the core in any solution to the 1:X challenge. Examples of dispersal of control include the student lesson planning tool (see Figure 2.6) that enables students to learn about the teaching process as they design and develop their own lessons. That tool extends classroom learning to non-classroom settings. Rather than driving a wedge between actual and virtual learning, it creates a self-similar continuum for learning that addresses the educational, social, motivational, and achievement-related goals (e.g., higher scores on standardized tests) of the Type-B approach. The examples show this to be possible because teachers and students share the same tools. Those tools support all-the-time feedback. This, in turn, makes self-organizing behaviors commonplace. It is unlikely that the goals will be met in a technologically determined online environment.

Assumption five: Improved education through edge technology improves student achievement. In the examples, edge technology serves as a mediating context for leveraging specific, well-researched practices in ways that improved teaching and learning. The improvements result in achievement gains (Bain & Parkes, 2006).

New Design

In this step, Bruce and colleagues turn assumptions into practice by designing and building applications, processes, and related products that enable their Type-B approach. Their efforts lead to three shifts in thought and practice through which studentship was reconceptualized, cognitive loads brought down, and new spaces and places created. The shifts serve as a broad *solution map* from which goals are established, pedagogies are identified, and potential difficulties with both are acknowledged. The map enables the *component building* through which specific pedagogical practices are *integrated* into specific cognitive tools and classroom practices. As they do they identify new commitments are related to redefined roles for teachers and students, the role of research and the centrality of ICT to differentiate content, teaching, management, and performance feedback.

The *e*dge technology described throughout the chapter shows the way in which commitments to practice (e.g., mastery and cooperative teaching and learning) define the technology. They serve as guides for designing the tools. The tools are then integrated into a shared schema for differentiated teaching and learning, providing an augmentative information-processing system that builds user capacity and deal with the cognitive load associated with differentiation.

New Trajectory

The assumptions and designs that enable teachers and students to establish the Type-B approach within and across classrooms at Bruce's school will, in subsequent chapters, be extended to all levels of an educational system. As it is, the questions of scale and ways for Type-B to gain further acceptance are taken up. The level-specific answers to both questions will show that *e*dge technology enables the requisite self-organizing and emergent behaviors for building capacity and defining roles.

SUMMARY

- The research and practice pieces needed to solve the puzzle for improving education have yet to be snapped into place to form a scalable and practical solution for the 1:X challenge.
- A primacy on teaching places a huge cognitive load on teachers, limits learning to classrooms, under challenges students, and consigns ICT to the role of automating existing practice.
- The Type-B approach uses *e*dge technology to connect the puzzle pieces in ways that make 1:X attainable for classroom teachers. It brings down their cognitive load by replacing their autonomously constructed schemas with a shared schema, reconceptualizing the role of students in dispersed ways, and extending learning beyond classrooms.
- Each change enabled by *e*dge technology is an expression of the schema that teachers and students share. When they use edge tools, they come together, build and distribute capacity, and extend teaching and learning.
- When this happens, the possibility of all students learning at higher levels in classroom settings can be realized.

CHAPTER 3

Schools

None of us is as smart as all of us.
—Ken Blanchard

*E*dge technology is instrumental in addressing the 1:X challenge at the school level. We show this by (a) using school-level examples to describe the challenge of creating a Type-B school, (b) discussing three shifts in the design of a school that are necessary for meeting that challenge, (c) describing the critical role of *e*dge technology in making those shifts happen, and (d) describing the form and function of a school that adopts those shifts.

EFFECTIVE ICT IN SCHOOLS: DEFINING THE PROBLEM

One of the most alarming research findings about education is the limited effect that schools have on student achievement (Hattie, 2009; Rowe, 2003). Since the research shows that good teaching effects achievement (Hattie, 2009), it seems logical that the activity of schools, by nurturing good teaching in classrooms, should produce a cumulative school-level effect size. The reality is quite the opposite. Schools contribute less than 10% of the variance in overall student achievement (Hattie, 2003, 2009; Rowe, 2003; Scheerens & Creemers, 1989). Regardless of the way they are managed, expend resources, configure classes, or establish student-to-teacher ratios, schools exert a limited learning effect overall and when compared to the more powerful effects attributed to the approaches used by individual teachers in their classrooms (Hattie, 2009).

Moreover, school leaders spend a disproportionate amount of their time pursuing low-power school-level solutions and reacting to day-to-day problems rather than providing leadership of the way teaching and learning happens in the school (Portin, Knapp, Alejano, & Marzolf, 2006). The resulting (and longstanding) failure of schools to effectively scale up good teaching is one more example of the "elephant in the room" described previously. Schools experience great difficulty building the shared cultures of practice necessary to become genuine professional learning communities.

THE PROBLEM WITH
TYPE-A SCHOOLS

The challenge of scaling learning effects beyond classrooms is illustrated in School Example 3.1, which summarizes the case of a department at a Type-A school facing a teaching and learning problem. The school has participated in the Trends in International Performance Study (TIPS-R) for 5 years. TIPS-R is used to benchmark the district's performance against international standards. This year, the school—a showcase for the district—performs poorly in the science section, with particular weaknesses in reasoning and problem-solving. Sarah, the school principal, reviews the findings and shares them with Bruce, the science department head. Sarah asks him to produce a plan to address the problem, making it an item on the agenda for the next science department meeting.

Prior to the meeting, Fred, a biology teacher with 10 years' experience, analyzes the test data using the school's student information system (SIS). He produces a report showing performance on TIPS-R is weakest for students with attendance, behavioral, and homework completion issues. Bruce asks department members to review the test results and Fred's analysis. Let us look in on the department as it considers the problem.

School Example 3.1: Science Department Meets

Bruce says, "Let's brainstorm some solutions." Anne, the 8th-grade integrated science teacher responds, "It would be a lot easier if science classes were tracked according to ability. Then I could work through the curriculum at a faster pace." Fred, who recently completed a workshop on peer tutoring, offers, "A department-wide peer-tutoring program would improve achievement." Chemistry teacher Ian says, "An extra-help club is needed. We could staff it with members of the department." Bruce recommends having weekly test-taking strategy and review sessions during the month prior to the test.

Before the meeting, Bruce had looked closely at the areas of poor performance on the TIPS-R and found that the text did not address the area of scientific problem-solving in a manner that was consistent and compatible with the TIPS-R questions. So, he suggests that the department may need to look at the texts and evaluate whether a change is needed.

When members of the department evaluate the outcomes of the brainstorming session, they decide to take up all of the suggestions except those offered by Anne and Fred. The group is reluctant to commit to Fred's peer-tutoring approach because they know little about this teaching method.

They agree that although Anne's tracking suggestion is a good idea, it would change the way the school and schedule was organized, so it was beyond the control of the department. They agree to pass her suggestion back to Principal Sarah with a recommendation for action.

Let us focus on five things that happen prior to or during the meeting. First, feedback about TIPS-R performance is top-down. A report arrives months after the students take the test. It is sent to Sarah, who forwards it to Bruce, who then engages department members. Moreover, the school's problem is defined and determined externally rather than from deep knowledge about what was going on within its classrooms. As a result, teacher ownership of the findings is low. They have moved on in the curriculum and so had their students.

Feedback is most effective when it is part of a timely exchange by persons engaged in the context from which the feedback emerged (Brinko, 1993). After such a large lapse of time, the TIPS-R results would have had to be tediously interpreted if they were to have any meaning for teachers and students. Research shows that delaying the reporting of results decontextualizes the feedback (Scheeler, Ruhl, & McAfee, 2004), thus making it challenging for the teachers to respond in timely and effective ways. For the department members, such delayed feedback on performance in the curriculum extends, not shortens, the cognitive distance between them and their students, because both students and teachers are now focusing on different curriculum goals and new teaching and learning experiences.

Second, students are not involved in the feedback processes related to the TIPS-R results. They are mere data-points, which reflect their limited role as consumers. Ironically, if more control for learning had been dispersed to the students, they could have contributed insight about the problem and participated in its resolution.

Third, research about the effectiveness of peer tutoring (Fuchs, Fuchs, Mathes, & Simmons, 1997; Kamps et al., 2008) indicates that Fred's suggestion is a potentially powerful pedagogical solution. However, his idea is not adopted because his colleagues do not know about peer tutoring. They are not negative about the idea; they just cannot act on it because they lack a shared research-informed understanding of the approach. Fred's attendance at a peer-tutoring workshop and subsequent interest in the approach are disconnected from the experiences of his peers.

Fourth, the suggestions that are adopted by the department do not reflect contemporary research and are unlikely to solve the problem because they have low educational power to influence student learning. A case in point is Anne's suggestion about grouping. Although it is intuitively appealing, research shows that tracking has little effect on student achievement (Hattie, 2009) and is inequitable for students (Oakes, 2005). Unfortunately, Anne and the other department members do not know the research. Even if they did, that knowledge is unlikely to be privileged in the autonomous construction of their teaching practice.

The department embraces extra-help and test preparation as their preferred remedies for TIPS-R, even though research shows that these time-honored approaches exert an even smaller effect on student achievement (Bangert, Kulik, & Kulik, 1983; Hausknecht, Halpert, Di Paulo, & Gerrard, 2007) than the other ones the department considers. These are the same approaches Bruce employs with reservation in his Type-A physics class. Now they are being considered for scaling across his entire department. Their implementation will generate more work for less return, perpetuate the role of student as consumer, and add to the cognitive and logistical load of teachers by forcing them to invest time and energy in practices that would not improve student learning.

Fifth, ICT figures in the resolution of the problem in limited ways. Fred uses the SIS to generate information about those students experiencing problems. At a general level, these data are useful. The information helps identify students who might benefit from extra-help and test preparation sessions. The data, however, are only distally connected to the kind of detailed lesson-by-lesson information about students' understanding and mastery of key ideas and curriculum objectives that is necessary for explaining students' successes and needs and for differentiating teaching practice.

A *distal* connection is distant or removed from the *proximal* or close factors that affect student learning. A *proximal* solution is one that is more likely to exert an effect on learning. The way a lesson is designed, whether the teaching approach reaches all students, whether a homework task is realistic, and whether an assessment task is accessible are examples of *proximal* influences on learning. Better student learning is more likely when *proximal* rather than *distal* factors are the focus of intervention efforts. For example, too much extracurricular activity may be identified as an excuse for a student's poor TIPS-R scores. Closer examination, however, may show a mismatch between the student's prior learning, expectations of the curriculum, teaching of the lessons, alignment of assessment with that teaching, and accessibility of homework. Each variable represents a *proximal* explanation of the student's performance. Although the student's involvement in extracurricular activities may have created a time issue, it was likely only *distally* connected to the real source of the problem. So, even if activities were reduced, the problem would not go away.

The proximal/distal distinction is important when determining the focus of efforts for addressing the 1:X challenge, how ICT can assist, and in predicting the likelihood that it will produce an effect. Fred's distal data does not address the proximal factors associated with teaching and learning. Hence, the data exerts a limited effect on the department members. This is evident in the way department members do not refer to the SIS data during their meeting and the minimal relationship between that data and the solutions that the department members ultimately agree upon.

Why did the science department only have distal information? The answer is the same reason that it cannot employ peer tutoring at scale. In a field where educational practice is autonomously constructed (Becker & Riel, 1999; Goodlad, 1984), there is no shared understanding of the factors and transactions that proximally influence learning. This is why the department members can easily agree upon the distal factors (e.g., attendance, behavior, and homework completion) that are represented in their SIS but find it more difficult, if not impossible, to represent proximal factors (e.g., differentiated practice, pedagogy, curriculum, and assessment) at scale. They have limited knowledge and no consensus about what those proximal considerations are or what they mean to individual teachers and how to employ the considerations in their construction of teaching (Becker & Riel, 1999). As a result, the school can only gather information about those things that are agreed upon at scale.

At the school, the SIS automates its Type-A practices and fails as an edge technology because the distal data it presents are of low power and limited use in addressing the 1:X challenge. The data cannot help the teachers extend and develop their capacities or shorten the cognitive distance between teachers and learners. The problem is not technological. *Education fails technology* because it cannot articulate high-power proximal teaching and learning transactions at scale that can then be empowered by technology to serve all students.

School Example 3.1 makes a few points obvious, including the department's limited capacity to solve problems and its lack of proximal solutions for classrooms. These points reflect a number issues that Type-A schooling has vis-à-vis scale, feedback, bodies of professional practice, and ICT. The department can only take distal action on low-power solutions that, according to well-found research, will not yield the desired outcome.

The department members' autonomous construction of their work fails them as they try to pool their collective intelligence (Gloor, 2005) in the absence of a shared schema. The cognitive load of each increases as they expend energy on low-return solutions that lengthen the edge between them and their students. Technology, in the form of the SIS, further confounds their efforts. It is easy to imagine a meeting between Sarah and Bruce at the same time next year, where, in the absence of proximal alternatives, they will continue with some permutation of the original plan.

WHAT MAKES TYPE-B SCHOOLS MORE EFFECTIVE

In Type-B schools, high-power proximal solutions reduce the load of teachers. School Example 3.2 shows the value of such a solution to science teacher Anne. In it, she uses edge technology to correct a problem with the science curriculum.

School Example 3.2: Anne Reviews Homework

Anne is using the Classroom Array to look into the performance of her students. Figure 3.1 depicts the view she sees.

Next to the field describing the percent mastery attained on the homework task, there is a series of red flags on the scrolling list view of students' homework. A flag appears next to the name of each student who did not master the homework last night. Clicking on it reveals content of the students' homework (submitted online) and their performance. A summary at the bottom of the list view shows overall class performance as well as the homework performance on the same task for students in other classes. The flag is projected on the layout when more than 10% of the class does not achieve mastery on the homework task or when the mean score falls below 80%.

Anne had received a number of emails from students about problems with the homework. The emails are validated by the feedback she gets from the Classroom Array—the flag appears next to her class summary and those of three other classes working in the same unit and module of the integrated science course. When she clicks on the flag, she gets a summary of the items with which students had difficulty. It identifies a link to the lesson plan that was the subject of the homework task.

Anne selects the link. It takes her to a mastery-teaching lesson she taught the previous day. She reviews the lesson and finds an omission in the guided practice for students. She reviews the homework task and finds

Figure 3.1. Classroom Array: Homework

NAME Student	HW CODE	% MASTERY		
John Davis	HW 39022	62	◖	
Maree Overton	HW 39022	61	◖	
Jack Highsmith	HW 39022	70	◖	○
David Martin	HW 39022	61	◖	
Kylie Manners	HW 39022	81	◉	
Frank Ovens	HW 39022	82	◉	
Jason Milliband	HW 39022	56	◖	
Steve Johnson	HW 39022	63	◖	
CLASS SUMMARY Teacher		% MASTERY		
Anne Adams		74	◖	
Frank McLean		69	◖	
Anne Thomas		63	◖	○
Wanye Simpson		81	◉	
Jason Miles		52	◖	

that two of the homework questions require students to generalize from a problem-solving concept that was not taught with sufficient guided practice during the lesson. Anne revises the questions, and adds the guided practice and the necessary components to the lesson. The task takes her 20 minutes to complete.

Anne sends an email to her peer teachers describing what she has done and suggests that they reteach the section of the lesson the following week. She could call a meeting about the lesson design problem, but she decides that an email will suffice. Her peer teachers helped develop the curriculum, have experienced the same school-based professional development (PD) program, and are working with a shared understanding of professional practice. Any of them could have made the adjustments. As a result, holding a meeting to discuss the problem and its solution is unnecessary.

Many things happen in the example. Let us focus on the five called out in the earlier example. First, the feedback that Anne receives about homework performance is immediate and emerges bottom-up from students, is made possible by the connections that the Array makes between Anne, the students, and her learning design. As soon as her students complete the homework task, the Array detects a subtle design problem in the curriculum. Instead of positioning the problem as a student performance issue, the Array enables Anne to view several proximal explanations for it.

Second, students are actively engaged in problem identification. Since teachers share a schema, they can disperse control to many students in many classes. So, when an educational design issue is causally related to a high stakes test like the TIPS-R, it can be resolved without a months-after-the-fact forensic analysis. Student engagement with the real problem is genuine and high-level.

Third, the curriculum that Anne uses is articulated in the A to B Toolkit. She and her colleagues developed it there. This is the unseen work of Type-B that is described in Chapter 2. It helps them identify and solve problems associated with the design of the cooperative and mastery lessons. Their cognitive load is reduced because problem-solving is a shared activity and solutions are scaled up for teachers and students.

Fourth, high-power, research-based practices that are proximal to the teaching and learning transactions occurring in her class underpins Anne's teaching. These practices included mastery teaching (Hunter, 2004), immediacy of feedback (Brinko, 1993), alignment of what was taught with what was tested (Hughes & Salvia, 1990), and an expectation of student mastery (Guskey & Schulz, 1996). Each improves teacher communication, heightens student engagement, and supports differentiated instruction. Collectively, they stand in contrast to the compendium of low-power, Type-A solutions (e.g., tracking, extra-help, and test preparation) that members put forth in their department Type-A meeting. Although the suggestions are well intended, none of them can produce the TIPS-R gains the department members desire. The solutions are too distal to the classroom transactions, are unrelated to the proximal feedback collected by teachers, and exert little effect on student achievement (Hattie, 2009).

Fifth, *e*dge technology enables Anne to solve her curricular problem. The feedback about homework performance that is generated through the Array gives her the proximal information she needs to make the necessary change. She uses it to drill down to the essence of the problem, connecting it to the lesson design. She literally sees the connection.

The more Anne uses the tool, the better she becomes at detecting and resolving problems. As she does, the A to B Toolkit serves as a shared repository that enables other teachers who use the toolkit to use her solution. They can adopt or adapt it. When they do, their cognitive load is reduced because they do not have to construct their own solution. Further, Anne's adjustment of the lesson design shortens the cognitive distance between her and the students by making their learning experience better. Anne spends 20 minutes developing her solution. When compared to the time-consuming science department meeting, the action plan produced, and the low-power solution that resulted, Anne's time is well spent.

The A to B Toolkit and Classroom Array turn cognitive structures (e.g., Anne's schema for differentiated classroom practice) into practical tools and components. They are the collaborative Type-B alternative to Type-A autonomous teaching. In 20 minutes, they help solve a problem that consumes much of Sarah and the department members' time. They make less of more, engage students more genuinely, and reduce the cognitive and work load of everyone involved.

THE SHIFTS REQUIRED TO MAKE
SCHOOLS MORE EFFECTIVE

To understand the difference between Anne's problem-solving and that of the science department requires an understanding of the three shifts that a school must make to become Type-B. Each shift involves migrating away from autonomous classroom practice. The first shift is to build a school-level schema comprised of specific commitments to a body of professional practice. The commitments forge a professional community that is capable of 1:X. The second shift involves embedding those commitments in the school's design for learning. Its design includes teachers' roles, the tools they use, and the way the school is organized, all of which reflect the school's schema in practice. In the third shift, the feedback that emerges bottom-up from the day-to-day transactions of teaching and learning inform all school-level decisions. The account that follows unpacks each school-level shift to describe why the shifts can only happen with *e*dge technology.

Shift one: Building a school schema for practice. A school-level schema is a set of professional understandings, beliefs, and commitments about teaching and learning. It translates a school's vision and mission into common actions that reflect those commitments (Bain, 2007). Its existence drives the form of a school and reflects the school's capability to design itself in ways that reflect and sustain its schema.

In School Example 3.3, Principal Sarah observes a science department meeting in her Type-B school. She uses tools from the A to B Toolkit to generate feedback to the department about its meeting processes and content. She uses the School Array to look into the way the department she is observing collaborates with other departments. An ICT director, who is visiting the school to see how the school uses ICT, is observing the meeting with Sarah.

Science teacher Anne leads the meeting. The department is committed to using a collaborative protocol in its meetings. The protocol helps focus the conversation, ensure universal participation, and, where needed, generate an action plan. Per the protocol, during the first 20 minutes of the meeting, the members "check in" with each other about what is happening in their teaching. Today, they describe student progress in the curriculum, problem-solving incidents, and the feedback they have all received from students, peers, and/or supervisors.

We look in on the meeting as Anne describes the solution she developed and how its development led her to identify a problem with the curriculum design. Using a computer and projector, Anne projects a layout from her Classroom Array feedback component, seen in Figure 3.2.

First, Anne reviews the feedback students provided her. Then she points to the lower than acceptable homework success and the tasks that were problematic (bottom right). She calls out the comments made by some of the students (top right). After that, she shows the lesson feedback she received from her colleague Fred, who had observed her delivering the lesson (left).

School Example 3.3: Anne and Sarah Use the School Schema

Fred says, "The lesson was going well until the students began their guided practice on analyzing water quality. As my feedback in the Array indicates, I could see that Anne noticed the problem during her lesson." Anne agrees, saying, "Yes, the problem you saw me experience was confirmed the next morning by the students' homework and emails. Most understood how a mastery teaching lesson should work and they were quick to detect the issue with the water quality lesson." Fred concurs. Anne then explains what she did to revise the lesson. Bruce says, "Along these lines, I think there are a couple of gaps in my projectile motion module. After seeing what you've uncovered, I think I should check them out."

Figure 3.2. Classroom Array: Lesson Feedback Tool

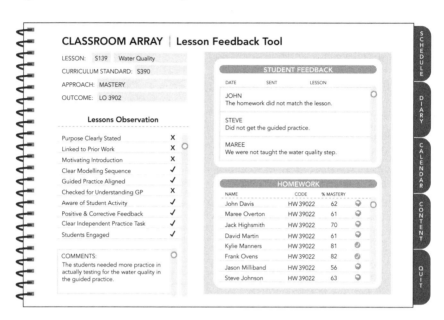

After complimenting Anne on her problem-solving, Bruce asks Sarah for feedback about the meeting. She had used the feedback component of the Array to capture her observations of the department's processes. Figure 3.3 presents a view of the tool she used.

Sarah explains, "After listening to Anne, I wonder whether we need to include an advanced mastery teaching workshop in the summer training program. What I am seeing here, and in other departments, is that we've moved beyond the basics of mastery teaching. We need something more—maybe an advanced workshop led by the department heads, less didactic than the original approach—we could use a problem-based learning model. What do you think?"

Department members quickly reach a consensus, affirming the need for advanced training. Sarah then compliments members for their use of the collaborative process. She makes special note of the need to link information from Anne's check-in to the department's curriculum action plan. She assures the group that by the end of the day, she'll post her feedback for departmental review and comment.

Figure 3.3. A to B TOOLKIT: Meeting Feedback Tool

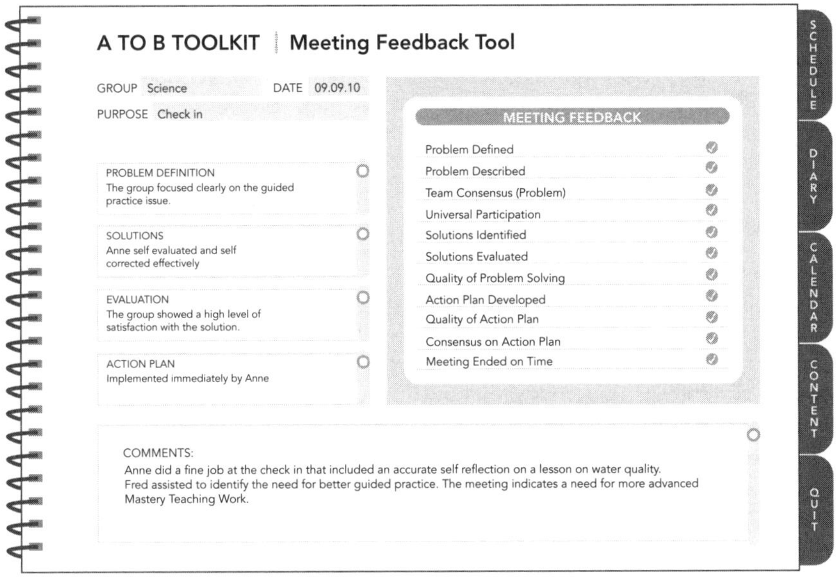

A school-level schema is about creating regularities in practice that bring down the cognitive load of stakeholders who work together. The transactions described above typify such regularities. One example is Anne using the feedback she received from students to refine her practice. Another is the lexicon of specific professional terms about their practice that the department members share (Bain, Lancaster, & Zundans, 2008). Still others include Fred's knowledge of Anne's pedagogical approach, Bruce's recognition of similarities across curricula, the department's use of a meeting protocol, Sarah's feedback about that process, and the consensus about a school-wide pedagogical issue. The regularities in the practice of the teachers indicate a shared schema. Moreover, their existence is reflected in the transactions across many levels of the school—from students providing feedback to Anne to Sarah providing feedback to the department. Although every stakeholder plays a different role, all are on the same page because of the school-level schema. School Example 3.4 presents Sarah's thoughts about the school.

School Example 3.4: Sarah Reflects

Before the change, I spent a huge amount of time chasing down problems that I could not resolve. In that way, this school was like every other—teachers pretty much did their own thing within the bounds of the state standards and curriculum guide. When we started our change process, we looked at what we needed to do differently. We identified some simple rules and made commitments to practices that teachers valued and felt were needed to do a better job of educating all students at the school.

After two workshops and a needs assessment, we asked our teachers the following question: If a pilot program based upon the commitments established in the workshops were launched, would you volunteer to participate? We had more than enough volunteers for our first year.

The pilot program put the rules and commitments about mastery, cooperation, and collaboration on the ground. They served as the basis for our schema. We started a training program that articulated the schema. Teachers worked in teams. They saw what the big-picture "mission things" looked like in practice. The schema just grew from there. We built the A to B Toolkit and the Classroom and School Arrays. They included components for giving and sharing feedback. The pilot scaled up.

The difference these steps made was remarkable. Now everyone focuses on differentiated teaching and learning. When I talk to the science department about a mastery learning workshop, they all get it—not just the one person who happened to attend a PD event outside of the school. Everyone has the knowledge and skill because of the way the school is designed. Everyone gets the solution because they share the need. We are all on the same page and you get fantastic collaboration as a result. This does not mean there is always agreement, just a common place to start. We have a foundation. Everyone shares a professional body of practice and they see the results of working together as a community.

The school is truly an emergent place. It all started with a schema and those commonly held commitments about what we do. Our teachers bring their unique interpretation of that practice and good things happen. My job is to keep this going in every classroom. The students, teachers, departments, and teams solve the real instructional problems. Parents no longer come to me about these things. They know that they will get much better, action-oriented professional answers from those directly involved. I don't have the superintendent breathing down my neck about items on the TIPS-R. When I see a need, I can ask the questions. Teachers like Anne and the students provide the answers.

A 5-year study comparing Sarah's school with 42 others supports her confidence about her school. It found that her faculty members believed their work environment was more collaborative and that they spent more time in constructive collaborative problem-solving activity (Bain & Hess, 2002) than their counterparts at the comparison schools. Another study showed that student, teacher, and administrator groups were each engaged with the schema and all implemented it with high levels of integrity over time (Bain, 2010). These findings show that a school-level schema is possible.

    Shift two: Enacting the schema-embedded design. Sarah's reflection illustrates a school-level schema for practice. She makes many references to the way it is enacted in the design of the school, including the *e*dge technology used to provide feedback, professional development, and assign responsibilities. Embedded design is the way her school creates the systems, methods, and tools required for schema enactment.

    Research on school reform makes clear that, all too often, the intent of a reform is not accompanied by the alteration of the way teachers teach and the way the school functions in support of the change (Berends, Bodilly, & Nataraj-Kirby, 2002). Moreover, the pre-existing form of the school often conflicts with the reform's intent. Both circumstances generate teacher overload and a high likelihood that efforts to change things will fail. In contrast, embedded design at the school level extends the capacity of the whole community to focus on those things it believes to be effective and thus brings down the cognitive load. It eliminates low-power distal solutions, and increases teacher and student connections that, in turn, disperse control for learning and minimize diffuse and unproductive efforts.

    Differentiated curriculum is a pivotal expression of the schema of Sarah's school. The process for developing it exemplifies how the school's embedded design enacts and evolves it. It is not something done the night before class or over a weekend. A case in point is the science curriculum. Sarah hires Bruce to develop the curriculum over a series of summers. Moreover, he and other teachers receive training about it as part of the school's summer institute. The A to B Toolkit is employed to articulate the school's schema for differentiation during training. The A to B Toolkit includes templates for designing research-based lessons, planning and building units and modules of instructions, and planning assessment activities. Using the toolkit is the way teachers learned about curriculum development.

    Bruce has to develop a module of instruction in order to graduate from the training institute. Subsequently, over 3 summers, he leads a science department team—all graduates of the institute—who develop additional modules for the curriculum. The department's curriculum is a "work in progress." For several years, Bruce and his compatriots teach the modules they have and approximate the missing ones as they work toward developing a complete curriculum. This is the *unseen* work described in Chapter 2. The A to B Toolkit helps it get done.

    The summer institute and curriculum development process give all faculty members a focused opportunity to experience the A to B Toolkit. Bruce's science department team assumes the role of lesson developers. As they use the tools with increasing sophistication, they apply the learning they derive from their professional development experience, instantiate their schemas for differentiated practice, and build capacity with the overall school schema and curriculum design. Edge technology enables their capacity building by embedding the teaching and learning transactions for better practice, more effective curriculum design approaches, and the elements of the school schema in the toolkit. It also helps Bruce build his skills as a master teacher and his abilities to lead others in creating the differentiated instruction that distinguishes Type-B learning environments.

The school's capacity is built bottom-up through the development of its schema and curriculum. All teachers create curriculum as part of their professional development. In doing so, they learn sophisticated instructional problem-solving skills like those demonstrated by Anne. While the teachers bring rich experience with content and teaching to the curriculum-building task, the school schema provides the necessary framework for them to collaborate and instantiate their views about the school's differentiated practice. The result is a collective intelligence and capacity that creates an *edge* for teachers and students.

The processes and interactions associated with the curriculum development approach described here produced over 2,000 hours of curriculum that crossed a number of subject areas (Bain, 2007). They shortened the edges in the school, those lines of communication between members of the community, and in doing so reduced the cognitive distance between its stakeholders. The school-wide curriculum development process makes their schema a school-level model of practice.

At the school, the less-is-more phenomenon plays out through its embedded design. The school implements those things about teaching and learning that it values and dispenses with those approaches that lack power and proximity in terms of their effect on learning. The design of professional development, curriculum development, career trajectory, and tools function reciprocally. Each is embedded in the other. The A to B Toolkit is used to design the curriculum. PD underpins the curriculum development model. In turn, the A to B Toolkit helps teach the way the curriculum is developed. Each is evident in the way Bruce's role in professional development and curriculum development is a requirement for transitioning to Master Teacher status. The toolkit, curriculum development, and PD model are embedded in each other and in the school's professional growth model and career trajectory.

Reciprocal embedding focuses the school's stakeholders on the things to which they are committed, including collaboration, cooperative learning, and mastery. The teachers build and then share high levels of expertise about the school's commitments because of the process of reciprocal embedding. As a result, solutions about teaching and learning needs and difficulties emerge bottom-up. One example is Sarah's suggestion about creating an advanced workshop for mastery teaching. It would have been easy for the same training or PD approach to occur year after year, even though, as with all schools, change never ends in a dynamic system. However, Sarah detects such a change and acts to avoid perpetuating training that no longer meets the school's more sophisticated needs.

Shift three: Generating feedback at scale. Feedback makes Type-B school-ing possible. It is the way Type-B schools learn about themselves through the "emergent" (Pascale, Millemann & Gioja, 2000; Gell-Mann, 1994) teaching and learning actions of its stakeholders. In Type-A schools, feedback only happens on key dates (e.g., tests or grade reports); at Type-B schools, it happens constantly via their teaching and learning transactions.

At Type-B schools, feedback is purposive, not summative and judgmental. It is how Anne learns from her students and shares what she learns with her peers. It is also how department members learn about their practice during her "check-in" and provide her with feedback during their meeting. Sarah learns from the feed-back she receivs from students and peers, the lesson design problem is resolved, and students learned more effectively.

As emergent feedback happens across the school, it informs what will happen there *next*. One example is Anne adjusting her curriculum in a way that alters the learning that students will experience *next*. Similarly, the *next* time her department peers build lessons using the mastery teaching approach, they, too, will apply her adjustment. Bruce will adjust his projectile module the *next* time he uses it. The same is true for Fred the *next* time he teaches. Likewise, Principal Sarah will alter the *next* professional development session.

Emergent feedback brings all stakeholders of the school together. It makes less of more by shortening the cognitive distance between each and all, all of the time. The connections it engenders makes it possible for learning to happen beyond the classroom at the scale of the school. It creates the *next* iteration of the schema in response to the changing conditions of the school.

HOW SCHOOLS CAN MAKE
THE SHIFTS THEY NEED

These three shifts make it possible for the classroom practices described in Chapter 2 to scale to the level of a school. They enable stakeholders there to work bottom-up. In combination, they create conditions for self-organization. Those conditions make 1:X attainable for them.

Sarah, instead of chasing problems, can be an instructional leader. She is, in the parlance of self-organizing systems, a "strange attractor" (Merry, 1995). She uses feedback to drive her school away from staying the same. Her analysis and capacity to see what is occurring across departments, teams, and the school as a whole enable her to bring questions to bear that will generate new solutions, ad-justing and altering tack, at times and in places that are proximal to teaching and learning, the school's core activity. She is an agent in a school where leadership is genuinely distributed (Spillane, 2006) and control is dispersed. Its emergent order is dynamic, the antithesis of the inflexible structures and top-down hierarchy that characterize Type-A schools. The professional practice, and school form it expresses, reduce the cognitive load of stakeholders, reconceptualize the role of students, and extend the spaces and places where learning happens. The bottom-up, self-organized participation it generates affect the whole school.

THE TOOLS SCHOOLS NEED TO TRANSFORM

Numerous references have been made to the way *edge* technology scales up when cognitive tools are used at the school level. School Example 3.5 presents a discussion between Sarah and the ICT director who is visiting her school.

School Example 3.5: Sarah Talks with the Visitor

"I could not do my job without our technology. I now spend most of my time helping teachers like Anne and department heads like Bruce generate emergent solutions to the challenges they face in classrooms. Technology makes it all possible. I use the A to B Toolkit to observe classes and meetings. I spend an immense amount of my time in proactive data-mining using the School Array. Here's the Lesson Feedback Tool from the School Array [Figure 3.4].

"Today, for instance, at a science department meeting, members discussed a problem with mastery teaching, one of the teaching approaches we use here. When I heard about it, I went to the Array. I checked every mastery teaching lesson that had been observed in the last year (top left). I could see the levels of mastery in a class, a department, or the whole school. If there were problems, I could look at any lesson (bottom center), the actual tasks involved, and whether they were undertaken cooperatively or individually. I could begin at the overview level as shown on the graph (top right) or the school report of the curriculum (bottom left) or drill all the way down to an individual lesson.

"I use this kind of analysis to work collaboratively with stakeholders here to decide how the school should grow, change, and evolve to meet the needs of all of our students. Take this Performance Summary layout from the School Array as an example [Figure 3.5].

"What you see here are two graphs. The first depicts school performance on standardized and curriculum-based measures. The second shows overall implementation of the curriculum as determined by feedback from students, teacher self-reports, and classroom observations. When I click on the trend line, I can drill down. By clicking on the grade lines on the second graph, I can look at the performance of any department and the curriculum implementation of every teacher based upon observation, self, peer, and supervisor feedback.

"At the bottom is a summary of students' performance in that subject for that grade level, including their homework performance, grades standardized test performance (ST), and the evaluation of their teacher (TF). I can begin with an individual student and work all the way up or drill down from the school level. This data changes all the time. It is similar at different levels of the school. What is gathered at the level of the school is simply the aggregation of student and teacher interactions. The data that is proximal or near to what goes on in classrooms is used all the time for feedback between teachers, students, and teams. It's not just numbers; I can see every reflection, comment, and narrative that is shared. The field at the bottom left is reserved for my analysis of the data described in the report. I can save the report and use the analysis when I attend meetings or give feedback in venues across the school."

Visitor: "Do you still gather the traditional information we usually see in School Information Systems?"

"We gather information on attendance, homework completion, and conduct. However, this tends to be more distal from what is actually going on in classrooms. Because the students have active roles in teaching and learning, we really don't need to keep track of missing homework to know whether they are engaged. That data are gathered as a simple by-product of looking into the actual transactions related to homework tasks, including how they link with the lesson designs and the students' performance. This is the conversation you and I observed at the science department meeting."

Visitor: "Do the students have tools?"

"Yes, and they are almost exactly the same as mine. It's the same for parents. They have toolkits and arrays. We do not show the students' identifying information, but parents can see how their student is doing in comparison to the class and school in every subject. The students can undertake the same kind of analysis that I described. They usually focus on their own classes. Our students have come up with some interesting educational design solutions. When parents come to teacher meetings, they do not discuss generalities. There are no surprises. They can see the teacher's gradebook at any time showing only their own child by name. They have a parent curriculum tool that describes the curriculum and how it works. They can then enter the curriculum proper and look at any aspect except for the assessment tools. Students use the tools to build their own lessons. This is a graduation requirement for our senior students."

Visitor: "Does transparency cause any problems?"

"It might if this data existed only for high-stakes summative purposes like tenure or student grade point averaging. This is not the case. All feedback in the tools is first and foremost an expression of what happens here every day. We use it all the time and are totally familiar with it—no surprises. As you saw in the department meeting, Anne was totally comfortable with Fred's feedback. It simply told us what to do next. Because the stakeholders see immediate and ongoing value, we do not seem to have problems around disclosure of information about teaching and learning."

Visitor: "You spend a lot of time in classes doing evaluation? Do you use different tools for that activity?"

"My colleagues in other schools think that since I spend so much time in classes I am always evaluating teachers. The truth is I do very little evaluation. I use the same A to B Toolkit that everyone here uses. It is how we provide feedback. You saw some of those tools in the science meeting we visited. The feedback component Fred used to observe Anne's lesson is the same one I would use to observe lessons. The meeting feedback tool I used is the same one that any member of the science department would use to give feedback about a department meeting. In the language used here, this is called similarity at scale. All levels of the organization use the same approaches.

"For example, teachers here build their growth portfolios [Figure 3.6] in the same emergent way students build theirs. Anne, whom you met at the meeting, will build a compendium of observed lessons, curriculum innovations, examples of the kind of curriculum problem-solving she described in her check-in, and feedback from students, peers, and administrators. Her growth is also an emergent product of the same feedback that makes the school work. She will build this using the electronic portfolio builder that aggregates her feedback received, reflections, and examples of practice.

"When Anne is ready to advance on the career path, she will submit that portfolio—no surprises. Our master teachers will review it against criteria that are known to Anne and all of the faculty members. Her transition to an advanced level works the same way as the process for students. She will be able to provide expertise to beginning teachers as they begin their journey. More than 35 teachers moved through our career path in the last 4 years."

Visitor: "Does all this feedback also apply to the school's leaders?"

"Absolutely—teachers, students, and parents provide feedback to the school leadership. This data is available in the School Array [Figure 3.7].

Here is one of the tools we use. Department heads and teachers use this tool to give feedback to leadership. The tool provides some insight into the role of leaders here—its focus on knowledge management, advanced problem-solving and expert knowledge of what the school is all about. See the explicit references to change (e.g., schema and solutions)? They are not about change for the sake of change, but are prioritized in this tool to ensure that leaders respond to the way the school grows and develops.

"With these tools, I bring stakeholders together through the sharing of basic information, the provision of feedback, and by enabling students to work together in and out of school. Around here, we call this *edge* technology. Everyone gains an edge."

Visitor: "This is all very impressive. Does it work?"

"This is a question we get asked a lot. You might think we would need a million-dollar grant and a team of university researchers to answer it. However, one of the benefits of our emergent feedback approach is that gathering the information to answer the question occurs every day by us just doing our jobs. The student feedback, the performance on curriculum and standardized tests, the observations in class, the reflections, the problem-solving are all designed to help us do what we do. They were not developed to make summative judgments, although when we need that information it is always available any time that we care to look.

"Here is what we have found so far: Since we developed the tools 5 years ago, more than 15,000 pieces of qualitative and quantitative data were generated, including 1,600 classroom observations and 12,000 student evaluations of teachers in a 5-year longitudinal evaluation. An 8-year study showed achievement effects of .58 and .70 (for students with learning disabilities) while studies of ICT use showed positive effects on teaching practice and student achievement.

"We are not at 2-Sigma, but are further along than any secondary school reform to date. For the most part, the data described above were gathered as part of the ongoing conduct of the school and used for problem-solving the design and process, the professional growth of faculty, evaluating student progress, and reflecting on school performance, as well as developing connections between the fidelity of implementation and the outcomes of the project. We know we have a lot more to do, although based on our review of the evaluations of other reforms, our findings so far are very encouraging."

(*Authors' note*: The data described here reflects actual change in school performance based on the findings of the Self-Organizing School project [Bain, 2007]).

Figure 3.4. School Array: Lesson Feedback Tool

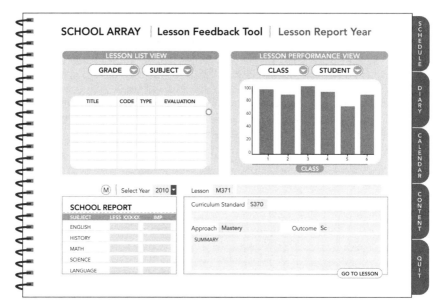

Figure 3.5. School Array: Performance Summary

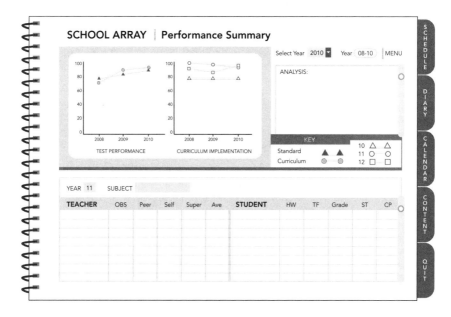

Figure 3.6. A To B Toolkit: Portfolio Builder

A TO B TOOLKIT | **Portfolio Builder**

FEEDBACK SURVEYS   Select Year 2007

REFLECTIONS

STUDENT	SELF	TEAM	PEER	SUPER
A A A A A	FALL WIN	FALL WIN	FALL WIN	FALL WIN

Average

Date	Sent	Title
Date	Sent	Title
Date	Sent	Title
Date	Sent	Title

BEST PRACTICE EXAMPLES

TITLE	URL	CODE

QUICK LINKS

- Curric Measures
- Standardised Test
- Lesson Observations
- Reflections

SCHEDULE | DIARY | CALENDAR | CONTENT | QUIT

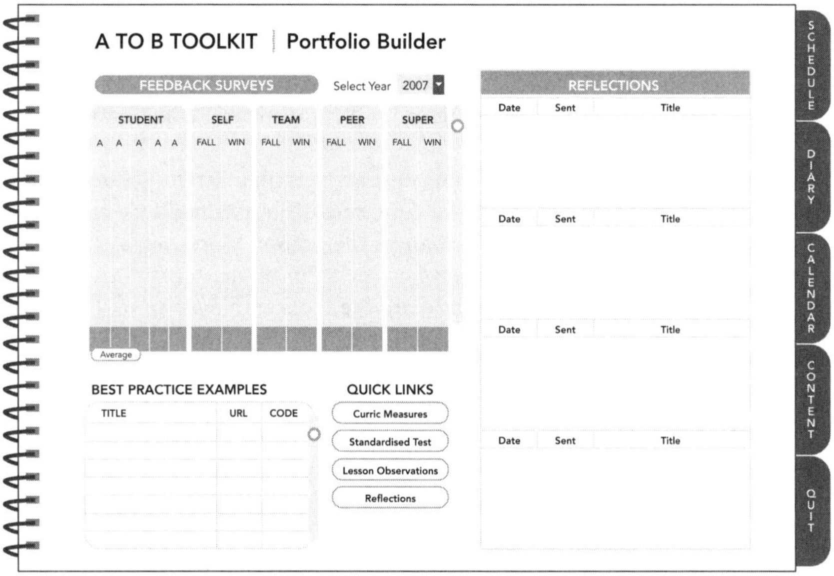

Figure 3.7. A To B Toolkit: Leadership Feedback

A TO B TOOLKIT | **Leadership Feedback**

LEADER NAME John Turk   DATE 10.05.10   ID 789544

SUPERVISION
- Provides insightful feedback in observations
- Uses collaborative process effectively
- Provides expert feedback on curriculum design
- Acts on feedback in a timely fashion
- Is assertive in sharing expectations

KNOWLEDGE MANAGEMENT
- Uses the School Array to identify key needs
- Synthesises information effectively
- Develops original solutions
- Can evolve the school schema

EXPERTISE
- Demonstrates expert knowledge of pedagogy
- Demonstrates expert knowledge of curriculum
- Demonstrates expert knowledge of assessment
- Demonstrates expert knowledge of differentiation

NARRATIVE:

SCHEDULE | DIARY | CALENDAR | CONTENT | QUIT

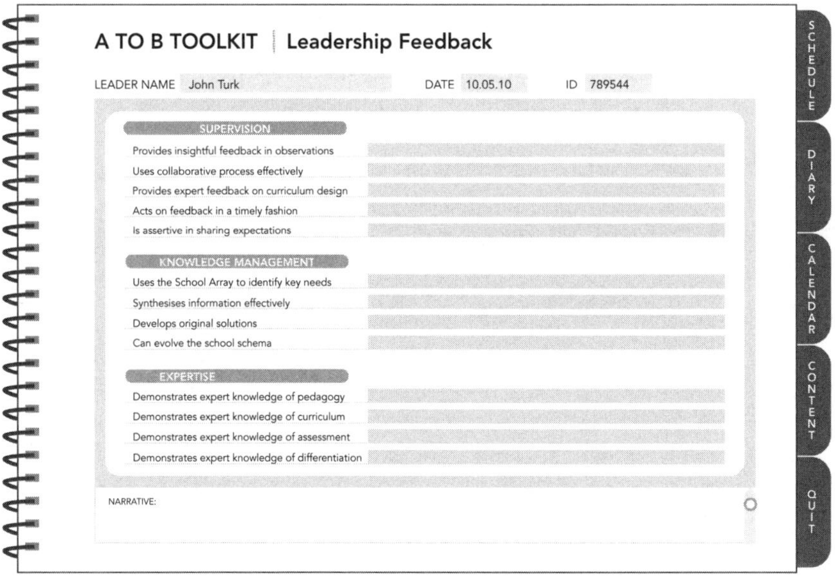

The discussion between Sarah and her visitor shows the way that the A to B Toolkit and School Array extend the capacity of the school by building the capacity of every stakeholder. Edge technology brings them together at the school level to build curriculum, share feedback, refine professional development, and advance on a career path. It gives the school an edge for meeting the 1:X challenge and instantiates a dynamic order for a dispersed collaborative effort around a shared purpose.

Since the research-based assumptions underpinning Sarah's school are represented in its edge technology, every time one of its stakeholders uses a tool, he or she connects, commits, and advances the school. Moreover, as the school changes, so do its tools. For instance, when the focus on mastery teaching at Sarah's school is expanded and refined, so are the tools employed to build, deliver, and share feedback about mastery teaching. In this way, they give the school's stakeholders a teaching and learning edge by shortening the cognitive distance between them. So, as they share feedback and work together, their problem-solving is a scaled-up iteration of the transactions that occur in their respective classrooms. This means that the successful practices used in one classroom are more likely to work in many classrooms.

USING EDGE TECHNOLOGY TO MOVE FROM TYPE-A TO TYPE-B SCHOOLS

Edge technology, by making Type-B schools more dynamic, articulated, and networked, makes self-organization and Type-B learning possible for everyone. The organizational structure that results is profoundly different from that of Type-A schools, whose structures are scaled-up versions of the hierarchical and centralized Type-A classroom described in Chapter 2. Figure 3.8 depicts a Type-A and Type-B network.

Figure 3.8. Network Migration

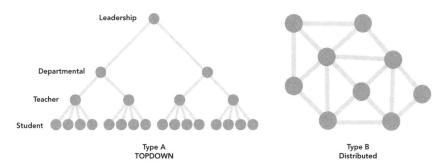

The edges that connect students, teachers, and school leaders are long and tenuous. Bottom-up self-organization is not possible because the nodes on the network are isolated and communication is poor. Change is transmitted from the top but not vice versa. School leaders' roles generate a cognitive overload and a painful disparity between what they believe they *should* do and how they actually spend their time. For them, everything starts and finishes at their desk. They do not have sufficient time to pay attention to teaching and learning, the proximal things of most importance.

In contrast, the Type-B school depiction represents what happens when the dispersed, flatter, classroom network described in Chapter 2 is efficiently scaled to the school level via *e*dge technology and the feedback it makes possible. In it, all classrooms are interconnected, stakeholders are in contact with each other, and they can act collectively.

HOW SHARED SCHEMA CAN TRANSFORM SCHOOLS

The three-step framework that was applied in the previous chapters serves as a lens for scrutinizing the key ideas presented in this chapter, the *e*dge technology that enables them, and the way both help the school-level support attainment of 1:X.

New Assumptions

Assumption one: Edge technology is the critical enabler for the school-level shifts that address the 1:X challenge. It enables Anne to detect and respond to a teaching problem in her lesson design and Sarah to understand the way the school's professional development needs are evolving as teachers build a more sophisticated understanding of mastery teaching. *E*dge technology instantiates the school-wide schema, enacts the school design, makes emergent feedback commonplace, and addresses the 1:X challenge beyond the classroom. The Type-B school where Sarah works can only be possible with *e*dge technology.

Assumption two: Edge technology exemplifies the way research on teaching and learning defines ICT at scale. Whether in the tools Anne uses to plan or monitor the feedback she receives about her lesson, or in the online protocol Sarah uses to observe the department meeting, the tools for stakeholders focus on a scaled-up and self-similar version of those found in Type-B classrooms. Research on differentiated teaching and learning, feedback, and collaborative process are embedded in each. They makes it possible for the stakeholders at Sarah's school to the generate day-to-day, emergent feedback for solving problems at all levels of the school, managing career progression, and determining what to do next.

Assumption three: When edge technology embodies a school's schema and design, it is impossible to separate learning "with" from learning "about" technology. It is an extension of the school's schema, design, and research-based practice. This is best illustrated in the way Anne uses feedback from students about their homework to revise her lesson. The tools generate the feedback Anne uses to identify a problem. She is able to use those same tools in an increasingly sophisticated way to revise her lesson. Since edge technology is the locus for school learning, learning about it means learning about teaching and learning.

Assumption 4: When expressed at the scale of the school, edge technology reaffirms a commitment to teachers, students, and schools as the core of the solution to the 1:X challenge. In this chapter we see the way students are engaged in providing feedback about the homework they complete, the way that feedback is employed by Anne to improve a lesson design, and the way Sarah uses the feedback to identify the need for improved mastery teaching. In each case students, teachers, and administrators employ the school's technology tools to resolve the 1:X challenge and evolve the school's schema. Edge technology serves what students and teachers do.

Assumption 5: The dynamic order, created by a schema and design, expresses in practice the high-power, proximal solutions that focus the work of the school on student learning and achievement. Together, this assumption and the four aforementioned ones create the conditions for pooling the collective intelligence of the community, supporting dispersed control and bottom-up self-organization. The agency of teachers and students is affirmed and magnified by the use of ICT as the key driving force in any school.

New Design

In this chapter, examples are provided of the design metaphor described in Chapters 1 and 2 and its three components: solution mapping, component building, and design integration. We position edge technology as a tangible expression of the school's design in response to the autonomous private practice of Type-A schools. We identify a school schema as the solution map for a school's design and the development of edge technology that will enact that design in the day-to-day life of the school. We show the way edge technology is integrated at scale in self-similar ways where students, teachers, and school leaders use similar tools to enact and evolve the schema. We show how edge technology can reconceptualize studentship, address cognitive load for teachers, and find new spaces and places at the level of the school. The examples of the ICT tools we describe show the way in which they could scale up a classroom schema for practice to the level of the school. The design of the educational technology becomes synonymous with the design of the school, integrating tools for the design, delivery, and evaluation of differentiated Type-B learning at scale along with tools that make constant emergent feedback possible.

New Trajectory

In the chapters that follow, we show that no Type-B school can be an island. All require the co-evolution of systems, professional organizations, and the ICT industry to be sustained over time and scaled up to influence the teaching and learning of large numbers of students and teachers. We show the way that the principles of embedded design, self-similarity and dispersed control, schema and self-organization can gain widespread acceptance within a system. We show how *e*dge technology enables the co-evolution of educational systems, including the way associations, policies, and products can address the 1:X challenge by supporting *e*dge technology and self-organizing Type-B schools at scale.

SUMMARY

- A shared schema is comprised of commitments to practice that are based on high-power, proximal research that are embedded in the design of the school and enacted at scale.
- Embedded design means that all elements of a school's schema are embodied in its tools, curriculum, professional development, and career pathways and then embodied in each other.
- The school's design is empowered by emergent feedback. It drives the school's response to the 1:X challenge and helps stakeholders determine what to do next.
- Emergent feedback is made possible by the *e*dge technology (e.g., A to B Toolkit and School Array) that articulates the school's schema and design.
- Since *e*dge technology turns a school's schema into tools, learning about technology means learning about the schema, the commitments it makes to teaching and learning, and the workable model of practice they represent.
- Education fails technology by expecting 1:X to be resolved in the absence of a schema, design, and emergent feedback. When a school's design lacks these features, ICT use is distal and low power.

CHAPTER 4

Transforming Districts

The real leader has no need to lead—
he is content to point the way.
—*Henry Miller*

How can school districts use *e*dge technology to assist schools in addressing the 1:X challenge? We show that (a) Type-B classrooms and schools are best served by Type-B districts, (b) district-level shifts that make this possible, (c) *e*dge technology plays a critical role in those shifts happening, and (d) a district functions differently as a result of it all.

THE ICT PROBLEM AT THE DISTRICT LEVEL

Being a district superintendent is widely recognized as a demanding, complex, and risk-laden job (Kowalski, 2005). Superintendent turnover can be as high as 30% annually and 70% over 5 years (Sharp & Walter, 2004). Although the educational effects of the superintendency are debatable, an undeniable gap exists between the time a superintendent typically holds the post and the time it takes for major teaching and learning reforms to take hold (Byrd, Drews, & Johnson, 2006; Natkin, Cooper, Fusarelli, Alborano, Padillo, & Ghosh, 2002; Snider, 2006; Urban Indicator, 2008/2009).

Superintendents report that improving student achievement is the highest priority and most challenging facet of their jobs (Byrd, Drews, & Johnson, 2006; Hess, 2002). Yet, despite the intense and often highly politicized pursuit of better student outcomes, districts are frequently criticized for their failure to affect the performance of students (Peterson, 2000, cited in Byrd, Drews, & Johnson, 2006). Waters and Marzano (2007) in an extensive meta-analysis found that district-level leadership only asserts modest effects on student achievement. The district has limited widespread influence on student achievement. The volatility, reactivity, and low effects that typify the district level of the overall educational system are symptoms of their inability to support classroom- and school-level resolution of the 1:X challenge.

District Example 4.1 illustrates these points. In it, school principal Sarah meets with Bruce to discuss the Trends in International Performance Study-Revised (TIPS-R). One year has passed since her school experienced student performance problems on the test. Recent results indicate that there has been marginal improvement on the science component and no improvement in scientific reasoning and problem-solving. Since Sarah's school fails to meet the district's TIPS-R performance goals, she is under considerable pressure from Superintendent James. Moreover, James receives many complaints from parents and board members about Sarah's school's performance. The complaints concern the international competitiveness of the district's curriculum and the quality of teaching at the school.

District Example 4.1: Sarah and Bruce Meet

Sarah says, "I'm more than a little frustrated by the recent results and criticism. Please tell me what has been done to address the problem." She flips Bruce a copy of a report from the SIS that identifies students who performed poorly on the TIPS-R. Bruce tells her, "I already have a copy." He then gives Sarah the action plan that his department implemented a year ago and says, "We ran the extra-help group all year and had pretty good attendance. Plus, I ran five sessions about test-taking that are mandatory for all students. They went well." Sarah asks, "How many students show up?" Bruce replies, "Five or six students usually come to each extra-help session, but they're not always the same ones." Sarah says, "That's a small percentage of the 9th-grade class." Bruce tells her, "It's voluntary and the needs of the students are so different. Any more would make it very difficult for the teacher conducting the session. We have to be careful here—a couple of teachers complained that the additional load is outside of the contract and have talked about going to the union."

Bruce changes the focus of the discussion, asking, "Has there been any progress on the tracking model that Anne advocated for during the science department meeting a year ago?" Sarah replies, "The vice principal looked into it, but it was just too difficult to schedule in science when so many other subjects are not tracked."

Bruce says, "I have decided to change the textbook at the beginning of next year when the new texts are purchased." Sarah asks, "What else can we do?" Bruce replies, "I think the text will make a difference. I will continue with the test-taking sessions and get the staff to try and improve attendance at the extra-help sessions. What about the class-wide peer tutoring that Fred suggested?" Sarah says, "James has freed up some additional PD funds. I will make them available for a workshop for your whole department; although the PD needs to be connected to the district's new 1:1 technology initiative." After an hour, Sarah and Bruce part ways with a slightly revised action plan and a commitment to meet again before the end of the term.

This conversation is a continuation of the school's science department meeting, described in Chapter 3. Despite their best intentions, the members could only identify low-power, high-load solutions that are distally connected to TIPS-R performance and do not affect learning and teaching significantly. A year after that meeting, some of their recommendations have been implemented. The outcomes (or lack thereof) they produce are predictable—big demands on the teachers' time with little gain in performance. To their credit, Bruce and his colleagues have worked diligently to improve TIPS-R performance. Their cognitive and overall workloads increase as they do, surfacing possible union relations problem in the process.

Failure to resolve the TIPS-R issue at the classroom, department, and school levels has causes the problem to escalate to the district level. Superintendent James feels pressure from the community and transfers it to Sarah. He defends Sarah and her team by reminding critics of the way the school has met its other goals related to performance on the state test. As he does, the critique intensifies because the successes in other areas are not reflected in performance on the TIPS-R. The PD on peer tutoring has been approved, but is not embedded in the school's schema for practice or design. Instead, it has been attached to the 1:1 computing initiative. As a result, peer tutoring gains limited traction in the department. The TIPS-R problem remains unresolved. Everyone is frustrated.

Difficulties arise when problems at or near the classroom-level cannot be resolved successfully. In their Type-A education system, Bruce, Sarah, and James share a profound problem—an inability to address teaching and learning issues with high-power, low-load, proximal solutions that can be scaled district-wide. They bring their expertise and influence to the problem without effect. Bruce persists with extra-help and test-taking strategies. Sarah diligently makes the district's goals a priority, asks for more resources, and revisits the department's action plan with Bruce. James budgets money for professional development, sets new goals, placates the board and community, and places additional pressure on Sarah. In the absence of problem-solving capacity, their efforts are ineffective.

WHY TYPE-A DISTRICTS DON'T WORK

The inability to resolve learning and teaching problems close to their source evokes a politicized interpretation of them. Such politicization drives districts toward more distal and unproductive debate. That debate invariably generates low-power solutions with little positive effect on student achievement. There is no better example of how this phenomenon emerges than the district-wide adoption of a 1:1 computer initiative. District Example 4.2 shows the way one such initiative set up the antecedent conditions for a fractious debate.

District Example 4.2: Board Agrees

School board chairman Alfred says, "Everybody is right behind the 1:1 computer initiative." James agrees, "Yes, it seems so." Alfred continues, "This is about the easiest decision we have made as a board. The state is providing the funds. The board and I gave unanimous support. All of the principals and a majority of teachers are excited about getting new computers and more training. Are our parents on board?"

James replies, "The company that won the contract conducted a highly successful orientation session for parents. At it, a new curricular vision and examples of computer applications in several subject areas were presented. The parents and broader community are excited. Our 1:1 initiative lines up perfectly with the goals set forth in the district's 5-year ICT plan."

Alfred says, "Please go over those goals." James refers the board to their board book for the meeting, the tab labeled "1:1 computing," and the page containing the following list:

- Teachers will improve student achievement by effectively integrating technology tools into their practice.
- School district staff will develop the technology skills to design learning experiences that challenge and enable students to use information technology.
- Computers will be available for student instructional use at a ratio of two students per computer across the district.

James says, "I feel the new computers make these goals accessible for us, especially those related to staff skill development."

Despite the apparent momentum, James knows thats the 1:1 initiative is a minefield. Similar 1:1 efforts in other districts have brought up more questions than answers. Issues include hidden infrastructure and staffing costs and a host of usage concerns that are often overlooked during the excitement of initial adoption and deployment. Moreover, the benefits seem limited and undocumented and the circumstances of the deployments are highly volatile. James read in a recent superintendents' association newsletter that 2 years after winning national superintendents' awards (for technological innovation, no less), two of his peers are fired due to ICT-related issues. District Example 4.3 provides highlights from a board meeting that takes place 1 year later.

District Example 4.3: A Reality Check

Alfred says, "James can you explain these results? Teachers don't seem to be using the computers to teach the kids, yet they complain about extra work and professional development demands. They say that overall they are using the computers for grading, accessing the school's information system, and searching for resources. Students are using them in some of their classes but not at all in others. What is going on with these teachers? The initiative was meant to transform the curriculum and improve our TIPS-R and Statewide Achievement Test performances. There's no change—I don't get it. The only goal we met is the one to improve access to computers! I am also hearing parent complaints about the slow turnaround time for repairing computers. What's going on?"

James replies, "Based on the experience of initiatives elsewhere, we know that changing the teacher culture takes time. Improving achievement test results also takes time. We're early on with the initiative. We need more time." Alfred tells him, "Maybe so, but this is expensive stuff. It seems we underestimated the total cost of this initiative." James answers, "Yes, there is a very real tension between the need for expending resources to maintain our larger ICT infrastructure and expenditures on ICT for classroom teaching and learning."

The inevitable rumblings about the questionable educational value, the overall cost, and return on investment of the 1:1 initiative are beginning in James's district. The research findings cited in Chapter 1 can help us unpack the above example. First, the goals in the district's ICT plan appear to have face validity. They are similar to the goals of many districts. Unfortunately, in the autonomously constructed world of Type-A schools, such goals have little meaning. Without a shared schema for what teaching practices and learning experiences mean, the goals are too ambiguous to be interpreted in valid and reliable ways. As a result, they most often lead to the automation of non-research-based teaching approaches. Alfred is correct to note that the only goal the initiative has met so far is altering the student-computer ratio. There is no doubt about the increase in computer numbers across the district. Access to computers, however, does not co-vary with the attainment of the other goals in the plan. This creates additional problems for James related to teacher time and workload.

Second, low and variable computer use (Silvernail, 2007), the preponderance of administrative use by teachers (Becker, 2001), variability in the student experience (Zucker & Hug, 2007), underestimation of the total cost of ownership (Hu, 2007), and the conflation of access with achievement typify the deployment of ICT in Type-A districts. Across James's district, the automation of existing practice, lack of achievement gains, and funding-related tensions (Rhodes, 1997) are having negative effects.

Third, it is unusual, and possibly ominous, that the district turns its educational vision for curricular use of the computers over to the company from which it purchased them. The district, it seems, has not only failed technology, but by transferring responsibility of its core activity to a vendor, has failed education!

After just 1 year, the infusion of ICT causes much pain throughout the district. The cognitive load on teachers increases as they are pressured to report greater classroom use after attending new training. Without a schema for teaching and learning and deep curricular embedding, the computers are just an added responsibility for most teachers. The 1:1 initiative proves to be another low-power innovation that adds to their work and makes no proximal contribution to their pursuit of the 1:X challenge. It is no different from the extra-help and test-taking sessions that the science department uses with little effect on the TIPS-R scores.

For James, the pushback from teachers, unaffected test scores, and implementation issues are compounded by growing community pressure. He, like superintendents elsewhere, begins questioning the role and value of ICT in his district (Shuldman, 2004). Although he knows that including ICT in school bond packages has been shown to positively affect their passage (Beckham & Maiden, 2003), the technology shine has clearly worn off for him and the district. He is overcommitted to an underperforming 1:1 initiative at a time when requesting more funds is likely to receive a cool reception, especially if he cannot show student achievement gains. As the initiative's limitations emerge, the traps and characteristics of the district's failed ICT strategy create a dangerous situation for James. The initiative has failed the core activity of the district, and in so doing, compromises its overall educational processes by creating management and budgetary issues and adding to the load of teachers without return in terms of student learning. The infusion of computers fails to address the 1:X challenge by not extending the number of locations where learning happened, shortening the cognitive distance between stakeholders, or building their capacities at scale. By failing to make the initiative a high-power, low-load, proximal solution for the students' learning needs, the inevitable politicization of the issues surfaces.

HOW TYPE-B DISTRICTS HELP TRANSFORM EDUCATION

The role of the district in Type-B education is different from its role in Type-A. In Type-B, the district supports the schema for practice of its many schools and responds to the 1:X challenge at scale. In Type-A, it does not. District Example 4.4 provides highlights from a meeting of the district's edge technology team that

James convenes to discuss a key goal of their annual plan. The goal is to increase the use of problem-based learning in elementary and secondary schools across the district and to show the effects of that use on student achievement on the TIPS-R.

Two years ago, a review of the district's curriculum and its performance on the Statewide Achievement Test and the TIPS-R showed that students were weak in applying scientific ideas and principles to novel situations. One year later, several teachers begin piloting a problem-based learning (PBL) approach to address those weaknesses. Their review of the literature shows that the PBL teaching and learning approach will assist students in problem-solving, building original solutions in context, and applying ideas to novel situations. However, their pilots at two elementary and two secondary schools do not produce enough improvement in student performance to warrant district-wide adoption. When the pilot team analyzes the experience, they find two flaws in their approach. The student role in PBL activity is not well defined and each student is not required to produce a substantive work product of his or her own. These flaws produce highly variable levels of student engagement in the PBL groups. Moreover, since the PBL lessons are not designed to be differentiated, they are a return to the one-size-fits-all curriculum that the district had moved away from years ago.

Six months later, the team reimplements the pilot. This time, they combine the principles of PBL with those of Cooperative Learning to ensure that there is sufficient task structure and clarity of roles (Slavin, 1991). Going forward, all students in the pilot will have to complete a report on their own after doing a group activity, and all activities will be differentiated. Not surprisingly, the results improve greatly and the team recommends that the approach, called Problem-Based Cooperative Learning (PBCL), be adopted district-wide.

District Example 4.4: James and Team Meet

James says, "Let's get started. I used the District Array to map the performance of any and all schools to examine every PBCL lesson taught in the pilot. I did this by mapping the lessons to curriculum-based assessment items that involve the application of scientific principles and the performance of the student participants in the pilot on the Statewide Achievement Test and the TIPS-R. My mapping confirmed your pilot group findings. They are compelling. What feedback do you have for me?"

Team members concur with James's assessment, noting the big change from the first pilot to the second. James says, "I understand a new software module is needed to accommodate PBCL. It will help teachers design and implement PBCL lessons as part of our district-wide curriculum. The project for building software will involve developing the layouts for designing PBCL lessons, developing the lesson-formatting tool, and integrating the new module with the existing suite of tools in the A to B Toolkit."

A team member adds, "Two teachers involved in the pilot have developed a beta version of the new module. It is a little clunky and time-consuming to use but is a great starting point for the group as they try and get a sense of the project."

James and the group members talk about the design of the PBCL tools, the scope of work for developing them, the way the project will be funded, and its integration with the district's A to B Toolkit and Plan Books. The meeting agenda has time allocated for examining the beta tools, developing a scope of work for the project, and building a plan using the district's protocol and standards for software development. After the meeting ends, the group has arranged to liaise with the district's professional growth planning team to explore the ramifications of the software project on their professional development efforts.

Many things happen in the meeting. Let us focus on four of them. First, the meeting is not about access to ICT or student-to-computer ratios. It is about scaling a proximal solution to a problem faced by all teachers from the school to the district level. As the scaling occurs, the school-level schema for teaching and learning that produces the solution also scales up. The PBCL solution that is presented and then refined through the pilots is the result of the design and implementation of a new pedagogy. All decisions about it are driven by the schema, the needs of teachers, and the research-based practice they use to modify the schema. Their work is done via the use of *edge* technology. The process of systematically developing the schema through problem-solving and pilot testing stands in contrast to the example of the 1:1 initiative and its unfounded presumptions about the effects of ICT access on learning.

Second, the emergent nature of the schema and associated design-driven change is readily apparent across the district. The first pilot, its revised iteration, and then the beta software emerge bottom-up, are driven by school-level stakeholders, and subsequently are supported at the district level. Such dispersal of control to the school and classroom levels contrasts starkly with Type-A, top-down approaches.

Third, by scaling the pilot district-wide, James plays a uniquely meaningful role that is made possible because of the district's emergent schema and the processes that had produced PBCL. The district-wide use of common tools brings down the load of all stakeholders. This means that the PBCL approach can be integrated with ease into the district's schema and *edge* technology. James knows about the pilots and related work, but does not manage it top-down. Rather, he lifts PBCL from the classroom and school levels to the district level. He can do this because he knew and understood the schema from which PBCL emerged and could employ the "schema knowledge" it generates to guide the scaling-up process. His efforts are proximal to those occurring at the school level. He is positioned to help build high-power solutions that extend the work undertaken there. He takes up PBCL and the software development for *all* stakeholders so their efforts do not have to be idiosyncratic acts of invention by *each* teacher in *each* school.

Fourth, *e*dge technology plays a powerful role in the district. Since the district is an emergent and self-similar representation of its classrooms and schools, James uses *e*dge technology to mine the performance of both pilots. In turn, he uses his deep understanding of the work of classrooms and schools—again, made possible by *e*dge technology, especially the District Array—to develop additional district-level components for the A to B Toolkit.

In contrast to his ominous sense of doubt about the 1:1 initiative, James is confident about spending additional funds for further developing the district's *e*dge technology, PBCL, and related professional development because they are inextricably linked with teaching and learning and produced demonstrable and proximal improvements. His confidence is confirmed in the second pilot and the data-mining he undertakes via the District Array. Investing in more *e*dge technology is not a speculative or idiosyncratic decision for him.

The creation of PBCL exemplifies how stakeholders are in charge of District-B, its curriculum, and professional development. They are a highly sophisticated community of practice that has a complex understanding of PBCL. Their curricular vision does more than demonstrate to their students what could be done with a computer. They moved far beyond the kind of curricular support that a computer company can supply. The roles they play, especially the role played by James, differ greatly from those they would have played in a Type-A district. There, James would have been unable to act supportively because his teachers would have been unable to act proximally at scale in high-power, low-load ways with the computers that the 1:1 initiative provides.

THE SHIFTS WE NEED TO MAKE
TO IMPROVE THE DISTRICT LEVEL

To understand the difference between James's ineffectual contributions to teaching and learning in his Type-A district and the role he plays in the self-organized PBCL problem-solving we need to acknowledge three essential shifts that distinguish District-B. One shift involves leveraging the benefits of a shared schema, dispersed control, similarity at scale, embedded design, and feedback to maximize, at scale, the high-power proximal solutions that the classroom and school levels generate. Those solutions address the 1:X challenge and make Type-B possible in many schools and classrooms. They require the district to do much more than assume a Type-A role—visioning, goal setting, and implementing data-driven decision-making—in which the district establishes the height of the bar that stakeholders must cross by setting standards and creating accountability measures. In Type-B, the district leverages the self-organizing capability of its classrooms and schools to help all schools cross the bar. This is obvious in the way PBCL builds on the district's existing schema and design. Two, the forces from outside the emergent system of classrooms and schools is reconciled with the action that occur within it. For James, this includes reconciling state policy and funding with the emergent schema and processes of a network of classrooms and schools. Three, district-level work is extended beyond the support of emergent initiatives like PBCL. James is a "strange attractor," a disruptive force on the system that lures classrooms and schools away from the tendency to keep doing things the same way. He knows that staying the same in the face of change is a prelude to "system failure" (Merry, 1995; Prigogene & Stengers, 1984).

Shift one: Leveraging process at scale. Chapters 2 and 3 describe the way edge technology makes research-based differentiated teaching and learning possible. The tools help stakeholders build deep and shared insights into the happenings in their classrooms and schools by designing and delivering lessons, generating and sharing feedback about them, and monitoring learning in timely ways.

In Type-B districts, the practices epitomized by Anne's reflection on her teaching, Eladio's empowerment of his students, and the problem-solving in Bruce's module are observable across classrooms and schools. Such a district-level view involves assuming a "helicopter perspective" whereby patterns of work that are not visible from the ground are visible at the altitude of scale. The perspective affords new and powerful sources of feedback for doing things better and possibly differently. A system-wide creative order makes the unseen patterns visible. It is a product of the schema and tools that stakeholders share and use. Repeated engagement with both generates a record of creative action that is unique to each, yet has sufficient commonality for patterns to emerge. This is illustrated when teachers share their understanding of PBL and use the tools to produce a common record of their actions. Even though they address different problems in different subject areas, the tools generates order and commonality of use. This means that the recurring problems of "task structure" and diminished "individual student accountability" (Slavin, 1991) become visible to them. In turn, their identification of these flaws leads to the creation of PBCL and a second pilot. If each pilot team member had constructed his or her own interpretation of PBL—as would have happened in Type-A—there would have been no cumulative sense of what each had done. No pattern would emerge. For Type-A, it does not matter how high the helicopter can fly. There is no pattern to see.

In Type-B, a key district-level role involves acting upon what is seen by leveraging and scaling-up successes, and helping stakeholders avoid reinventing existing but unrecognized good ideas or missing them altogether. Schema, embedded design, tools, and sophisticated problem-solving processes provide the district level with intelligence about the needs of the classroom and school levels. The accumulation of intelligence helps it better understand their instructional issues, deploy resources, and extend their innovations. Such a role is the antithesis of the top-down, standards-accountability, goal-setting, and transmissive data-based decision-making model that Type-A districts typify. They have deficient processes for generating self-similar records of action so emergent patterns cannot be easily observed and acted upon. The science department's invention and implementation of its TIPS-R response and the limited relevance of the SIS data in generating that response is a case in point. By way of comparison, PBCL emerges from the creative order of District-B.

The distinction between Type-A and Type-B districts is illustrated in District Example 4.5. In it, James welcomes a new member, Sylvia, to the board. Sylvia is new to the area and has no prior involvement with the district. She previously served on the board of a larger school district in another city. During her service there, Sylvia promoted the idea of an earlier start to the school day for high schools. She had read some research that showed students were overcommitted at school and were sleep-deprived as a result. Diminished sleep was correlated with drops in student achievement. Sylvia is keen to make a major contribution in her new role. So she arranges to meet with James to discuss a study showing that student achievement improved across her former district when school started an hour later.

District Example 4.5: Sylvia and James Meet

Sylvia says, "The study showed that when the district went to a later start time the high school students performed significantly better on the State Achievement Test." James nods in acknowledgment, then asks, "Were there any differences across kids who began the day earlier because of different bus routes or their levels of extracurricular involvement?" Sylvia indicates that she was unaware of any data in those areas. James asks, "What about absence, illness, homework completion, and performance in the curriculum beyond the standardized achievement tests?" Sylvia replies, "As far as I know, the study did not look at those factors."

James asks Sylvia to pull her chair up to a large computer screen where he has logged onto the District Portal and District Array. He enters a query on all high school students by bus route, ranked from the most distant from the school to the closest. Sylvia watches carefully as James explains what he is doing. He tells her, "The school day for those students in the most distant route begins 1 hour earlier than for those nearest." He also runs a query on attendance for all students, absence related to illness, and extracurricular activity. He drags homework completion and homework, grades into the query, as well as recent grades and achievement on the state test. He selects the report icon on his multilevel query and generates a series of line graphs that show the relationship between the bus route variable and extracurricular activity and attendance, sickness, class performance, state test performance, homework completion, and mastery.

James says, "Interesting—there is no discernible relationship shown on any of the graphs." He then queries the tools about whether there are any differences in performance and sickness for students who engage in high levels of activity and who can be categorized as near or far on the bus route. Sylvia watches carefully as the screen refreshes. James hits the summary button and a series of tables appear that show no difference for each of the factors. James walks Sylvia through the graphs and tables, explaining how they are linked to his previous questions, and tells her what is going on in each while summarizing the bigger-picture implications.

James says, "Looking at what we have here overall, I think we would expect to see a different picture if the kids were having problems. Even the kids with the heaviest extracurricular involvement who live the farthest away are managing their schedules and, with the exception of this bump during flu season, are staying pretty healthy and performing well."

Sylvia replies, "That's a remarkable tool you have there; I see that my homework was a little incomplete!" James tells her, "Yes, it helps me get the kind of information I need to make decisions. Ironically, I expect the main reason for the findings we saw here had much less to do with the factors we punched into the database and much more to do with the curriculum and teaching and learning in this district." He explains the difference in the level of stress and time taken with homework when a curriculum is differentiated, the role that students play in the learning process, and the alignment of in-school and out-of-school work with that role.

A number of things happen in the above exchange. First, Sylvia genuinely wants to make a difference. However, her supporting information is weak and incomplete. The study she cites shows a relationship between performance and start time but no causal attribution. In her prior experience, big ideas got political traction with limited evidence. So, when James seeks to fill in the blanks in the relationship between start time and achievement by asking questions, Sylvia is unprepared.

Second, because District-B has a schema and embedded design, James can generate the data necessary to fill in the blanks for Sylvia. He can inform their conversation with information about patterns of student performance, attendance, and travel. Third, *edge* technology makes the detection of those patterns an emergent process for James. The findings emerge from the rich data about the performance of the district available to him through the District Array. Sylvia is impressed with the technology and James's facility with it. Fourth, James does not take a position about school start time that Sylvia could construe as adversarial, overly judgmental, or kneejerk. Instead, the self-informative analysis he conducts shows Sylvia that her case for an earlier start time does not hold up for District-B. As a result, Sylvia steps back from her proposal. If James had not had edge technology and could not show the patterns in student performance, Sylvia might have persisted, turning her advocacy for an intuitively appealing change into a political battle. Fifth, James helpes Sylvia understand that the factors that drive the manageability of student workload are those that differentiate and align students' needs with the curriculum.

James realizes that Sylvia's start time proposal would massively affect the district's schedule. He has no problem making such a change if it can be shown to exert a high-power, proximal effect on student achievement. But looking into the district informs him that the need for Sylvia's initiative will produce no such effects. James uses the tools, feedback, and knowledge of District-B to fill the vacuum that politicized debate might have filled if an unresolved or poorly understood educational problem had received district-level consideration. The power he derives from looking into process at scale creates the opportunity for Sylvia and him to have a deeper, more productive conversation about teaching and learning.

Shift two: Reconciling forces for change. Addressing the 1:X challenge through research-based practice, collaboration, teacher effectiveness, authentic assessment, differentiation, and technology are resonant drivers of contemporary educational policies. Few, if any, local, state, or federal policies for the improvement of education conflict in principle with the form and function of the Type-B paradigm. However, for the Type-A paradigm, policies are poorly designed, distally connected, and bluntly applied to the students and teachers they are intended to benefit.

Sylvia's proposal for changing the district's policy about school start time might have foreshadowed such bluntness if it had not been mediated by a proximal understanding of what is actually going on. A disastrous implementation of an unneeded, low-power, distal policy could have resulted.

Reconciling forces is the second shift that a district must make. It involves the intersection of Type-A thought and policies with the complex sophistication of Type-B classrooms and schools. In Type-B, the district level navigates that intersection, ensures the proper flow of resources, and mitigates the disruption and diffusion that Type-A policies might cause Type-B practice.

In District Example 4.6, James reconciles the state's certification policies with District-B's professional development program. In an attempt to improve the quality of teachers in the state, the commissioner of education had changed the requirements for continuing education programs. A cornerstone of the new policy is an "approved provider clause" that establishes the state as the certifier of all professional development and continuing education providers. The state's universities are the preferred providers—a move intended to improve the quality of professional development and strengthen the district-university partnerships. For any program to receive professional development funds from the state, it has to be certified by the state.

Each year, District-B conducts two district-wide elementary and secondary school institutes. At the institutes, teachers learn the practices and processes that underpin their school's schema, design, and any practices common to both. New teachers attend an institute with an extensive multisession program. Shorter, ongoing institutes are held for current faculty to receive updates about practices such as PBCL. The district utilizes leading experts in the field to develop highly customized training modules for the institutes. The experts target specific areas of the schema that all teachers share. An expert teaches the first iteration of such modules. An aspiring or current master teacher from within the district teaches subsequent iterations.

Teaching in the institutes is a requirement for reaching master teacher status on the district's career ladder. A review of the modules is undertaken every 2 years. Changes to them are driven from within the district or by new research findings from outside. The dynamic design of the institutes is guided by the embedded design principle described in Chapter 3, which invokes a commitment to make those things a school believes in part of its design. It uses contemporary research evidence that shows PD is most impactful when it is research-based, deeply connected to the local context in which it is applied, evaluated beyond measures of teacher satisfaction with the experience, builds leadership capacity, and focuses on developing pedagogical and content knowledge (Guskey, 2003).

Despite having such a well-established and research-informed PD program, District-B does not meet the state's new requirements. Its strong in-house delivery approach does not comply with the approved provider clause. Unless the program connects with an approved provider, it will not receive state funding. James's colleagues at the state office are aware of the institutes and their rigor and reputation, but they are still constrained by the clause.

District Example 4.6: James Captures Resources

James calls Annette, the Dean of the Education at the local university, with whom he has served on several accreditation panels. He tells her, "I want to explore the possibility of involving your faculty in the delivery and evaluation of our institutes, I'm also interested in determining whether the institutes might comprise a graduate credit package for your Master in Education program."

Annette responds, "That certainly makes sense. We are always looking for legitimate collaborations. Your program has a good reputation and we would be happy to be involved. Of course, we do need to look closely at the details of what we offer versus what you are doing. I think it would bring us closer together. It'll also help our faculty meet its goals for faculty-district collaboration."

James says, "We've been working on modules that combine problem-based and cooperative learning. I know some of your faculty has expertise in those areas and could help us design and teach the first iteration." Annette replies, "Yes. We just made an appointment in inclusive practice, and I'm sure she'd be glad to help out. Also, other faculty members could review your existing modules, since that will be a requirement in the new guidelines. A review process will also help develop the credit package. I think our involvement in the institutes, along with the awarding of credit, should satisfy the new state certification requirements. It could also create some additional possibilities." James answers, "I agree. There is real potential here. Let's get together soon to look at the new requirements and work on an action plan."

The exchange between James and Annette highlights a number of disjunctures, challenges, and opportunities related to his efforts to reconcile a Type-A state policy with James's district's Type-B practices. First, the policy is driven by the state's well-intended attempt to improve the quality of continuing education that teachers receive. Although the policy seeks to influence the quality of content and the presentation of professional development, it does not address the contextual factors that influence the efficacy of those programs. The policy is distal to the continuing education problem, and thus low in power. Second, the institutes at District-B are an emergent expression of the research on PD and are proximal to the needs of stakeholders in its classrooms and schools. Moreover, the institutes have a high level of local delivery, customized design, and embedding in the broader design of the district's schools. This includes the way schools are organized and function, how teachers progress career-wise, and how edge technology is used. Third, although the new policy is benign in terms of PD effects, it is a challenge for the Type-B district that James leads. Ironically, his district's rigorous institutes are ineligible for PD funding. In order to obtain the funds, James has to reconcile an external Type-A force (i.e., state policy) with the emergent requirements (i.e., research-aligned PD) of the district.

James wants to implement the new PBCL training district-wide via the institutes, but he needs funding. So he collaborates with the local university and his friend Annette. Their collaboration can become a mutually interdependent relationship in which the university, by incorporating features of District-B's program into its work, will prepare pre-service teachers who will be attractive to Type-B schools, including those in James's district. The collaboration might also attract additional practices, research collaborations, and practicum opportunities. It might even develop a Type-B education faculty in direct support of the district.

Shift three: Strange attraction at district-wide scale. James, in his district-level role, uses emergent feedback and data to make decisions about PBCL and school start time, and to reconcile the institute approach to PD with a state policy. He responds to emergent issues identified at the board, school, and classroom levels, and in doing so, he evolves the district-level schema.

James also functions as a driver or source of change, playing the strange attraction role defined in Chapter 1 and personified by Sarah when she disturbs the equilibrium of her school by refining its PD focus on mastery teaching. District Example 4.7 presents highlights of James in his role as strange attractor in relation to parent involvement at District-B.

Parent involvement is a key tenet of the district's design. Parents have their own edge Plan Books, just as teachers and students do. Parents use the Plan Books to provide teachers with feedback about instruction, comment on curriculum, and access a broad range of information related to student performance. James recognizes that the level of access to classrooms and schools that parents have via their Plan Books is being underutilized at the district level. Ultimately, the district's budget and funding for new initiatives is subject to community approval. However, the kind of emergent bottom-up decision-making by teachers and administrators that drives the district's budget planning do not involve parents. James believes this is a missed opportunity. He feels that engaging parents in school-level goal-setting and planning will build support for the district's budget and capital initiatives. He develops a protocol for a parent town-hall meeting to be used to set goals in each school. James raises the protocol as an agenda item at a meeting of the district leadership team attended by the school principals.

District Example 4.7: James the Strange Attractor

James says, "I've placed a special item on the agenda for the leadership team to consider. I think we need parents to be more engaged in the broader strategic work of the district. I am proposing that we hold a town-hall-type meeting in each school that will allow you to present data on your schools' performance and needs and enable parents to get on board with meeting those needs."

James says, "I will attend and help facilitate each meeting. Let's go over the protocol that I've laid out in this PowerPoint presentation. As you can see, I am using the tools available in the parent Plan Book to show how we are doing. I know some of you have reported a reduction in parent use of the tools. I think we can use the town-hall meetings as an opportunity to reinforce the importance of parents using that tool in addition to our broader agenda of strategic parent engagement. Let me explain the steps of the protocol."

James says, "I think the town-hall meeting approach represents an opportunity to share each school's needs with parents in ways that can reflect their perceptions and engender their support." Sarah interjects, "This makes sense overall. But we do need a tight action plan for the conduct of the meetings and we need to clarify the role you will play in collaboration with the principals." James agrees and finishes his presentation, then turns the meeting over to the leadership team. The group uses its collaborative process to respond to his proposal. They have an extensive discussion on how the town-hall meeting should be implemented, and develop a clear plan of action.

Why are James's parent engagement efforts a source of strange attraction? He sees the static role parents play and the equilibrium condition that the parents' passivity fosters in the district's schools. He is concerned about four things. First, although the district has provided parents with Plan Books they can use to engage with the educational process, at most schools the parents' use of the Plan Books is limited. Second, while most parents are engaged in a general conversation about their child's learning, their engagement is passive. Neither the feedback parents provide nor the schools' use of it to plan and problem-solve extend to the district level. Because he has not observed any actions being taken to address the situation, James doubts that school principals are aggressively seeking deeper engagement from parents.

Third, James envisages parent engagement as a positive disruption that will bring additional perspectives to school and district decision-making. He believes that the current situation represents a lost opportunity for garnering parent views and building support for the district. Fourth, James's parent engagement protocol extends the role of parents. Parent input will embed the role of parents in the design of their children's school. Greater use of the Plan Book will generate additional input building upon existing feedback about the performance of the school in a positively disruptive, not chaotic, manner. He uses the leadership team meeting to build support for the protocol. The collaborative process used at it is the same as the approach used by teachers and students. James built a rationale and case for his parent proposal at the leadership meeting and helped ensure that the solution would not be foisted upon the principals.

James's actions on behalf of parents illustrates the way that a district-level leader in a Type-B district can attract support for evolving a district's schema in ways that reflect the values and principles on which that schema is based. James helps schools avoid equilibrium that might have caused stakeholders to be less responsive to the changing circumstances under which they operate.

HOW SHIFTS IN THOUGHT WORK AT THE DISTRICT LEVEL

A schema, self-similar design, and common tools shared by a district-wide community of practice can foster the self-organizing and problem-solving capacity that make a powerful new role for ICT possible. Three shifts make the district level an iteration of the beliefs, values, and design principles embedded in its classrooms and schools. This is why District-B could act responsively and proactively in relation to the patterns in the emergent feedback it receives. It is how James can lead learning at scale. He and the board act responsively to the high-level extant performance patterns of the district by helping teachers and schools to scale up their emergent needs and solutions.

This capacity to respond and lead is empowered by the scaled-up view of teaching and learning they possess because they use *e*dge technology. Such capacity empowers James as he reconciles the external policy forces that might affect the behavior of his schools and teachers. It is what makes James and the district level sources of strange attraction, uniquely positioned to have a perspective that disturbed the equilibrium of schools and the district overall. What James does with and for District-B echoes what Sarah did with and for School-B. Both disperse control and acts in self-similar ways. They share the same processes for collaborative problem-solving and shared decision-making.

*E*dge technology makes the shifts possible. James, using the District Array, looks deeply into the work of stakeholders at the schools. He detects their needs and responds accordingly. For instance, the Array helps him recognize when and where action is necessary for scaling PBCL district-wide. It extends his decision-making capacity, builds his understanding of the way the work of classrooms and schools could scale to the district level, and shortens the cognitive distance between the district and parents. No matter how many times James might visit a school or meet with teachers or parents, he will always be closer to all members of the community because of *e*dge technology.

THE ICT TOOLS THAT ALLOW
DISTRICT LEVELS UPPORT FOR SCHOOLS

In the examples of the district-level supporting the classroom and school levels of a Type-B system, we refer many times to the *e*dge technology used to interrogate problems, detect patterns of performance, and create sources of strange attraction. Figure 4.1 presents the layout of the Plan Book James uses to perform these functions.

Figure 4.2 depicts the District Array that James used to problem-solve the student sleep issue. The array includes layouts for district and individual school performance on teaching practice, problem-solving, curriculum progress, and student achievement based upon standardized, curriculum, and portfolio measures.

Figure 4.1. District Level Plan Book

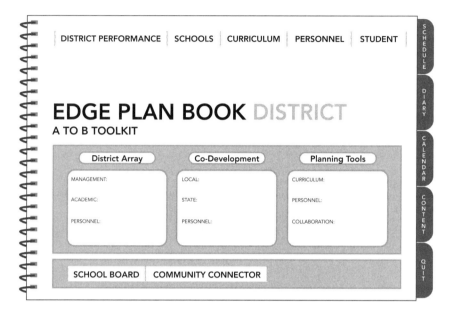

Figure 4.2. District Array

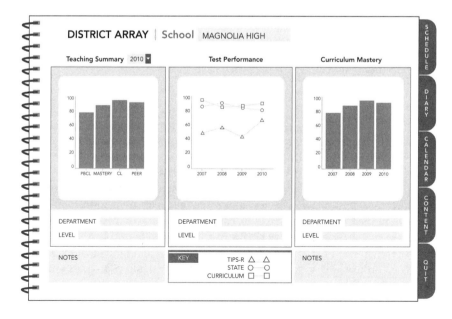

Figure 4.3 depicts a query field that James uses to undertake the data-mining and problem-solving that he does during his conversation with Sylvia about the possibility of changing school start time. Board members and other district-level leaders have access to the same tools and can engage in their own data-mining and problem-solving.

James also uses the Co-Development Tools to connect the policies that are driven at the district from outside with the emergent self-organizing system that he leads inside it. For instance, the tools help him reconcile the district's professional development efforts with the state's drive to improve continuing education. Figure 4.4 presents a tool that James can use to link sources of funds with the factors (e.g., differentiating and aligning student needs with the curriculum) that he and Sylvia determine will help students better manage their respective workloads and the needs identified by teachers, students, parents, and school leaders within the district.

Figure 4.3. District Array: Query Builder

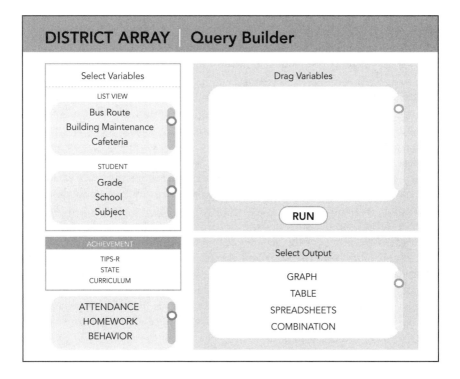

Figure 4.4. District Co-Development Tool

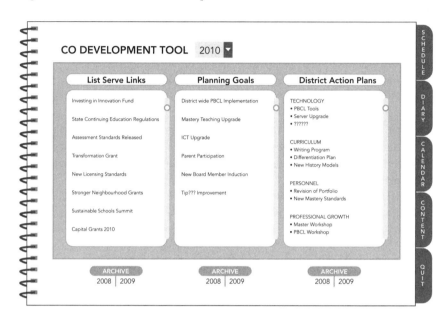

Just as the classroom and school tools described in Chapters 2 and 3 create an *e*dge by bringing teachers and students together, district-level tools have the same effect for James by shortening the edges of the network. They create an *e*dge at scale. They focus the entire learning community on its core activity and shorten the cognitive distance between its stakeholders. In this way, District-B is a scaled-up representation of the interactions occurring in all of its classrooms.

By way of contrast, the Type-A district structure represents a scaled-up version of the hierarchical and centralized Type-A classroom and school described in chapters two and three. The Type-A structure regresses to a top-down flow of information and decision-making as unresolved problems scale up. The network structure elongates the distance between the students and teachers, classrooms and schools and schools and the district. The Type-B district, on the other hand, represents a leveled extension of the free-flowing school network described in chapter three. Each of the tools described here leverages the shared schema and design that exists in District-B's schools, making leadership connected, solutions responsive, and creating an interface with the Type-A system that exists beyond the Type-B district.

SHARED SCHEMA: UNITING DISTRICT, SCHOOL, AND CLASSROOMS

Let us now revisit the three-step schema framework that was applied in previous chapters to examine the key propositions of this chapter.

New Assumptions

Assumption one: Chapters 2 and 3 show the ways in which the 1:X challenge could only be resolved with ICT. Edge technology creates the conditions to make a different kind of classroom and school possible. In this chapter, we show how *e*dge technology makes it possible for the district level to capitalize on the emergent order that exists in those transformed classrooms and schools at even greater scale. *E*dge technology makes it possible to see needs, identify patterns of success, and build solutions with a resonance that emerges from the distinctive self-consistency and similarity across the district's schools. *E*dge technology in the form of the district-level tools serve as a vehicle for generating the insight that makes it possible for James to act with confidence at scale, whether he is responding to the emergent needs of schools or determining where to act as a source of strange attraction.

Assumption two: The edge technology described in this chapter exemplifies the assumption that the role for ICT at scale must be defined by the research on teaching and learning. The example of the process employed to develop the tools for PBCL epitomized this connection. Because the tools described in this chapter are a scaled-up version of those used in classrooms and schools, they are underpinned by the same research-based design assumptions related to curriculum, pedagogy, and school organization. The only differences between them are the power and field of view provided by a district-level lens.

Assumption three: We show the way learning with ICT becomes indistinguishable from learning about it. James's use of the tools informs his knowledge of the district as well as his knowledge of the tools. This is why he can inform and assist others, including the school principals and board members.

Assumption four: James's lens shortens the distance between the district leadership and the individual members of the community, making dispersed control possible. James can drill down to look at an individual class, a piece of curriculum, a parent's feedback, and a student record shortening the distance between him and the individuals who originally generated the information. Deep access and a wide view makes it possible for James and the board to serve as a source of strange attraction in the district through a sensitive engagement with what he knows because of his *e*dge technology. Whether in service to dispersed control or strange attraction, ICT becomes the way the district gets things done, positioning its leadership to work in ways that are relevant to addressing the 1:X challenge.

Assumption five: The edge technology James uses connects all of his efforts at scale back to the contributions of individual teachers, students, parents, and school leaders. In doing so they enable everyone to maintain a tight, concerted focus on student achievement. The knowledge they create and produce represents the solution to the 1:X challenge.

New Design

James and the stakeholders at District-B use the design metaphor described in Chapter 1: solution mapping, component building, and design integration. Their *e*dge technology is positioned as an emergent, scaled-up expression of Type-B classrooms and schools. The schema and tools of the classrooms and schools is the *solution map* for the district level and the design of *e*dge technology at scale. Edge technology is integrated at scale in self-similar ways. It generates the record of action from which patterns of continuity and discontinuity in the performance of classrooms and schools emerged. This leads to further *component building.* Edge technology also plays a critical role in scaling up a classroom schema for practice to the level of the district. The tools such *design integration* makes it possible the district level contribute to it becoming a scaled-up expression of the way each classroom and school addressed the 1:X challenge.

New Trajectory

This chapter shows how Type-B classrooms and schools can be supported by Type-B districts. Subsequent chapters position the district in a broader context in which it co-evolves with associations, policies, and businesses to meet the 1:X challenge. The self-similar district-level representation of classrooms and schools is shown to reshape the role of professional associations, the way policy is developed, and the way businesses serve the field of education.

SUMMARY

- Teaching and learning problems that are not resolved at their source are unlikely to be resolved at scale by low-power, high-load, distal solutions.
- When a district shares a schema with its classrooms and schools, its gains power by viewing the patterns of work done in each from the altitude of scale.

- Edge technology shortens the edges between stakeholders at various levels of the system. This increases the likelihood that they will enjoy shared understanding, collective action, and better results.
- In a system driven by bottom-up feedback, district-level leaders must do more than just respond. They must use the helicopter perspective to become a strange attractor that disturbs the equilibrium of the overall system.

CHAPTER 5

Associations and *Edge* Technology

*People seldom improve when they have no other model
but themselves to copy after.*
—*Oliver Goldsmith*

Why do membership organizations have limited effects on the overall performance of the educational system? We answer this question by (a) reviewing the nature of Type-A associations and groups, (b) showing that they are incapable of supporting the work of their members, (c) explaining why such associations and groups maintain Type-A, inhibit 1:X, prevent Type-B, and do not support 2-Sigma at scale, (d) presenting three shifts in thought that make Type-B associations and groups possible, and (e) showing how Type-B groups better serve members and educational improvement at scale.

THE PROBLEM WE FACE AT
THE LEVEL OF ASSOCIATIONS

Over the past 3 decades, many organizations have involved themselves in efforts to innovate, reform, and change various levels of the educational system. They often contributed leadership, offered expertise, and mobilized support for such efforts (Glaser, 1993). Of the organizations that made such contributions, most fit into two general categories—professional and advocacy.

Professional associations, sometimes called trade associations (e.g., Council of Chief State School Officers, National School Board Association), inform, support, and unite people who do the same type of work and have similar jobs (Sheridan, Stephens, Cimini, Watson, & Talbot, 2007). Advocacy groups (e.g., Committee for Educational Funding) influence public opinion and/or policy (VeneKlasen & Miller, 2007; Wong, 1999). Both types of groups vary considerably in size, influence, and motive (McLaughlin, 2009). Their scopes can be international, national, regional, local, or a combination of these (Glaser, 1993). Some even combine professional and advocacy functions (Schott, 2006).

Every educational stakeholder has at least one professional association representing the role he or she plays in the overall educational system. For instance, school superintendents have the American Association of School Administrators (AASA, 2010), education-department technology directors have the State Educational Technology Directors Association (SETDA, 2010a), and so on. Likewise, nearly every issue has its own corresponding advocacy group. For instance, the International Society for Technology in Education (ISTE, 2010a) promotes more and better ICT use in schools. Since every stakeholder and issue has corresponding associations, it is not surprising there are hundreds of thousands of education associations and groups worldwide (Gale, 2010). It is surprising that associations and groups, however, despite their best intentions and resources dedicated to particularized interests, generally fail to meet the needs of their members (Cavaney, Wash, & Holleyman, 2007), influence issues (U.S. Congress, 1998), or positively affect education overall (Cheung, 2009).

The failure is evident in four ways. First, when education associations and groups champion laws that would benefit their members, the misguided conceptualization or incomplete implementation of the laws that they champion often impede benefits from the laws accruing for members at scale (Deschenes, Cuban, & Tyack, 2001; Herring, McGrath, & Buckley, 2007). Few groups, if any, achieve their hoped-for outcomes. Second, during the past 3 decades, the educational funding increases that have been sought by associations and groups for their members nearly always proved unattainable due to the field of education's lack of consensus on how best to educate all students to high levels of learning or proved financially unsustainable because of competing agendas and limited funds (Brimly & Garfield, 2007). Third, the inclusion of ICT—computers, the Internet, and software—in the work of associations and members only occurs at limited scale (Becker, 1999, 2001). Fourth, even when associations and groups did contribute to efforts to bring more students into the educational system (Glaser, 1993; Herring, McGrath, & Buckley, 2007), questions about the efficacy of the system into which students are brought remain unanswered (Deschenes, Cuban, & Tyack, 2001; Gordon & Graham, 2003).

WHAT IS WRONG WITH TYPE-A ASSOCIATIONS

To understand why this happens, we need to examine the outcomes that present-day associations and groups seek for their members. They aspire to represent the interests and needs of membership, contribute to an overall agenda for bettering education, build capacity of members for advancing that agenda, and carry out activities for that strengthen the association or group's relevance and power in the educational system (Sheridan, Stephens, Cimini, Watson, & Talbot, 2007). Most groups engage in five common activities. First, nearly every association and group convenes meetings and holds conferences that provide opportunities for members to spend collaborative time together and provide the hosting association or group with a means to gain revenue (Mina, 2000 Talbot, 1990). Second, associations use various means of communication—such as newsletters (Beach & Floyd, 1998), Websites (Whitaker, 2007), blogs (Loewenstein, 2008), social media (Evans, 2010), and webinars (Clay, 2009)—to inform, motivate, solicit, and educate members (NEA, 1969). Third, associations sometimes conduct research (Portis & Gargia, 2007; Wilson & Peterson, 2006). A few even publish journals, such as the Journal of Scholarship and Practice of the American Association of School Administrators (AASA-JSP, 2010) and the Education Journal of Digital Learning in Teacher Education of the International Society of Technology in Education (ISTE, 2010d). Fourth, some groups promote specific practices for members to use, programs for them to attend, policies for them to follow, and/or laws for governments to enact. Associations that have an ICT orientation typically push for funded government initiatives that increase student and teacher access to ICT (C2K, 2010; DEEWR, 2010; USDOE, 2010a; Partnerships for Schools, 2010). Fifth, since the stakeholders of associations and groups are often required by their profession or the government to meet continuing education and/or certification requirements, some associations and groups offer professional development for members (Jacobs & Glassie, 2004). A few even manage the certification process for their members (ASCA, 2010; ASLHA, 2010).

Thousands of education related associations and groups around the globe perform similar functions. Collectively, they generate and spend hundreds of millions of dollars, convene thousands of events, send countless communiqués, report a great deal of research, advocate for their priorities, and offer training to their members. They do this in the name of their members for the sake of improving education (Cavaney, Wasch, & Holleyman, 2007; Gale, 2010; Masemann, Bray, & Manzon, 2007; Sheridan, Stephens, Cimini, Watson, & Talbot, 2007). Association Example 5.1 presents a staff meeting at one such organization, the fictional Association for Education Technology Professionals (Association-A).

Association Example 5.1:
Association-A Plans Its Annual Conference

Herb, the executive director of Association-A, sits in the chair at the head of the table in a conference room packed with staff. Today is the day that Herb finalizes the agenda for the 24th Annual Conference and Workshops of Association-A. As members of the staff make their reports, Herb's personal assistant takes notes.

Tricia the association's director of events and planning goes first. She tells the group, "I'm exhausted. Four of us spent the last 5 days reviewing proposals for concurrent sessions. We recommend that Herb approve 40 of the 129 proposals submitted, the ones that best reflect a balance of hot topics, sponsors, members, and geography. Eleven of the sessions feature new products or research about recently released products. Each has a corporate sponsor. Also per Herb's request, board members will lead seven of the concurrent sessions. If any of you want to look at the proposals, check out the workroom, I've stacked them there."

Tricia continues, "We sent out an email survey to members, other stakeholders who've attended our past meetings, and vendors who've sponsored sessions and rented booths. Not many members responded, so we anticipated their needs. We did receive high returns from vendors who wanted to be formal presenters. There will be four pre-conference workshops, each eligible for continuing education credit and recertification purposes. Two are topical—standardizing data systems and minimizing implementation costs. The other two feature corporate sponsors who offered up a day of training about their new products."

After thanking Tricia, Herb asks, "What day do I give my state-of-the-state speech? This one will be my 10th. I've spent 6 months collecting jokes to tell." Tricia replies, "You'll be up on day 2. I promise to laugh." He then calls on conference planner Jan to report. Jan says, "Big news! Luke Bull is our keynote speaker. Of the five possible choices in our online poll, he got the most votes. He even campaigned for the slot."

Business manager Pat reports, "The board meets on the first day of the conference. The seven board members who are doing concurrent sessions will be there. The other five will call in. Herb will present the association's budget and preview the new publications being released on day 2. The latest issue of our *Teaching Technology Journal* will be featured. It contains case studies of the 1:1 laptop programs in five districts. Herb, do you plan to brief the board about what you are doing to restore funding for the Enhancing Education Through Technology (E2T2) grants?"

Herb answers, "Yes, I will. Our software indicates that year over year we've lost 20% of our member-schools and conference registrations are down 13%. I'm hoping to offset lost revenue by getting more corporate sponsors and selling more booth space. Julie, how are we doing on those fronts?" Julie replies, "We have 10 new sponsors and booth rentals are up 17% from the past year."

Before ending the meeting, Herb and the staff sort out logistics for the Internet kiosk donated by a corporate sponsor, finalize the entrée and dessert selections for the banquet, and review the ceremony for the distinguished-member-award winner Herb selected. After adjourning, Pat summarizes the meeting in an email that she sends to the listserv, posts on the association's blog, adds to her Facebook page, and posts on Twitter.

We can see seven attributes in Herb's meeting that provide insights into how Association-A works. First, it is controlled hierarchically. Herb runs everything. Second, the association is distally connected to the lives of its members and the classrooms, schools, and districts in which they work. It has no view into those settings. So, amid ever-changing circumstances, the association has limited capacity to adapt in ways that better serve, retain, and/or attract members. Third, in the association's design and operation, members are affiliated to the work that the association does but are non-collaborative parts in the association's work processes, they are low-power components. The association does *for* members, not *with* them. Herb controls the budget, session selections, awards, lobbying, and more. Fourth, Association-A has neither schema nor commitment to shared practice. So the work that some staff does is not connected to the work that other staff do and all the work of the staff is disconnected from the work of the association's members. The work is reactive, just like the work its members do in the classrooms and schools. The day-to-day work of the association's staff and members is distal to the association's advocacy for ICT and the ICT professionals. Herb scrambles to restore funding for E2T2 (USDOE, 2010a), but has no mandate from his members about the importance of those grant funds in the ICT related work that members do. Fifth, the organizational network of the association makes communication with members difficult and generates little usable data about what members do in their work and how the association might aid members' efforts. The network has long edges. Leadership is distanced from members; work is determined via delegation of tasks rather than shared schema. The relationships are self-serving; Herb gives the "state-of-the association" speech; board members get preferential treatment for leading concurrent sessions, and so on. Sixth, the feedback generated by the surveys that few members or venders respond to is idiosyncratic and disconnected from the association's goals and those of its members. For instance, the selection of sessions and speakers is driven by sponsorships and popularity, not the day-to-day realities facing members. Seventh, ICT plays an ancillary role. It automates some functions (e.g., conference registration) of the association but not others. Staff still reviews session proposals manually, Internet kiosks are still ad hoc components to the conference, and social media because it is used in a post-the-message-and-hope-someone-reads-it mode still passively communicates the business of the association to its members. The connections between the association, staff, and members are distal and low-power just like the Type-A classroom, school, and district settings in which members work. Because the linkages among staff and members are non-meaningful, unproductive, and reactive, ICT neither serves the association nor its members at scale.

What do the seven attributes indicate about Association-A's capacity for representing members and bettering education? They show it to be "orderly" (Prigogine & Stengers, 1984), "quiescent" (Currie, 1974), and "dissimilar" across members and staff (Cross & Sudkamp, 2002). It functions to preserve the status quo. It has much action, but little forward movement. The association exists in a state of equilibrium. Herb and the staff oscillate from one annual conference to the next, one hot issue to another. Not much change and few tangible effects are produced by the efforts of Herb and staff. Things are done as they have been done for years (Herb's 10th state-of-the-association address will differ little from his first). Members and staff are affiliated, but not connected. Staff and members are independent from everyone and everything else. Technology is not a key element in the design of the association, a driver for its continuous improvement, or a shared tool for staff and members. Not surprisingly, the staff does not bother to bring their computers to the planning session.

The design, operation, and activity of Association-A represent a pattern of non-support for members and educational innovation, reform, and change at scale. This point is made clear when, during the planning session, Herb and staff do not once reference common educational goals, member needs, or performance measures. Association-A is incapable of representing its members well.

WHAT MAKES TYPE-B ASSOCIATIONS MORE EFFECTIVE

Must education associations and groups be run the way Herb runs Association-A? Must they contribute so little to overall efforts to improve education? Must they lack the capacity to attract support for educational innovation, reform, and change? Definitely not. The example below introduces a different approach. One in which the stakeholders (e.g., Herb) are the same as in the earlier example, but the association's design, operation, and activities have changed. Association Example 5.2 looks at a conference planning session at Association-B, the former Association-A, which continues to represent educational technology professionals.

Association Example 5.2:
Association-B Plans Its Annual Conference

Association member Bruce, executive director Herb, conference planner Jan, business manager Pat, events director Tricia, and membeship coordinator Julie sit at a table in the conference room. Herb opens the Meeting Tool in the Association's section of the A to B Toolkit that he accesses through the Association's portal. He asks Jan to facilitate the meeting and offers to time-keep. Jan makes introductions as Bruce plugs his laptop into the overhead projector, gets online, navigates to the portal, and then clicks on the Member Schools Performance Array. Everybody at the table and on the conference call bridge is logged on to the portal.

Looking around the room Jan asks everyone "Ready to check in? How are we progressing with our goals?" After recording and summarizing the responses of the group, she asks, "What does the latest data indicate about problem-solving incidents at the member schools?"

Bruce smiles shyly, and replies, "I analyzed the performance evaluation data from our 400 member schools. It shows that during the past 6 months, the schools undertook 1,798 problem-solving activities. A subcommittee cross-referenced those incidents with the feedback from teachers and their peer observations of their classrooms conducted during the same timeframe. Another subcommittee reviewed the feedback from parents and students. My analysis of both indicates 129 curricular design issues. All of them fit into one of three categories: differentiating cooperative learning, improving the Array, and refining and advancing the content of the A to B Toolkit." Tricia says, "My working group used Bruce's analysis to design the workshops and concurrent sessions for the annual conference."

Herb answers, "When I reviewed the same data and cross-referenced it with other efforts under way here, two policy issues emerged that will surely affect our schools. One, our model must fit the new requirements for getting professional development funds from the education department. Two, the low rate of career progression among our master teachers means we must strengthen the advanced curriculum development component of the career path. I think we should hold workshops that target both issues."

Herb continues, "This year, my state-of-the-association speech is being replaced with a panel of members discussing the Advanced Mastery Teaching workshop that school principal Sarah pioneered. In my intro of them, I'll talk about what the data from the Array indicates about the big picture for 1:X and ask members to keep using the A to B Toolkit to generate examples of how they resolve classroom and school incidents. When the panel ends, we'll present the 2-Sigma Awards. According to Member School Performance Array, 15 schools earned the award. Last year's winners will present the awards this year."

Business manager Pat replies, "The board has decided to meet on day 1 of the conference. They will have a facilitated discussion about the progression of member schools to 1:X, the impact of changes made to the association since their last meeting, and the implications of the data that Bruce just reported. They'll also be briefed by fellow members about issues—money is a big one—that members asked us to track, participate in breakout sessions led by teacher Anne, principal Sarah, and teacher Phil, and receive executive summaries of soon to be released publications."

Pat goes on to say, "Also, the board wants Herb to report about how the Funding Work Group is influencing the reauthorization of E2T2 to make that grant program conform to our latest data about what member schools need to make their 1:x exemplars more commonplace. The board is pleased with how Herb is leading members and officials in Washington, DC, to co-develop the E2T2 solution, while we are waiting for the solution to be finalized we have a waiver in place to that ensures funding continues flowing without interruption."

Membership coordinatior Julie offers, "We have 79 new member schools, 30% year-over-year increase in pre-registrants, a 15% increase in exhibitors, and 25% increase in members. Three of the new exhibitors will be demonstrating the new software and services they developed from the work they did with Bruce and his fellow physics teachers."

At the end of the session, Bruce clicks the send icon on the work session template. Instantaneously, everyone at the session receives a summary of the information that was shared and decisions that were made. Each person takes a moment to review everything and then rate the quality of his or her contribution to the effort.

Let's look at Association-B using the same seven attributes we applied earlier to Association-A. First, the primary design characteristic of Association-B is dispersed control. Decisions are made with and through members. Herb leads the overall association as a member of a team. Second, stakeholders of Association-B have a common understanding about the professional practices of the association and have a plan of action for having those practices occur at scale. This is the schema that they share. Hence, staff and members have extensive capacity to *see* into data about member's classrooms, schools, and districts and to *respond* to what they see occurring in those settings. The staff and members are proximally connected; the design of their network of which Association-B is a part has short edges because the flow of information and feedback occurs multidirectional across the now more flatly organized association. For instance, the annual conference is informed by the 1,798 problem-solving incidents that have been culled down to 129 curricular design issues, and then synthesized into the three categories that subsequently become the foci of the workshops and concurrent sessions at the conference. The tight connection between the conference and the problem incidents is an intentional consequence of how Association-B is designed to respond to member feedback. As individual members change and develop, the association's design allows for collective and interconnected change and development. Its edge technology brings about emergent feedback, which helps make the association high-power, low-load, and responsive to the educational challenges that members face daily. Third, all members and staff are active in the affairs of Association-B. The processes they use reflect a common schema, design, and operation that are scaled up iterations of the designs, processes, and tools members use. In this way the processes that the tools enable are essential to the individual and collective work that all the association's stakeholders do. Association-B is about its members, whereas Association-A is about itself and its leader Herb. Fourth, Association-B has proactive, focused, emergent, and proximal advocacy for its members. It attracts new members and retains current ones to the association and proactively provides them the knowledge, expertise, skills, and advocacy that they need (but may not have realized they need) to meet their 1:X and 2-Sigma goals. It also pulls members and staff closer to the problem being solved. For instance, when Herb proposes solutions for two emergent problems (e.g., funding changes and career path), he provides an invaluable service to members, one that only he, with his view and experience across levels, could provide. Fifth, since everyone associated with Association-B shares a common schema, they are able to form collaborative relationships. The collaborative approach (e.g., report outs using the Array and Toolkit) that they employ for conference planning is the same one that members such as Bruce, Sarah, and James use in their respective classrooms, schools, and districts. Likewise Association-B and its members use a multilevel monitoring approach to track progress toward 2-Sigma. The multi-level data that is monitored makes making directional changes uneventful (e.g., adding workshops and concurrent sessions) for the association. Each stakeholder's work informs the work of Association-B and its members, reduces their loads, and advances their shared schema. Sixth, the design and processes of Association-B enable the timely and informative feedack that make self-organizing activity possible across the many levels of the educational system. Such feedback reduces the distance between members and staff, problems and solutions, and the effort expected and effort needed for meeting the 1:X challenge and attaining 2-Sigma. Seventh, edge technology is essential to everyone and everything associated with Association-B. It is part of the association's overall design and operation and represents the schema, aids stakeholders' co-development, strengthens their decision-making, and reduces their cognitive load.

What do the seven attributes indicate about Association-B and its capacity for representing members and improving education overall? They show Association-B it to be dynamic and forward moving. Its staff and members are proactive, interconnected agents who share control of their association. They contribute, create, implement, and refine the schema that is shared by several levels of the overall educational system. Edge technology reflects that schema. It enables the timely feedback of members and staff that informs and guides all their activity.

Because of its design and operation, Association-B plays an essential leadership role in the work of its members and is a strange attractor that drives purposeful change throughout all levels of the system. Although the association is physically removed from its members, the association still makes proximal, high-power, and load-reducing contributions to them. For instance, it aids members by identifying and addressing the issues of funding for professional development and the low rate of career progression among master teachers. Not surprisingly, its membership numbers are higher year over year. Tricia worked at Association-A and now works at Association-B. In Association Example 5.3, Tricia relates her experience working with each.

Association Example 5.3: Tricia Reflects on A and B

"Three years ago, I nearly quit my job as director of events at Association-A. Organizing the annual conference was a nightmare. Keeping everyone happy was impossible. Herb drove me nuts. If he read something in the newspaper, he would want me to organize a session about that topic. Business manager Pat was just as bad. When he got a call from a board member, he would tell me to create a new session even if there was no space. Whatever I did, sessions were never good enough. After the conference, I cried when I read the bad evaluations.

"Now, we do things differently. Our processes are computerized and available through the A to B Toolkit. Members use the same Toolkit in their schools and classrooms. I daily query the activity and feedback from member schools using the Array. I feel connected and engaged with what happens. The Array gives me real-time information about how things are going for our members. That information shows me what to do to help them. Our meetings are run the same way that member schools run their meetings. We include leaders and teachers and they include us in their meetings. So, when we put the annual conference together, we easily determine what sessions to offer. Members expect us to bring sessions to them that are relevant to them. And we expect them to bring more members to Association-B.

"Now I get emails from members expressing gratitude for what they experienced at the conference. I feel like I am truly making a difference. Plus, the vendors who chose to attend self-select. They know that if they have something genuinely useful, then our members will want it, but if they have old technology or outdated ideas, there won't be any interest."

Tricia's experiences at the association show what it means to represent and attract members at scale and support their attainment of 2-Sigma. Much of the difference that Tricia recounts comes from the unseen aspects of Association-B that affect her behavior and reduce her job related stress and frustration (cognitive load). The unseen aspects are twofold. One unseen aspect is the processes and tools that comprise Association-B's design and operation. The other aspect is the way the design and operation of the association mirrors the processes and tools that its members use elsewhere. Both aspects bring the association (including Tricia) and its members closer by shortening the network edges of the members and staff's communications across the multi-level educational system. The shorter edges are evident as Bruce and Herb gather, analyze, and cross-reference member schools' data prior to the conference planning session. Their findings drive the planning and ensure that the conference includes proximal, high-power concurrent and general sessions that match member needs and attract registrants and exhibitors. Their findings also bolster staff confidence that the experiences of attendees will be relevant to their day-to-day work. In this way, the conference that Tricia and the staff produce is a genuine response to member needs.

SHIFTS IN THOUGHTS NEEDED TO IMPROVE ASSOCIATIONS

How does Tricia find working at Association-B less demanding and more rewarding than working at Association-A, even though the former iteration of the association had a more orderly design and operation? Tricia finds this to be the case because stakeholders transformed the staid, isolating, and stress producing Association-A into the dynamic, participatory, and stakeholder-enabling Association-B. Three design and operational shifts helped bring about the transformation. First, stakeholders shifted from centralized to dispersed control of the association. They realized that more of the Type-A Herb-in-charge leadership was akin to more of the Type-A principal-centric schools at which they had worked. Since the approach failed to represent classrooms at the school level and schools at the district level, members knew it could not represent them at the association level. Such representation would only be possible if control of the association is dispersed. Second, such dispersal is possible because the association's work is done using the same practices, processes, and tools that members employed in their respective work settings. Members knew that shifting control from a staff-centric to a stakeholder-centric model necessitated a more essential role for ICT, one that is profoundly different from the peripheral contribution that ICT made to Association-A. ICT must generate, reflect, and analyze the feedback that guides and manages Association-B. So, ad hoc ICT use was replaced with the edge technology that is used throughout all levels of the system. Third, stakeholders knew that the cognitive load that limits individual stakeholders from generating greater effects on learning in their school and district settings could be reduced by shifting some of the individual member load to Association-B where its shared schema makes load reduction possible

Shift one: Dispersing control to stakeholders. The Type-A design of most education associations and groups gives operational control of them to one person (e.g., executive director) or a small group of persons (e.g., board of directors), and that control is codified by articles of incorporation, charters, and bylaws (French, 2009). He, she, or they subsequently (a) set the association's mission, (b) plan for mission attainment, and (c) manage the personnel and resources for doing so (Pakroo, 2009). Such efforts nearly always include the development of documents that contain explicit aspirations for representing members and achieving lofty goals (Graham & Havlick, 1994). Association Example 5.4 includes excerpted samples from the mission statements of three representative education associations. Note: The *emphasis* seen in the excerpts has been added.

Association Example 5.4: Excerpts of Mission Statements

The mission of the American Association of School Administrators is to support and develop effective school system leaders who are dedicated to the *highest quality public education for all children* (AASA, 2010).

[The International Society for Technology in Education] *advances excellence in learning and teaching* through innovative and effective uses of technology (ISTE, 2010B).

State Educational Technology Directors Association (SETDA) . . . serves, supports and *represents* the interests of the educational technology leadership of state education agencies in all 50 states, the District of Columbia, the Bureau of Indian Affairs, American Samoa, and the U.S. Virgin Islands (SETDA, 2010a). (emphasis added)

The mission statements above, much like the documents that guide most Type-A associations and groups, assume that attaining representational and educational aspirations is possible without a collective schema and a design for making aspirations happen. As shown with District-B's Technology Plan, unless terms such as "learning experience," "technology tools," and "well-researched practice" are explicitly defined, then mission statements are destined to be distal and low-power. Moreover, associations and groups assume that their guiding documents give them sufficient capacity for realizing their aspirations if they "serve" members, have "core beliefs," "agreed upon goals," "strategic plans" in place, and use technology in "innovative and effective" ways. Explicit in such documents is verbiage describing organizational structures, financial provisions, staffing roles, and so on. Association Example 5.5 presents descriptions for a senior staff role that were excerpted from documents of the three organizations for which the mission statements were previously presented.

Association Example 5.5: Examples of Role Descriptions

Executive Director [of the American Association of School Administrators]
. . . Serves as national spokesperson and advocate for public education, superintendents and other school system leaders. Provides thought

leadership in the education arena through public appearances, media interviews, and published articles. Is the chief executive officer for the association and staff liaison to the AASA governance structure (AASA, 2010).

Chief Executive Officer [of the International Society of Technology in Education] . . . Primary responsibility is to carry out Board Policies as adopted by the Board of Directors and to act as official staff liaison to the Board of Directors. The Chief Executive Officer also (1) provides staff leadership and executive management for the organization as a whole, and delegates those responsibilities of management as shall be in the best interest of the organization; (2) acts as the official spokesperson for the organization; (3) signs legally binding agreements and contractual obligations on behalf of the organization; and (4) implements the strategic plan through leadership for planning, implementation, and evaluation of the organization's services, programs, and other activities (ISTE, 2010c).

The Chairperson [of the State Educational Technology Directors Association] shall be the chief executive officer of the organization. He/she shall preside at all meetings of the Board of Directors. He/she shall have general supervision of the business of the organization and shall be responsible for having all orders and resolutions of the Board of Directors carried into effect. As authorized by the Board of Directors, he/she shall execute on behalf of the organization and may affix or cause to be affixed the corporate seal to such other duties and do such other acts as are prescribed by the Board of Directors. He/she shall work in partnership with the Executive Director to carry out Board decisions (SETDA, 2010b).

These role descriptions assume that if the head of an association or group does whatever the description says he or she is supposed to do, then the representational and educational aspirations of the organization will be attained (Barbeito, 2004). The language that the descriptions use presumes that persons and strategy are synonymous (Huselid, Becker, & Beatty, 2005).

Three factors show why the logic underlying this and the previous assumption about attaining representational and educational aspirations without having a shared schema are flawed. First, the mission statements and corresponding role descriptions are disconnected. The missions aspire to represent members and improve education, but the matching role descriptions are mute on both points. Representation and improvement are distal in both. Second, when mission and role statements are distal to each other, organizations generally gravitate to more centralization of control, not less, and more self-invented action (e.g., the way Herb in Association-A mode planned the annual conference in a self-serving manner) than responsiveness to member needs and interests (Schermerhorn, Hunt, & Osborne, 2004). Distal mission statements and role descritions engender low-power activity that can be confused with design, operation, and outcome (Abrahams, 2007). Third, when design and strategy are conflated with role, the demands made of the person(s) responsible for leading the organization and attaining the aspirations that are contained in mission and role documents often are greater than her, his, or their capacity to accomplish (Kouzes & Posner, 1987). The load placed on leaders who are in such a circumstance is too high.

If an organization does not have an explicit mission and corresponding operational structures (e.g., organizational chart) and processes for mission attainment, then the efforts of all and any stakeholders will appear to lead to the fulfillment of the mission. However, such ambiguous circumstances will limit the organization to Type-A centralization of control and distal, low-power, and high-load activity. This is why associations and groups rarely realize their membership and educational aspirations and lack sufficient control, schema, and design for doing so. They increase rather than reduce the cognitive load of staff and members. At Association-B this is not the case. Association Example 5.6 presents an excerpt from the mission statement for the fictional association.

Association Example 5.6: Mission Statement

Association-B is a tax-exempt, not-for-profit professional association that exists for maximizing the learning and achievement of every student at schools that pay a fee to be a member of the association. All stakeholders of the association believe every child is capable of learning two standard deviations above her or his predetermined aptitude and that every teacher is capable of helping a classroom of students attain such levels of learning. In pursuit of that goal, the organizational design of the association reflects a commitment to a collaborative member-centered approach based on research-proven practices for organizational development, mastery teaching,cooperative learning, and differentiated instruction. Consistent with its design and commitment, the association shares goals, processes, practices, and tools with members in an intentional and results-oriented manner. Its shared schema and embedded design produce proximal, high-power, low-load solutions for members.

Association-B's mission statement explicitly addresses responsiveness, control, and capacity. Moreover, its statement is designed to be complementary of the various roles (e.g., teacher, administrator) that members play. For instance, Association-B is explicitly committed to supporting members as they collaborate to meet the 1:X challenge and attain 2-Sigma. Association Example 5.7 presents excerpts of the role description for its executive director.

Association Example 5.7: Role Description

The executive director of Association-B is responsible for overall performance of the association through the achievement of its goals and those of member classrooms, schools, and districts. The Member School Performance Array, a tool that connects Association-B and member schools, measures performance of stakeholders who work in those settings. The executive director will demonstrate breadth and depth of understanding of the field of education with particular emphasis on the areas of cooperative development, instructional design, and capacity building in classrooms, schools, and districts.

Specifically, the executive director will (a) use and model processes inherent in the design and operation of the association and member schools, (b) monitor association processes such as linking conference planning to member needs, member and staff use of the processes, and performance of member schools, (c) provide positive and corrective feedback to staff and members about performance, (d) work collaboratively with persons at all levels of the network to continuously improve performance and processes, (e) monitor trends and identify emerging issues to be addressed, (f) provide leadership in the selection, development, and application of ICT to attainment of common goals, and (g) foster best practices in an informative and instructive manner.

A portion of the compensation that the executive director receives will be determined by her or his attainment against specific performance aspects of the association's schema that is shared with its members.

This role description differs greatly from the ones presented earlier. It is unambiguous, committal, and explicit. It calls out the executive director's responsibility for advancing and refining the schema that the association and its members share, provides measures of their performance, defines areas of emphasis, and identifies specific behaviors. Not surprisingly, the work Herb does at Association-B, when compared to the work he did at Association-A before it was reconfigured, is less stressful for him and his colleagues.

Responsibility at Association-A rested squarely with Herb, who, spent much time controlling concurrent sessions, board members, corporate sponsors, lobbying, and dessert selections. Although Herb (and association executives like him) periodically delegated tasks to staff (e.g., telling Tricia to create new sessions), he kept control over most things and paid little attention to things that—if he were truly committed to realizing the association's aspirations—should have occupied more of his time (e.g., association process and member performance). However,

Association-A had no capacity for dealing with such things in substantive ways. Its conference planning illustrates this point by being a mishmash of topics, sponsors, member proposals, and geographic representation that arguably reflects members' needs. Its contents and program were, as Tricia recounted, too distal from members to have any effect on them and on education overall. Association-B and its annual conference meet the challenge of meeting members' educational needs that Association-A had failed to meet. Association-B is configured differently. Herb plays a different role in it. Association Example 5.8 presents highlights of Herb's remarks at Association-B's new member orientation session.

Association Example 5.8: Herb Welcomes New Members

"You are the foundation upon which Association-B rests. We get the results we get because of the normal work you do in your classrooms that is supported by the schema, embedded design, and edge technology we share.

"You are here because some way, somehow you realized that if you do more of what you've been doing, most students will continue to be poorly educated. I know, because I once had that same realization. Today is about getting familiar with the Type-B approach. Based on the feedback from the folks who previously joined Association-B, we've found it best to have three sessions—one about the normal work you do at your level, another about the work that is done across the network, and a third about how Association-B supports you in both. In each session today, you will experience processes and edge technology, interact with persons who play roles similar to the ones you play, and then do some problem-solving. At the end of the day, you will understand the A to B Toolkit, Member School Performance Array, Co-Development Tool, and share a schema with the association that supports your efforts at your school.

"We'll build on the work we do today via weekly webinars hosted by the association. To set the stage for today's sessions, I'm now going to introduce you to our schema and the common goals. Please click on the icon for the A2B Toolkit."

Herb, using the schema, design, and tools that Association-B shares with its members, models the cooperative relationship between the association and its stakeholders. He behaves this way because of the design principles (e.g., role description) that underpin Association-B to its members proximally by dispersing control to them. Each member is similar because they use the same approaches and edge technology.

Association-A was hierarchically controlled and designed for operational efficiency (Daft, 2007). However, the association's mechanistic nature that produced those operational efficiencies limited its capability to react, respond, and adapt to challenging and changing circumstances in a timely manner (Pearce, 2010). That is why, when Herb and Tricia worked at Association-A, they could not respond to the needs of its members.

Shift two: Fostering similarity of stakeholder activity at scale. The memberships of Type-A associations and groups are quite different. The work of those associations and groups, however, is more alike than like the work of their members (Drucker, 2006). Although Herb and his counterparts at other Type-A associations focused on different issues and had different memberships, they went about their work in the same way. Their working in the same ways is apparent in what the term *system* means in Type-A and Type-B education.

Type-A education defines the word *system,* using the scientific method (Fitzpatrick, 2004), as something divisible into components, each examinable and reversible that when added together describes its whole (Lemke, 2006). Everybody and everything has a place, purpose, and time (Brafman & Beckstrom, 2006). In education, this means that students are products (Jones, 1997), teachers are assemblers (Naney & Chalkey, 2009), businesses that might someday employ the former students of those teachers are purchasers (Davis & Botkin, 1994), and associations and groups are contributors (Zucker, 2009). Each piece of the whole of education is a step on an "assembly line" (Connolly, 2003). The steps on the assembly line are linear, sequential, analyzable, and reversible (Tolliday, 1998). The step for associations and groups consists of the convenings, communiqués, research, advocacy, and training they do. None of the activities of association and groups, however, reflects a final educational product or whole process. Their activities are not proximally connected to their members or to other network levels. Their staffs are dissimilar to each other and to members. Their activities and roles—regardless of how well they are carried out—have no direct effect on the whole of education.

In Type-B education, *system* is characterized by the interactions of its components and the nonlinearity (Bertalanffy, 1973) and irreversibility (deGroot, 1952) of those interactions. In this parts-reflect-the-whole depiction the players, places, purposes, and times are indistinguishable from each other. All are similar at every level and at scale. Knowing one part means "knowing all other parts" (Rapoport, 1986). Further, having the features of the system embedded at all of its levels makes levels of the system similar to the entire system (Gleick, 1987; Merry, 1995).

When classrooms, schools, and districts change to the Type-B approach, the *what, how,* and *why* they do things differ from the *what, how,* and *why* things are done in the Type-A approach. That is why as stakeholders such as Bruce, Eladio,

Anne, Sarah, and James become adept with the Type-B approach, they realize that Association-A is distally connected to them. It does not and cannot reflect and support their needs. It is easy to see why. Bruce, Eladio, Anne, Sarah, and James have changed. Each now possesses a more sophisticated knowledge of teaching and learning (e.g., PBCL). Each has a different, more collaborative relationship with her or his peers. Some of them may even be on well-defined, highly professional career trajectories (e.g., master teacher) at districts with missions that articulate a common schema for practice. The schema they share changes their relationships with ICT, curriculum, students, and peers. They have grown accustomed to being proximal to educational problem-solving, sharing control, and approaching their respective responsibilities in similar ways. Reversing course is inconceivable because they have a profoundly altered worldview of education.

Shift Three: Members and associations co-evolving. Self-serving behaviors, such as avoiding problems to seek person reward, lead stakeholders to ignore problems, miss opportunities, avoid big issues, and embrace distal, low-power, high-load solutions (Rus, 2009). A case in point is Herb, who sought to offset the revenue with additional corporate-sponsorships and booth-space sales. Rather than seek the underlying cause for Association-A's decline, Herb opted to co-exist. If stakeholders had not changed Association-A, it would have co-existed, paid its bills, employed Herb and staff, benefited board members, hosted many annual conferences, and provided Herb with a lot to crow about during his big speech. Such co-existence, however, would have occurred at the cost of the real needs and interests of members and lost opportunities to affect education at scale. Co-existence is the concurrent, but separate, existence of two or more persons. Persons who coexist do not meaningfully collaborate to solve common problems. For instance, over time, although Herb's self-serving and co-existing behavior might have solved Association-A's immediate financial problem, it would have poorly served the Association and its members. Fortunately (for Herb and the association), stakeholders took charge of the association and redesigned it to use a Type-B approach.

Type-B education disperses control, supports processes and practices that are similar across levels, and enables schema sharing. Association-B extends these characteristics by having a design that fosters conditions for members and staff to easily and meaningfully collaborate. Such conditions do not readily occur through the Type-A approach because in it stakeholders have too many differences (Cañas & Sondak, 2008), are often at working cross-purposes (De Lia & Fredericks, 2005), and frequently compete for relevancy, resources, and power (Lessem & Palsule, 1997). Stakeholders explicitly and implicitly seek self-advantage, often at the expense of colleagues (Reina & Reina, 2006). That is why Herb and Tricia had to give board members plum spots on the conference program. The self-serving conditions engendered by Association-A's design made them rely on their individual schemas which pushed them to compete and seek self-advantage. Seeking self-advantage did not help Herb and Tricia solve the problems they faced (e.g., declining membership and revenues). It only puts them into cognitive overload.

For associations and groups, "co-evolution" (Durham, 1991) is a better alternative than "co-existence" (Stradling, Newton, Bates, & Hearder, 1997). In a co-evolving system, each stakeholder shares a common goal with other stakeholders, even though they might be competitors. They evolve together. They adapt to the adaptations that each other makes. Co-evolution makes an association's stakeholders more responsive to each other and increases the chances of success for all, and as a result, they grow and develop. This was the case with Association-B, whose successful conference helps members succeed, too. Likewise when members leverage the association's services to meet the 1:X challenge, their capacities are extended. As their 1:X attainments increase and more schools attain 2-sigma, more schools are attracted to Association-B. This shows that when they are connected in co-dependent ways, all levels of the system co-evolve within and across levels and get better at what they do.

Association-B, like the schools and classrooms of its members, is in a constant state of dynamic change. Since the work of its members and staff is emergent and the targets of their efforts are ever-changing, Association-B and its stakeholders have to co-evolve. This means they must be proximal. Conference planning, schema, design, and problem resolution are indistinguishable. For instance, this year, the Association-B's conference focus, thanks to Herb, is Mastery Teaching; next year, it will be some other timely and important area of concern. The conference meets stakeholders' interests and needs. Members, as the increased registration numbers reflects, find the association to be attractive. The members and their association, by co-evolving on a dynamic ever-changing landscape, are surfing the "edge of chaos," a place characterized by reinvention and creative adaptation (Pascale, Millemann & Gioja, 2000).

Co-evolution occurs when stakeholders share feedback, control, schema, and cognitive tools with other stakeholders. Such sharing reduces the stakeholders' cognitive load and supports the normal work they do (Garnsey & McGlade, 2006). The design and operation of Association-B enables stakeholders to do the intensely collaborative work required for taking up the 1:X challenge of its members and the field of education. Association-B is a vehicle for building its members' capacity for taking up the 1:X challenge up and meeting it. Association-B's capacity to self-organize enables the precise behaviors of stakeholders that makes 1:X more readily attainable for them. What happens in member schools, affects and informs what happens at Association-B. Likewise, what happens at Association-B affects the work in schools and in all levels of the educational system. The self-similarity within the association drives "self-similarity without" (Cohen & Havlin, 2010).

Association-B's capacity for bridging to other levels of the educational system means that it can directly affect the policy arena, for instance the government program that Superintendent James seeks out that oversees funds for PD or the business that designs and builds educational ICT products that his district might purchase. The parts-reflect-the-whole-system to which Association-B and all stakeholders belong is more "complex" (Gleick, 1987) and "less orderly" (Prigogine & Stengers, 1984) than the Type-A assembly-line system in which the parts-add-up to a whole. What in the latter are low power, self-serving distal member affiliate parts, in the former are members that are proximal to the association in ways that give it powerful capacity to respond to the changing circumstances of both Association-B and its members. In short, when associations and members co-evolve, all stakeholders and the educational system benefit. Association Example 5.9 presents a case of co-evolution at Association-B.

Association Example 5.9: Herb Helps Co-Evolve Physics Curriculum

Association-B has several curricular working groups. Bruce and his fellow physics teachers comprise one such group. Herb identifies that management of cooperative learning—a key instructional strategy employed at the association's member schools—including the placement of students and the assessment of their performance in cooperative learning groups, is load producing for many of its members. Herb finds that teachers generally like the approach, but are concerned about how students use time in groups and the way their levels of engagemnt affect their learning. Herb meets with Bruce's group. The members confirm what he has discerned and agrees to help him solve the problem.

On behalf of the member schools, Herb approached a company run by Isabella that has previously developed software for Association-B. Her company agreed to develop a plug-in that will make it easier for teachers to manage placement, assessment of students' cooperative learning, and monitor their progress using cooperative learning in their courses. Herb arranges for Bruce's group to beta test the plug-in. Four weeks later, Herb hosts a video conference during which the group discusses the value of the plug-in. Their feedback results in recommendations for improvements. Isabella's developers revise the plug-in accordingly. It is installed in the A to B Toolkit at every school via a push process managed by the technology director at the association through which the plugin is loaded on the association's servers then automatically updates the software at all member schools. At the annual conference, a special track of sessions is added for teachers to experience the best practices for use of the plug-in. The working group of physics teachers facilitates the sessions in that track.

Herb and the physics teachers solve a problem that has vexed many teachers. In turn, their common need and the solution they develop to meet it drives self-similarity across the whole network of the educational system. As Herb and the teachers solve the cooperative learning problem they and Association-B co-evolve. Their role as members evolves too. The solution to the problem and the new role for members reflects the processes in place at other levels of the educational system. In turn, those processes lead to less cognitive load for Herb, the working group, and other teachers. Association-B attains better results— more registrants, sponsors, exhibitors, responsiveness to members, and contributions to education overall. All do less but get more. The changes that make Association-B possible mean that its members do not have to change much in order to attain better outcomes at their respective level of the system. Association Example 5.10 presents an excerpt from the description of the evolved role of member at Association-B.

Association Example 5.10:
Role Description for Association Member

Association-B operates in a dynamic and co-evolving manner. As a member, you have a stake in the association and it in you. The normal work you do at your level contributes to the normal work others do and the work of the association. You have a responsibility for being an active and contributing participant in all processes. This includes (a) using the processes and tools of Association-B and member schools, (b) monitoring your and the association's performance, (c) providing feedback about that performance, (d) working collaboratively with persons at all levels of the network, (e) monitoring trends, and (f) fostering best practices. This means you must be an expert in our shared schema, its components, and embedded design.

The role description draws from what stakeholders do every day in classrooms, schools, and districts to define what they do as members of Association-B. It reflects an expectation that members be active in the formulation, implementation, and evolution of the association's schema. Whereas in Type-A associations members are responsible for raising funds, recruiting members, and attending events, in Association-B, members are expected to serve their level (e.g., classroom) needs and all other levels. This means it is impossible for them to play their role without fundraising, recruiting, and attending. Their extended engagement in the association's operation and design drives the association's overall contribution to education. Plus, as members become more adept at playing their more dynamic role, they contribute to the reconceptualization of roles at other levels. Not surprisingly, at a time when membership and relevancy of associations and groups are waning (Putnam, 2000) and overall education performance is flat lined (OECD, 2008; UNESCO, 2008), Association-B is gaining membership and clout.

HOW MAKING SHIFTS
IN THOUGHT WORKS IN PRACTICE
FOR ASSOCIATIONS

By making three shifts and taking up the schema and design of its members, Association-B becomes similar to its members (and they to it), self-organizing, and more member-centric. The three shifts show the way for education associations to truly represent their members in ways that make 1:X common and 2-Sigma attainable at scale. The examples show how an association might respond to the emergent feedback of members. They also sho members such as Bruce stepping up to play a more active and meaningful role in Association-B and and staff such as Herb stepping over by dispersing control to them exemplify such responsiveness.

Research shows that flatter organizations with dispersed control across stakeholders are more responsive and adaptive to changing circumstances than hierarchical ones (Daft, 2007). At Association-B, Bruce and his fellow stakeholders literally and figuratively have places at the table and a measure of control over the association's actions. Data from (and about) members informs the actions that the association takes.

Research also shows that organizations controlled flatly and organically are more capable of rapidly reinventing themselves as challenges and opportunities arise (Burns & Stalker, 1961). The design and operation of Association-B makes 1:X and 2-Sigma much easier for stakeholders. The load associated with achieving 1:X and 2-Sigma is lessened for individual members because their association shares common schema, tools, and processes with them. Since its stakeholders share control, they can work on different things, such as solving the cooperative learning problem or planning the annual conference; yet by using common processes, they maintain laser-like focus on their 1:X and 2-Sigma goals. Stakeholders, the edge technology of their association, have the capacity to direct the association to make specific shifts. By shifting, Association-B more completely represents its members. Association-B becomes something its members are part of; Association-A, on the other hand, remains something they are subject to.

THE TOOLS ASSOCIATIONS NEED
TO SUPPORT STAKEHOLDERS

The edge technology used at the association level of the Type-B educational system, includes the (a) Member School Performance Array, (b) A to B Toolkit, and (c) Co-Development Tool. Figure 5.1 presents a layout from the Array. At Association-B, staff use the Array to look into the performance of their member schools.

The 2-Sigma benchmark field on the top left of the layout shows how schools are performing against the 2-Sigma standard, all students learning at levels two standard deviations above their aptitudes. It depicts the numbers of schools that have attained Sigma, 1-Sigma, and 2-Sigma. The fields on the right of the layout show member schools' professional development and problem-solving priorities such as refining the feedback tools (1-Sigma) and advanced differentiation of instruction (2-Sigma). The benchmark field shows the proportion of schools at different stages of 2-Sigma attainment. Association staff uses this field to identify the member schools that have attained 2-Sigma and to plan the induction ceremony at which those schools will be recognized and welcomed by the representatives of the schools that previously attained that distinction. Staff also uses the data to plan ways (e.g., career paths for master teachers) to assist members in their 2-Sigma pursuit. They use the professional development and problem-solving professional development fields to identify priorities for the annual conference, determine continuing education offerings, and scope out software needs. For example, the data in the field represent the way PBCL and advanced mastery teaching emerges through the data reported in the Array from member schools as a priority of the association. For instance, Sarah found advanced mastery teaching to be a professional development need at her school. Subsequently, it was identified as a need at the district, and then at other districts. Eventually the need for help with mastery teaching became an issue that Association-B took up. By using Array to identify new problems and take actions that solves the problems of members, Association-B is a source of strange attraction. Its schema evolves, and as it does, the overall educational system coevolves.

Figure 5.2 presents an Association Page from the A to B Toolkit that is used for co-development planning. It shows the activities occurring at associations member schools. The A to B Toolkit helps staff reconcile the information about those activities with the information about policies and funding

Clockwise from the top left, the layout shows the policy and legislation connector, feedback about the annual conference, calendar for professional development events, and school-level solutions. In the Policy and Legislation Connector a change in the state requirement to become a principal is depicted. Staff use the connector and the calendar sections get details about how specific professional development sessions meet the state requirements to be a principal. In this way,

Figure 5.1. Member School Performance Array

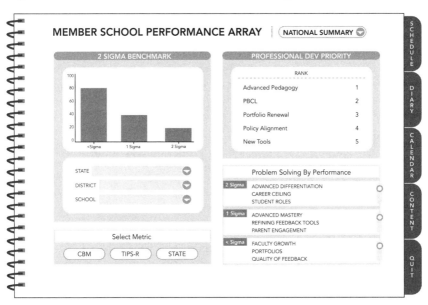

Figure 5.2. A To B Toolkit: Association Page

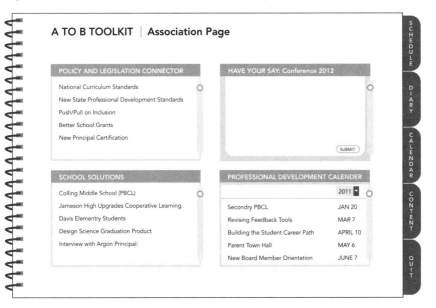

the member's certification requirements are matched with appropriate resources and activities. The Association Page is the same one superintendent James uses at the district level. It helps him reconcile the needs of his Type-B district with the realities of Type-A policies and practices.

SHARED SCHEMA: HOW ASSOCIATIONS CAN SUPPORT OTHER LEVELS IN EDUCATION

The three-step framework previously applied to other levels of the educational system is applied here to examine the key propositions about the role edge technology plays in education associations and advocacy groups.

New Assumptions

Type-B associations represent and benefit Type-B stakeholders across and within all levels of a multi-level educational system. Much of that advantage comes from the edge technology that enables such representation and the load-reducing and power-increasing advantages it affords members of Type-B associations.

Assumption one: Type-B classrooms, schools, and districts require an association to serve its members in complex, responsive, and supportive ways that make 1:X and 2-Sigma more attainable for the members who work in those settings. Such service to members is only achievable with edge technology. For example, edge technology makes it possible for Association-B to genuinely represent the need of its members at its annual conferences because the A to B Toolkit helped make members behavior patterns (e.g., need for PD)more visible. Staff and members use of edge technology drives the emergent processes, such as feedback loops about performance, that lead to continuous improvement of their association, their annual conference, and their work settings. Edge technology has *intended* consequences. Its use leads Association-B's stakeholders— with each mouse click on the A to B Toolkit and Performance Array—to become more committed, knowledgeable, and sophisticated in attaining the goals (e.g., 2-Sigma) that they share with other stakeholders. As mouse clicks accumulate, the stakeholders, association, and the various levels of the educational system became more proximal, powerful, and load reducing.

Assumption two: Research on teaching and learning defines the role for edge technology in an association that aspires to represent Type-B stakeholders and impact education overall. The application of ICT in education rarely intersects in an integrated manner with the extensive research about increasing the academic performance of learners, the quality of instruction of teachers, the effects of classrooms, and the benefits of a robust curriculum (Bain & Parkes, 2006). Edge technology makes Association-B capable of enabling stakeholders to identify educational problems (e.g., mastery teaching) and co-develop high-power, proximal, research-based solutions (e.g., PBCL); one example is the way the professional development solution Sarah uses at her school informs Assoication-B's annual conference and member schools. This means Association-B can drive co-evolving behaviors, support good practice at scale, and further refine the design and operation of the association. Over time, the members' role is reconceptualized and opportunities for further development and career advancement emerges for members

Assumption three: At Association-B, doing the work of members through edge technology is indistinguishable from staff and member learning about edge technology. This is the difference between the Type-A Herb saying, "We must work to save the E2T2 program so our members have more money to buy more ICT," and the Type-B Herb saying, "Our members need edge technology because the research-based transactions of teaching and learning are embedded in the software applications we use for representing our members. The E2T2 grants make it possible for our members to buy the ICT they need." In Herb's latter statement, access to edge technology is a basic requirement for Association-B's stakeholders to do their jobs. When this requirement is met, then edge technology enables stakeholders to integrate themselves into the association and other levels of the network that comprises the educational system.

Assumption four: In Type-B associations and groups, access to edge technology is a simple yet fundamental requirement for dispersing control and generating the feedback for getting things done. Meeting the 1:X challenge necessitates that associations with their members. Edge technology enables co-evolution because as members and staff use it to do their normal work they generate, analyze, and act on the understanding it fosters about member schools (and their association). They individually and collectively progress toward goals, identify best practices, and make directional changes when necessary. This is the case with Herb and the physics teachers who co-evolved. The normal work that they did increases the association's capacity to support all memebers and to adapt to their changing circumstances. Every action taken by every stakeholder improves her or his performance and that of the association.

Assumption five: edge technology serves as a mediating context for Type-B Associations leveraging well-researched professional practice to enhace teaching, increase learning, and improve student achievement. Such performance increases are the logical extension of stakeholders at all levels of the educational system using the same tools and processes to solve the same education problems. Edge technology enables Type-B associations and groups to assume the challenges of their members and navigate the patterns of complexity that are associated with 1:X and 2-Sigma that their Type-A counterparts cannot.

New Design

Efforts to improve education at scale benefit little from the contributions of Type-A associations and groups (Darling-Hammond, 2010; Ravitch, 2010). The big ideas reflected in the above assumptions do not reside in the design and operation of such organizations. That is why when stakeholders turn Association-A into Association-B they had to completely redesign the association. The stakeholders made those design changes using the same three step framework used to change other levels of the system.

Solution mapping is the first step they took. Association members (along with Herb) mapped their understanding of the challenges inherent in their being represented at scale, improving education overall, and attracting other stakeholders to their collective efforts. The solution map that resulted articulated their new commitments to control, scale, and mutual interdependence through co-evolution. In that map the roles that members and staff play and the work each does were profoundly altered. For example, the control of the association was dispersed across members, processes and tools were made similar, and a shared schema was adopted. These shifts create the conditions for co-evolution that align the association with its members' goals of 1:X and 2-Sigma rather than with the self-serving needs of Herb, board members, and staff.

The conditions for coevolution contributed to the *component building* through which stakeholders clarify, define, and articulate what they know, want to do, and how they would do it at Association-B. Specific plans, policies, processes, and products such as the association level versions of the A to B Toolkit and Member School Performance Array emerge and further defined Association-B. The stakeholders make role descriptions for Herb and the members. They drew up an explicit mission. Members become active agents in the association, participated fully in its decision-making processes, and agree not to seek self-advantage. Similarly, the association's guiding documents lay out the way the association would support members behaving in the non-self-serving way.

Stakeholders use their solution map and components to engage in *design integration*. They assign responsibilities and actions to specific persons. Knowledge, commitments, and roles are translated to actionable, and measureable assignments that contributed to member schools attaining 1:X and 2-Sigma. For instance, Herb is to model the processes inherent in the schema that all members share, monitor those processes, and provide corrective feedback about both. In this spirit, Herb sacrifices his 10th annual state-of-the-association speech on the altar of dispersed control for the purpose of better serving its members.

New Trajectory

Thanks to the 3-step framework and the edge technology it produces, Association-B is on a trajectory to transform itself and its members. Its assumptions, solution map, components, and design are embedded in its edge technology. For instance, the Member School performance Array helps members and staff track their progress toward the common goal of 2-Sigma and helps them prioritize the work they do through Association-B in pursuit of that goal. The common goal of 2-Sigma replaces the self-serving goals that prompt members to change their association from a Type-A to Type-B approach and becomes the yardstick used to measure Association-B's performance. This change is no minor accomplishment. Type-A associations and groups rarely, if ever, intersect with the everyday realities of their members. That is why edge technology is so essential to Type-B associations. Association-B, by putting edge technology in a mediating role increases the power and lowers the load of its members and makes 2-Sigma possible for them all.

SUMMARY

- If professional associations and advocacy groups represent the scaled-up activity of the work that their members do in classrooms and schools, then those associations and groups can play a key role in efforts to improve education overall and attain 2-Sigma at scale.
- Scaled up activity entails associations and sharing the schema that their members share.
- That shared schema makes dispersed control, similarity at scale, and co-evolution possible.
- When members are part of the self-organization of an association, then the design and processes of that association can connect the intent and action of all stakeholders.
- Associations that empower their members in self-organizing ways by dispersing control to members, using the practices and processes of members, and shifting some of their cognitive load to the associations serve as attractors and enablers of co-evolution across all levels of the educational system.
- Edge technology enables, supports, and enhances such co-evolution. It generates the feedback necessary for an association to directly and significantly affect student learning at system widsystem-wide scale.

CHAPTER 6

Policy Shifts

A policy is a temporary creed liable to be changed, but while it
holds good it has got to be pursued with apostolic zeal.
—Mohanda K. Gandhi

The field of education's lack of consensus about which educational practices to take to scale is curtailing policymaking that drives, supports, and refines Type-B education and limits the role that *e*dge technology can play in the educational policymaking process. Using examples derived from actual policymaking, we show that (a) Type-A policymaking reinforces Type-A classrooms, schools, districts, and associations; (b) Type-B policymaking reinforces the Type-B analogs of the classrooms and so on that are capable of meeting the 1:X challenge and 2-Sigma at scale; (c) three shifts that make Type-B policymaking possible, (d) the conditions that the shifts create drive policymaking that emerges bottom-up from the work that teachers and students do in in their Type-B classrooms and schools and stakeholders do with their Type-B associations, and (e) all are enabled by *e*dge technology.

THE PROBLEM POLICYMAKERS FACE
IN REFORMING EDUCATION

Sue is the first-term governor of a mid-sized state with a declining population, challenged economy, and lagging education system. She is engaged in a competitive election. Election day is 43 days away. A recently released state-by-state comparison of educational performance shows that her state has slipped five places during the 4 years she has been in office. Her rival uses this fact to claim that she is ignoring the state's educational needs. In response, Sue's campaign manager arranges a series of meetings for her with educational thought leaders—high profile theorists, researchers, association heads, and practitioners—from across the state. Policymaking Example 6.1 shows Governor Sue reflecting with her manager about her meetings with the thought leaders.

Policymaking Example 6.1: Governor Sue Reflects

"Too many children aren't completing school and our state is not getting the educational results needed to compete economically with nearby states. Every day at every town-hall meeting, I hear this. You arranged for me to meet with several of the best and brightest educators in the state. They said the same three things education advocates always tell me: Step up with more money for teachers, more computers for students, and more charter schools. They always seem to want more, more, more, but never offer up any evidence that what they're asking for will keep more kids in school, help them learn better, and make the state be competitive. This feels hopeless. What am I going to do?"

In one form or another, Governor Sue's reflection about her recent conversations with the thought leaders—in which she is told that more stuff equals better education for more students—happens regularly in council rooms, statehouses, congresses, and parliaments around the world (Hanushek & Lindseth, 2009; Squire & Moncrief, 2009). In those policymaking venues, no issue has received more attention than education during the past 3 decades (Didsbury, 2003; Ravitch, 1983; Weston & Walker, 1987). However, all that attention failed to translate into effects on teaching, learning, and student achievement (CSAW, 2007; Darling-Hammond, 2010) because the field of education, despite conducting incalculable amounts of research, cannot agree about a foundation of research-based practice on which policy could be built (Weston, 1987).

To understand why the field of education has no consensus, and why Governor Sue is so exasperated with the thought leaders she met with, requires us to look back to the 1980s, when education became a top priority for countries that believed a well-educated citizenry was advantageous economically, politically, and socially (Pittas & Gray, 2004). The links established between a citizenry being well educated, a country's future, and the quality of its educational system (Brown, 1996) gave rise to general questions about the performance of students, such as how well students performed on standardized tests, and specific questions concerning the implications of the overall performance of schools, districts, states, and countries and debate about what actions should be taken to improve the performance of each (Fuhrman & Elmore, 2004). When answers to the questions indicated that education performance was lagging, concerns were sparked about a rising tide of mediocrity (NCEE, 1983), winning the "brain race" for economic superiority among countries (Kearns &

Doyle, 1988), the changing nature of work from industrial to service economies (Dawkins, 1988), and administering schooling to produce "excellence" (Picot, 1988). In turn, the answers to the questions prompted unprecedented scrutiny of almost every aspect of educational systems worldwide (McKenzie, Mitchell, & Oliver, 1995). At the policy level, these circumstances drove an unprecedented number of attempts by policymakers to reform education (Ravitch, 2000; Toch, 1991). No level of the educational system was left unaffected by such policymaking (Elmore & Fuhrman, 2001). Their policies, however, failed stakeholders and the field of education because they were more of the same distal, low-power, and high-load solutions that had been used before and had created the circumstances that policymakers were now seeking to change.

The education field's lack of consensus about what practices had the greatest effect on learning and well-documented examples of successful large-scale engagement with such practices left policymakers confused about the best way to improve education (Kirst, 1984; Kirst & Meister, 1985). As public pressure for improvement intensified, policy arenas became battlefields for particular educational ideas, approaches, and philosophies (Ravitch, 2000, 2010). No policy proved capable of generating widespread support among educational stakeholders (Goertz, Floden, & O'Day, 1996). Although education was once a common denominator within and across nations, it became a divider as stakeholders picked sides (Kunin, 1995). Some stakeholders supported more of the existing policy approaches, while others sought new ones (Cuban, 1990). Whether the approach they supported was old or new, the approaches produced few improvements and few, if any, fundamental changes in the design and operation of classrooms, schools, and districts (Gordon & Graham, 2003). Not suprisingly, well-intentioned, often rhetorically intense policy efforts produced few wide-scale and sustainable educational performance gains in student graduation rates and achievement test scores (Lieberman, 1993). The vacuum created by the field's ambiguity about practice was filled by policymaking that was highly politicized and mostly focused on more, more, more of the same.

Not surprisingly, after nearly 3 decades of politicized policymaking, education performance remains flat lined with graduation rates and test scores unaffected (Hanushek & Woessmann, 2010; NCES, 2006, 2005). This current day state of affairs has several universal characteristics, including a status quo in which (a) few students are well educated (Goldin & Katz, 2001), (b) ICT's potential is ignored (Collins & Halverson, 2009), and (c) policymaking for changing such circumstances is ineffectual (Cummings & Williams, 2008). The state-of-affairs is the elephant in the room that remains there because policymaker engagement with the 1:X challenge is low and policymaker expectations remain high that enactment of additional low power, distal policies will improve things. Governor Sue has reason to be exasperated.

WHY TYPE-A POLICYMAKING FAILS

Five characteristics of Type-A policymaking make resolution of educational problems rare. First, proximal, high-power educational practices that the research shows have the greatest effect on learning and teaching hardly ever get considered because the field of education cannot agree about what those practices are and consequently do not provide policymakers with examples of how such practices might be enabled and supported across the educational system. Instead, practices that are distally connected to student learning and achievement (e.g., remuneration, computer access, school type) have been the foci of policy and surrogates for the proximal, high-power solutions (e.g., research-based teaching and learning approaches, feedback, and cognitive and meta-cognitive strategies) (Hattie, 2009) that research shows do make a difference. This is unfortunate since proximal solutions, because they have greater inherent capacity to directly affect student learning and achievement (thus are easier for policymakers to support and defend), are better policy drivers than distal solutions.

Second, issues seldom receive policymakers' attention at the optimal time of need and opportunity for rational resolution (Eyestone, 1971). Students not graduating high school, for example, have been prevalent since the establishment of comprehensive high schools in the 1950s. It was not until the 1980s, however, that low graduation rates received policy remedies in the form of laws and funds for dropout prevention programs (NCES, 1989). By then, countless students' lives had gone sideways. This characteristic delay is evident when James, then Sarah, and then the departmental colleagues receive the TIPS-R scores many months after students have taken the test. By the time the TIPS-R report arrives, James can do nothing more than pressure Sarah to do better. She, in turn, runs around the school, reacts, but cannot do much by way of an appropriate response. When she flips the TIPS-R report to the department, members of the department seek to address the problem with an assortment of instructional and curricular approaches. None of the approaches, however, is capable of addressing the problem. The low-power approaches that are proposed mean that James and his team cannot redress TIPS-R. This is the case for most policymakers—an educational problem becomes apparent after the fact, with no rational solution available.

Third, external events sometimes elevate one issue over others on the policy-making agenda. For example, in the United States during 1950s and 1960s, court rulings (e.g., *Brown v. Board of Education*) and the civil rights movement sparked the passage of policies for equalizing education that increased student access to high-quality schools and established greater government involvement, more funding, a more standardized curriculum, and more school-level programs (Kirst & Wirt, 1969). The legal and social circumstances that influenced the policy agenda were external and latent to the policy arena and did not emerge from educational policymaking. Moreover, the policies that resulted have not had a proximal effect on learning, teaching and learning outcomes. James experiences similar circumstances with 1:1 computing, as does the department with TIPS-R. The solutions that are offered up by the department members (e.g., more computers, extra test preparation) are not directly connected with the circumstances that had elevated the problem in the first place. Such solutions are like a bumper sticker looking for a car.

Fourth, elections frame and advance policy issues (Reese, Gandy, & Grant, 2001). During campaigns, the interactions between the candidates, voters, and the media contribute to raising awareness, building coalitions, and setting agendas. Through such interactions, some issues become prominent on the policy agendas of victorious candidates. A few issues may even be the pivot point of the election (Van Dyke & Mc-Cammon, 2010). This was the case with Sylvia, James's newly elected board member, who made the school start time her top agenda item. Similarly, the election made education prominent on Governor Sue's policymaking agenda.

Fifth, Type-A policymaking has neither an appraisal function for measuring whether the policy affects the problem it is supposed to solve nor capacity for emergent feedback from the stakeholders whom the policy is intended to benefit. Type-A policy making ignores the impact it is supposed to have. Hence, this type of policymaking is incapable of altering course or mobilizing attention and support if and when needed.

Let us further examine Governor Sue's case to see how she engages with the Type-A policymaking process described above. Policymaking Example 6.2 presents an excerpt of Sue's victory speech on election night.

Policymaking Example 6.2: Governor Sue Looks Ahead

"Thank you, thank you, thank you for re-electing me governor of this great state. Tonight is about celebration. Tomorrow is about getting to work to make our state stronger. During the hard-fought campaign, as I traveled from town to town, one issue more than any other was in the hearts and minds of the hardworking people who supported me—EDUCATION. I stand before you now to affirm that I heard the message you sent to me. That's why my single-minded focus in the upcoming legislative session will be enacting a policy that ensures each and every child in this state attains significantly higher levels of learning. They are our future, and the future is now!"

Governor Sue, thanks to a big nudge from the voters, moves education to the top of the state's policy agenda. Having done so, her immediate goal becomes addressing the education crisis sufficiently enough to satisfy her supporters who re-elected her end the educational crisis in the state. She starts her new term by agreeeing with her legislative counterparts to form a blue-ribbon task force comprised of the thought leaders she had met with during the campaign. She knows they represent the views of the field and hopes that despite this they can help her and the legislators identify sustainable and research-based educational practices that if scaled to schools statewide will end the crisis. They charge the task force with holding hearings, gathering information, making recommendations, and issuing a report that she hopes will guide her policymaking and end the educational crisis. Policymaking Example 6.3 presents excerpts of testimony that two (of many) education advocates provides to the task force.

Policymaking Example 6.3: Return of the Experts

Dr. Rose says, "Thank you, Madame Chair. Copies of my full statement are being circulated. Briefly, I'm a professor at the nearby university and conduct research about teacher attitudes. I met with Governor Sue several times last fall to discuss ways my research might help her solve the crisis. In our meetings, I explained how I had surveyed and interviewed teachers who had 1, 5, or 10 years of classroom experience. My sample consisted of 10 teachers in each group. The Nonesuch Foundation funded my study. My findings indicate that 47% of 1st-year teachers believe students and parents undervalue their work, and 64% of 5th-year and 71% of 10th-year teachers express similar beliefs. Further, 83% of the total group believes a relationship exists between student performance and teacher value. These findings support a possible recommendation by this task force that increasing teacher compensation will increase their value and thus improve student test scores."

Chairperson replies, "Thank you, Dr. Rose. We'll now hear from Dr. Nelson."

Dr. Nelson says, "Thank you, Madame. Chair. I, too, met with Governor Sue during the campaign. She sought me out because I am a vice president of community affairs for ABC Ltd., a leading educational consulting and training company. Among other things, we sponsor research about teaching, learning, and achievement. We're in year 8 of a 10-year qualitative study of the effects of school culture on teacher satisfaction and student achievement. We've been following 15 teachers—five primary, five middle, and five high school. Our preliminary findings indicate that salary levels are a poor predictor of teacher and student performance. Amount of experience, quality of teacher preparation, and in-service training received are better predictors. More investments in these areas will make the crisis go away in short order. I request that the task force reflect this point in its report."

Chairperson answers, "Thank you, Drs. Nelson and Rose. So if I hear you correctly, your testimony makes three points. One, you don't agree about what should be done to fix the crisis. Two, the recommendations you make have limited generalizability due to research problems with design and methodology. And, three, you have no suggestions for how progress toward resolution of the crises might be appraised."

The first of the five characteristics of Type-A policymaking is evident in the testimony. The members of the task force do not discuss high-power, scalable, research-based practices. Instead, despite being asked to address the education crisis, Rose and Nelson disagree about its causes and its resolution. They also completely ignore any appraisal of the nature of the crisis and how that appraisal links to the solutions they propose. Their connoisseurship of the crisis consists of posturing punctuated by education-speak. By not taking up the crisis—speaking directly about the crisis and its causes and nuances—they unleash another elephant in the room, and this one has even bigger potential for negative impact on a far greater scale.

Creating a task force like the one described above is a political tactic frequently employed in educational policymaking (Peterson, 1983). Such a task force invariably involves publication of a rhetorically intense report replete with requisite recommendations, platitudes, and fabrications of data that frames the problem to be solved in a politically advantageous way for the chief sponsors of the task force (Baines, 1997). The well-meaning souls who participate in a report's development are then referenced on its acknowledgment page and singled out as being representative of the interests and needs of this or that stakeholder group (Deal, 1985). As de facto representatives of their respective groups, they deliver talking points about the report at assorted convenings and confabs (Ginsburg & Wimpelberg, 1987). A flurry of newscasts, op-eds, panels, and speeches often echo the points they deliver (Passow, 1984). When the flurry of attention subsides, each person goes back to her or his work setting, doing more of what they did there before the flurry occurred (Plank & Ginsburg, 1990). The report becomes the justification for a bill that the legislature considers. Legislators hold hearings, advocates and detractors weigh in, everyone postures and compromises, and perhaps a bill gets passed (Lindblom, 1968). This is the process that Governor Sue and her legislative counterparts set in motion when they created their task force.

Let's check in to see how the recommendations that the Task Force makes are playing out in the state's legislature. Policymaking Example 6.4 presents excerpts from a hearing that the House Education Committee holds about HB-471, *Save the Teachers and Improve Our Schools Act of 2011*.

Policymaking Example 6.4: Committee Considers HB-471

Chairperson Charles says, "Today, we continue deliberating about the future of education in this state. Many of you know that I am on the record questioning the need for taking up this issue now. My constituents tell me their schools are just fine. They say there is no crisis. Moreover, I think the media contrived the whole thing to advantage the other party during the election. Also, since I don't put much faith in achievement tests, I don't worry much about state-by-state comparisons. Nonetheless, I've heard from my leadership that a bill must be on the floor for a vote within 60 days. Minority Chair Smith, opening remarks?"

Representative Smith replies, "Thank you, Mr. Chair. At this time, I ask that a statement from Governor Sue be entered in the record. It indicates that she is following our deliberations with keen interest. She, however, does not believe the potpourri of policies that HB-471 puts forth will solve the crisis. She looks forward to appearing before this body next week to outline her proposal."

Chairperson Charles answers, "Thank you. Now let's hear an overview of the bill."

Representative Jose speaks next, saying, "Thank you, Mr. Chair. A written version of my testimony was submitted for the record. Briefly, the recommendations of the blue-ribbon task force that this committee helped form are the basis for my bill—HB-471. It revises existing state code to provide more, and might I add much needed, funding for making our teachers' salaries competitive with those of nearby states. Specifically, it provides for the teachers in targeted districts who take one of three state-led professional development courses to get a certificate of compliance and a bump on the salary schedule. It also provides start-up grants for charter schools, additional standards for math and science curricula in low-performing schools, summer school programs for youth in large cities, discounts for students to purchase computers, and a Teacher Support and School Improvement Commission to annually report about progress on each of those component of HB-471. The date of initiation for the HB-471 is July 1, 2013. The date of full implementation is June 30, 2015. Notwithstanding other legislation, reauthorization occurs concurrently."

Chairperson Charles replies, "Thank you. Quick question, what sponsorship do you have for HB-471?"

Representative Jose tells him, "In addition to the task force members, all members of the Education Betterment Caucus of the House are co-sponsors. Also sponsoring HB-471 are the teachers' associations at the 11 biggest districts, Charter Schools Now (an advocacy group), and three technology integrators from my district. All helped write HB 471. As for my friends across the aisle, I sent a letter to each asking for their support. To date, none has responded. By the way, I've included several reports with my written testimony."

Representative Smith says, "Thank you. Obviously, you don't have enough votes to go forward and you don't have any research for us to appraise the value of HB-471. I'll have my aides review the reports you reference. I suggest you and I discuss this matter offline. One more question:

Since the things that HB-471 provides for—such as professional development, charter schools, educational standards, and computer purchases—are already being done in one form or another, in districts across the state what feedback have you received about their impact on learning and teaching?"

Representative Jose answers, "Correct. Everything in HB-471 is presently possible under existing code. All are being done in some schools. As for feedback, I've received letters about many of the provisions. All the letters say the practices are having an impact. I don't, however, have any hard data to back up those claims."

Chairperson Charles says, "Thank you, Representative Jose. This committee stands adjourned until 1 week from today when we'll receive testimony from Governor Sue."

Many things happen in the hearing about HB-471. Let us use the five characteristics of Type-A policymaking to cut through its muster and bluster. First, HB-471 is a distal, low-power policy that provides for more of the same practices (e.g., professional development, charter schools, standards, and computers) that are already possible under existing laws and have not affected the educational crisis to date. If Chairperson Charles and the committee members examine the literature about the practices HB-471 promotes—remuneration, unfocused professional development, charter schools, standards, and so on—they will know that to be the case. However, because they have no clear directive from the field of education and share no schema and embedded design with them, HB-471 is the best policy they can conjure up. Second, HB-471 is neither timely nor rational. Big intervals existed between its proposal, initiation, full implementation, and the educational crisis that precipitates it. Between enactment and implementation, the state's educational decline will continue unimpeded. Third, the external events (e.g., state-by-state comparisons) that elevated education on the policy agenda did not emerge from the field. Rather, as chairperson Charles points out the events are concocted by Sue's opponent, embellished by the media, and pushed by special-interest groups. Fourth, during the campaign, Governor Sue's opponent frames and advances the issue of education by accusing her of ignoring the state's poor educational performance. Sue, in turn, by taking up the accusation, accrues political capital that she can use if re-elected. Representative Jose, as Representative Smith points out, has little capital, and what he does have comes from bartering for votes. Thus, his policymaking is more of the same policies already in place. Fifth, the bill and the policymaking that produce it have no capacity for appraising the impact of the policies and policymaking or capacity for having feedback emerge directly from the stakeholders whom the policies and policymaking affect. This means that neither the policy nor the policymaking has capacity for refinement, a point made evident by the actions of the task force chair and Chairperson Charles. As Governor Sue is about to show, Type-B policymaking works quite differently.

HOW TYPE-B POLICYMAKING CAN IMPROVE EDUCATION

Type-B policymaking is the antithesis of the policymaking described above that is incapable of resolving the state's educational crisis. Although the task force agrees that the state has a problem, its members—representing the field's lack of consensus and using the Type-A approach—cannot agree about how to resolve their lack of consensus and the state's problem. The task force's report is a compendium of testimony that reflects the non-consensus of its members. Not surprisingly, HB-471, the bill it spawns, is piecemeal, distal, low-power, high-load, destined to fail, and quite possibility will make the crisis worse (Pogrow, 1996). Policymaking Example 6.5 includes excerpts of Governor Sue's testimony to the House Education Committee concerning HB-1, *The Educational Reconceptualization Act of 2011*.

Policymaking Example 6.5: Governor Sue's Testimony on HB-1

"Mr. Chair, thank you. I come before you and your esteemed colleagues with some trepidation. Your public criticisms of HB-1 have been disconcerting. Fortunately, the strength of conviction derived from what I experienced during and after the campaign gives me confidence to stand before you with the backing of the electorate and a bill that solves the very real educational crisis they expect us to end.

"I was once skeptical that genuine, wide-scale, research-based educational improvement is possible via the highly politicized educational policymaking process. That changed when Herb, one of my thought leaders, arranged for me to visit District-B. There, I engaged with Superintendent James, Principal Sarah, teacher Bruce, and others. All their classrooms and schools had master teachers, students learning cooperatively, and a design that enabled both. What they did was amazing, simply amazing. It made me yearn to be a student again.

"I was ready to see what I saw because I knew they shared a common schema, that means they had a formal understanding about what they would do in classrooms and schools and how they would do it in each, a curriculum that is differentiated to accommodate the differences and needs of individual students, and edge technology, a term that describes a special category of software tools. I learned about each when, prior to my visit, Herb and I went online with Association-B's Member School Performance Array. With it, we generated a report comparing the performance of District-B's classrooms and schools with that of other member and non-member districts. Also, we used the A to B Toolkit to generate curricular exemplars of what I would likely see in Bruce's classroom. We viewed real-time self-report data from Bruce's students about the units and modules they were working on. I learned how he was adapting his instruction based on their performance and feedback. So, when I sat in Bruce's classroom, I knew exactly what to look for, what words to use, and which questions to ask. I could see that all students and teachers received the educational support they needed when they needed it.

"Afterward, when James, Sarah, Bruce, Herb, and I debriefed, we used the Array and Toolkit as a basis for discussing the practices that I had experienced at District-B and Association-B and the effects they had on students and teachers. For instance, I learned that the TIPS-R scores and overall achievement for Sarah's school had improved dramatically. In fact, if the school's performance was the performance of this state, we'd be number one in the world!

"Everything I experienced in District-B and Association-B was similar and subject to rigorous, yet supportive, feedback-based performance appraisal. Their shared framework or *schema*, as they called it, and embedded design enabled this to occur. HB-1, now before you, is a practical reflection of what I experienced. It codifies the schema, design, feedback, and technology required to make all schools in our state like District-B. It provides a way for them to attain 1:X by using the change process that is playing out in District-B and Association-B. Through that same process, all districts will establish Type-B design standards for their schools. This will ensure that research-based practice is brought to scale across the state.

"Also, HB-1 provides grants for schools and districts to undertake change processes, to establish professional development institutes, and for transitioning to the edge technology that will generate the feedback and performance data that will guide their efforts. Please note that HB-1 will extend edge technology to this body as well. That means you will have access to the same data about this state that James can access for his district. The standards that HB-1 establishes are exacting, although, based upon the experience of District-B, we know they will solve our educational crisis.

"As I close, I want to make three quick points about HB-1. One, upon its enactment, the benefits I just described will begin accruing immediately in every classroom, school, and district throughout the state. Two, the impact of HB-1 will be easy for us and our constituents to appraise because the schema, design, and tools we'll share will give them and us the capacity and functionality for doing so. Last, the feedback processes that HB-1 facilitates at all levels of the system will help us meet the 1:X challenge statewide. Moreover, the processes will inform and guide refinement of our policies and policymaking. In sum, HB-1 empowers everyone.

"Mr. Chair and committee members, I ask on behalf of this state's citizens, all the teachers, and students in our schools, that you reject HB-471 and approve HB-1 and send it to the floor for a vote."

The five characteristics—consideration of proximal, high-power, research proven practices at an optimal time that responds to specific sets of events such as an election and produce measureable results—utilized earlier to examine the hearing about HB-471 are used below to deconstruct Governor Sue's testimony about HB-1. First, HB-1, unlike HB-471, is a high-power and proximal solution for the state's crisis. Because Governor Sue presents insights, examples, and references to data that are informed by her interactions with the processes and tools of District-B and Association-B members of the committee can give HB-1 a balanced and informative consideration. Members can judge HB-1 vis-à-vis its potential for resolving the crisis. Second, Governor Sue's testimony and the policymaking it invokes are timely. HB-1 commences upon enactment at the end of the current legislative session, accrues immediate affects, and is appraised from then on. Its implementation and appraisal are proximally linked to the current educational crisis facing the state. Moreover, its provisions can be unvaryingly applied in all classrooms, schools, and districts; none will be deprived or disadvantaged. Third, the events associated with her interaction with Herb and subsequent visit to James's district assert an emergent influence on HB-1 and the policymaking associated with it. Governor Sue tells the committee how *e*dge technology helps her prepare for appraising the learning in Bruce's classroom and the impact his and other practices have on TIPS-R scores and overall achievement. Fourth, the recent election frames and advances the policymaking—a point underscored by Governor Sue when she says she is doing the work that the voters told her to do. Fifth, HB-1 has explicit appraisal functions to measure its impact on the educational crisis. Feedback about HB-1's affect and refinement of HB-1 and the policymaking associated with it are built into its design. Hence, the educational course that HB-1 sets for classrooms, schools, and districts in the state can be altered as circumstances change.

The policymaking for HB-1 differs dramatically from that for HB-471. Representative Jose's bill, HB-471, reflects the top-down piecemeal approach of more-more-more, whereas Governor Sue's bill, HB-1, demonstrates the bottom-up possibility of educational stakeholders contributing to the whole system. Only HB-1 is capable of addressing the education crisis. Herb is familiar with the Type-B approach, District-B, and Governor Sue. Policymaking Example 6.6 presents excerpts from his testimony to the committee.

Policymaking Example 6.6:
Herb Testifies For Governor Sue's Bill HB-1

"The voters of this state, by re-electing Governor Sue, sent a message that they expect education to improve and they expect it done ASAP. Having been involved in several educational turnarounds, I know the work that such turnarounds entail. "Briefly, the crisis resolution you seek will not occur by doing more of the same. I learned that the hard way at our association. Ultimately, it took a combination of a shared schema, embedded design, and feedback processes to dramatically improve the performance of the association and its member districts . . . of which District-B is one.

"Here's how it happened. First, we dispersed control of the association to members. Second, we implemented the processes employed in member-districts and adopted their shared schema. Third, we adopted their edge technology. When we did these three things, we began co-evolving with the association's memebers. The design and operation of the association and work of its members became proximal. High-power, low-load processes are built into the design of how we now do our work so they are commonplace for me and the staff. In fact, many of our recently hired employees and new members know no other way of working. Realizing 2-Sigma at all member schools is our common goal. Since the changes were made, association performance has been remarkable. Membership and participation has skyrocketed. So has the number of member districts achieving and sustaining 2-Sigma.

"I am convinced that if you use HB-1 to scale such practices, 1:X will become the norm, and 2-Sigma will be attainable statewide. Please note that the improved performanc of Association-B and its member schools happened in spite of the distal, low-power, and non-research-based policies, such as HB-471, put forth by this body. Superintendent James and District-B are exemplars of this phenomenon. Much of what we do evolved from the schema, embedded design, and tools that their perseverance produced."

"If you pass HB-1, there will be no need for stakeholders to do such work-arounds or to reinvent what District-B has already created. Because you and your constituents share a schema, tools, and feedback processes, you'll be self-similar. This body will co-evolve with our association and all the state's classrooms and schools. As you improve, we'll improve, and vice versa. Please do the right thing by passing HB-1."

Herb's testimony offers insight into why Governor Sue, despite facing tough criticism from her political opponents, comes confidently before the committee. The life changing "gestalt shift" (Perls, 1969), that she experiences at District-B profoundly alters her view of education and policymaking. Specifically, she understands how the district's shared schema, design, and edge technology drive the bottom-up emergent feedback that generates improved student and teacher performance in classrooms and schools by making it easier for teachers to deliver high power instruction in ways that lower their cognitive loads and meet the 1:X challenge. Moreover, she understands what this means for her state.

When Governor Sue juxtaposes her experience at District-B with the Type-A policymaking she is familiar with, she readily notices the differences. She realizes that policymaking must create policies that remove rather than add load, enable rather than inhibit innovation, and release rather than restrain the growth of research-based practice. The policymaking that comes up with the first bill, HB-471, is inadequate. It establishes a lowest common denominator for educational practice and performance. It inserts policies into the assembly-line educational system and fosters expectations that miracles will spontaneously happen.

Governor Sue wants to enable the ever-expanding "boundary of performance" (Carter, 1989) and "continuous improvement" (BQF, 2001) that she experiences at District-B and Association-B for all stakeholders. For instance, when she sees that teachers provide formal feedback to other teachers and students providing feedback to other students lead to improved performance for all, she realizes that she needs a policy that is different than the Type-A policies that isolate teachers and students. She wants policies and research-based practices to naturally connect stakeholders at each level in simple yet profound, timely yet lasting ways that benefit their expertise and experience. After enacting such a policy, her next challenge is to prove that HB-1 had solves the crisis.

Typically, Type-A educational policies answer questions of impact of the policy on educational practice through the use of cost-benefit analyses (Zerbe & Bellas, 2006). Such analyses almost always prove ineffectual because they depend on data that is hard-to-come-by because if the data exists then special processes and permissions are often needed to obtain it and if it does not exists then data must be generated. That data are often subject to different, sometimes contradictory, interpretations (Verenez, Krop, & Rydell, 1999). In many ways, such analyses are unnecessary because HB-471 and policies like it are predicated on solutions that are not directly linked to the problem to be solved so will never return benefits no matter how much more money, technology, standards, or training they provide. Such policies are doomed to fail from the start. No analysis of impact is needed.

The politically charged and nuanced nature of Type-A policymaking causes many leaders to avoid the type of educational challenge (i.e., solving the state's crisis) that Governor Sue took on, preferring instead to routinely serve up distal, low-power, and high-load educational policies that deliver action but not results to their constituents. Governor Sue succeeds by going where other leaders fear to go and solves the crisis.

SHIFTS IN THOUGHT NEEDED TO
TRANSFORM POLICYMAKING

Governor Sue and the educational stakeholders who support her approach to solving the state's educational crisis make three shifts in order to create and pass HB-1. One shift changes stakeholders from policy consumers to policy contributors. They become proximal to the policymaking process and to the crisis. A second shift changes policymakers from problem creators to problem-solvers. Getting results, not more action, becomes their modus operandi. A third shift changes the basis for their policies from data collection to results reportage. This makes policymaking more about what is happening, than what has happened.

Shift one: Stakeholders becoming contributors to the policymaking process. HB-471 shows the way that Type-A policymaking relegates educational stakeholders—the persons with the most at stake in classrooms, schools, and districts—to the sideline at critical junctures during policy development, implementation, and refinement. They are expected to consume whatever the policymakers put on their plates even if it has been shown not to work. In contrast, the policymaking for HB-1 makes stakeholders active contributors. It draws on the everyday circumstances they face in their classrooms, schools, districts, and associations to inform the policies that will affect their work. District-B and Superintendent James make this shift, becoming contributors rather than consumers. Two weeks after Governor Sue testifies about HB-1 to the House Education Committee, James provides his testimony. Policymaking Example 6.7 presents excerpts from it.

Policymaking Example 6.7: Superintendent James Testifies for HB-1

Chairperson Charles asks James, "So, you are telling me that every stakeholder, at every level of District-B, contributes to every decision that is made there?"

Superintendent James replies, "Yes, Mr. Chair, that is correct. We share a schema that defines and guides the teaching and learning that occurs in our classrooms and is embedded in the overall operation and design of the district. That schema is the result of an on-going process through which we co-evolve in ways that help us attain 1:X. The edge technology we use makes us all contributors because it helps us generate and share real-time information; as we do normal work, our common tools generate feedback that informs and refines the work each of us does. We started with students and teachers. Then parents and administrators joined in. Recently, the Chamber of Commerce began engaging. Contributing is such a part of what we do at District-B that it is reflexive for most of us and attractive to others."

Superintendent James says, "Let's cut to the chase. I'm here to ask you and the committee to pass HB-1. Currently, many laws impede our efforts and require us to do work-arounds. That is why we demand the opportunity to contribute meaningfully to the processes through which the policies that affect us are made. HB-1 makes that possible and means work-arounds won't be necessary for having all students benefit from 1:X all the time."

James makes it clear that all District-B stakeholders contribute to the processes and policies that affect their schema, design, and practices. Their contributions lead to improved instruction, learning, and student achievement. Over time, their contributions broaden, not narrow, the range of contributors. First, students and teachers shift from being consumers to being contributors. Then parents and administrators shift. Eventually, the Chamber of Commerce shifts as well. At Association-B, Herb experiences similar shifts, when the contributions of the physics teachers he convenes end up attracting corporate contributors. In each instance, *e*dge technology by engaging stakeholders in meaningful ways and eliciting their feedback about how to make things better amplifies their contributions, scales their practices, and accretes their knowledge. The shift to being contributors would not have happened without *e*dge technology.

Shift two: Policymakers becoming problem-solvers. Policymaking and problem-solving should be synonymous (Lindblom, 1968). For HB-471, they are not. Process and people limit both.

To understand the disconnect between policymaking and problem solving, we need to deconstruct the rational chain of events that produce HB-471. Identification and clarification of a problem (e.g., plummeting performance) are linked to analysis (e.g., the task force report) that in turn is linked to the bill. At face value, such links appear to be orderly and productive (Elster, 1991). However, deeper review shows many gaps. For instance, Representative Jose, in typical Type-A mode, seeks to help a few stakeholders to get salary increases, a few schools to get grants, and some districts to get summer school programs (mostly in his legislative district). Moreover, the task force seeks to present the fragmented interests of the field. Neither Represetative Jose, Governor Sue, nor the task force can solve the state's educational crisis because they *are* the problem. This is further evidenced by how Representative Jose's trading of distal solutions (e.g., startup grants) for votes fans the flame of the crisis by diverting support away from its resolution. The task force's disjointed report adds even more fuel to the fire. Representatives Smith and Jose are at the center of the policymaking milieu surrounding HB-471. Policymaking Example 6.8 provides an excerpt of a recent conversation they had about HB-471.

Policymaking Example 6.8: Representatives Smith and Jose Meet

Representative Smith says, "Thanks for dropping by my office. I want to talk with you about HB-471." Representative Jose replies, "Indeed. I'm here to ask for your vote. You do not seem to care much about the education crisis but you do seem interested in getting more salary money to your teachers and more programs for your schools before the next election. Perhaps we can work more of each into HB-471." Representative Smith answers, "Tell me more."

When voters put education at the top of Governor Sue's policy agenda, and she puts it atop the agenda of the legislature, Representatives Smith and Jose default to what they know—policymaking that motivates them to co-exist. They, and other stakeholders, seek more of the largess that HB-471 affords, more grants, more programs, more requirements. Their self-serving behavior and limited knowledge of educational practice at scale make them incapable of doing anything else. As they did do they know, the policy they create encourages other stakeholders to co-exist, too.

Because Type-A policies are so distal to research-based practice, they readily lead stakeholders to default to co-existence. For instance, the Adequate Yearly Progress provision of the No Child left Behind Act (USDOE, 2002) incents schools for improving test scores (USDOE, 2010b), not teaching or learning. This is why the educators whom NCLB it supposed to benefit buy who care more about teaching and learning than test scores have come to revile the law (Meier & Wood, 2004). The same is true for Race to the Top (USDOE, 2010c), assignment of passing and failing grades to specific schools (PSK12, 2010), voucher programs for public and private schools (Friedman & Friedman, 1980), privatized management (Hill, Pierce & Guthrie, 1997), and open enrollment within and across school districts (Bierlein & Mollholland, 1993). Each policy fails to adequately connect the problem to be solved, the stakeholders who are suppose to solve the problem, and policies that address both because none of the policies are informed by definitive research. The absence of supportive data fosters highly personalized and politicized distal processes that are incapable of positive results. Such divisiveness inhibits the collaboration, change, and growth that is necessary for actual solving educational problems such as for attaining 1:X at scale.

Policymakers who use the Type-A approach co-exist with the elephant(s) in the room and provide leadership that is not based on research and best practice. That is why Representative Jose's bill, HB-471, sets high-stakes outcome standards and requirements that are insufficient to drive genuine change in classrooms and schools. By way of comparison, Governor Sue's bill, HB-1, focuses on the way the problem is to be solved, how research informs that solution, and the way schools can be designed differently so all students will learn at high levels. HB-1 sets standards for the design of schools that are proximal to student learning.

Shift three: Turning the data that stakeholders generate into reportage.
HB-1 is derived from the salient data that stakeholders generate. When, how, and why such data is utilized is *reportage*. The gathering of that data is *data collection*.

As the worldwide technological revolution advances so does the quantity, quality, and types of data collection. Unified reporting is a common part of the business intelligence and knowledge management fields of practice that are attracting sizable followings (Hannig, 2002). Business intelligence uses reportage to improve process and operational effectiveness by identifying critical trends, enabling speedy delivery of actionable data, and informing decision making. Knowledge management analyzes reportage to identify, create, represent, distribute, and adopt insights and experiences for the purposes of shrinking the cycle time for innovation, benefiting from intellectual capital, and coping with the deluge of unstructured information (Alavi & Leidner 2001). Data reportage and collection play increasingly important roles in the organizational development of many disciplines such as medicine, manufacturing, and media (Brown & Duguid, 1998). In these fields, both are embodied in persons and/or embedded in processes that benefit individuals and groups alike. Neither, however, contributes to the making of HB-471. Both, however, are key to the creation of HB-1. Policymaking Example 6.9 presents more testimony about HB-1.

Policymaking Example 6.9:
Experts Testify

Chairperson Charles says, "We'll now receive expert testimony from Dr. Rose and Dr. Nelson."

Dr. Rose begins, "I've visited District-B, studied School-B, and reviewed the performance reportage from both. The results attained there are quite significant. And I might add that the District Performance Array used by Herb and the stakeholders of Association-B made accessing and analyzing the reportage very easy. Even without deep knowledge of the district's Type-B approach, the Array and A to B Toolkit made it easy for me to connect student learning to teacher performance, curriculum problem-solving, and the evolution of the professional development model in the district's schools. They helped me map the way the district responded to its TIPS-R problem with PBCL and the effects that approach had over time and at scale. The reportage I accessed made the various statements about the Type-B approach that I'd heard from stakeholders much more impressive and reliable. I recommend that HB-1 be enacted ASAP."

Dr. Nelson testifies, "I agree with Dr. Rose that you should pass HB-1. Our company sponsored a study of District-B, other districts like it, and Association-B. Based on that research, which was greatly enhanced by access to the Array and the A to B Toolkit, I agree that the design employed there should be replicated statewide. The reportage helped us see the proximal connections between the mission, design, methods, research, and tools that comprise the Type-B approach. Moreover, we have concluded that it would be much easier to take what District-B is doing to statewide scale than do what Representative Jose proposes in HB-471."

Chairperson Charles replies, "Thank you, Drs. Rose and Nelson."

The testimony of Professor Rose and businessperson Nelson about HB-1 derives from the emergent reportage they interact with via Performance Arrays and A to B ToolKit that District-B and Association-B use. Their testimony contrasts with that the testimony they provided earlier about HB-471 in which they did not agree about the educational crisis facing the state and its possible resolution. Their subsequent testimony about HB-1 is in total agreement. The difference between their first and second testimonies is how edge technology and the reportage it generates informs their second testimony by helping them see the same problem, experience the same solution, and arrive at the same conclusion (HB-1 could solve the state's educational crisis).

The testimony of Rose and Nelson illustrates how policymaking for HB-471 is not advantaged by reportage but testimony for HB-1 is. The testimony for HB-471 is more about data connoisseurship than use. As such, it is one dimensional and low power. That is why Chairperson Charles' recounting of what he had heard from constituents is given so much credence. It is similar to the manner that Anne and her science colleagues consider the TIPS-R problem via distal solutions that generate no power so. How did what Governor Sue, Superintendent James, association executive Herb, and experts Rose and Nelson shared become HB-1? Policymaking Example 6.10 presents Governor Sue taking up that challenge.

Policymaking Example 6.10:
Governor Sue Directs the Legislative Counsel to Draft HB-1

"The bill you're drafting, HB-1, is unlike any that has ever been drafted before. To get started you must do four things. One, create a new section for the state code that preempts and defines all existing laws pertaining to education from a Type-B perspective. Two, develop a preface to the section that sets forth definitions of key Type-B concepts that the law will enable. Concepts must include *cognitive load, cooperative teaching, differentiated instruction, dispersed control, co-evolution, proximal, schema, scale, self-organization, similarity,* and so on. If you have questions, call Herb at Association-B. He understands each and can explain them to you.

"Also, the preface must include role descriptions for each stakeholder— be sure to include students and parents—and specific language about the changing natures of the spaces and places such as classrooms and schools in which they do their work. Three, write a preamble that clearly describes the educational crisis facing the state and the problems, such as self-serving programs and poorly researched solutions that have created it and how the law will solve it. Four, describe the specific changes that will be undertaken to replace the current educational approach with the Type-B approach. This should include timelines, responsibilities, measures of progress, and so on. Contact James should you have questions. He has district-level policies you can adapt for our purposes. When you see them, look for the co-evolutionary behaviors they make possible. Thanks in advance for making this a top priority. My scheduler will arrange for us to meet 2 days from now."

Governor Sue's directions for drafting HB-1 rejects the piecemeal, destined-to-fail co-existing approaches that HB-471 embodies and that are common in Type-A policymaking. She makes clear that HB-1 supports the high-power, research-based practices that are proximal to the stakeholders and the educational crisis. The bill has new definitions, reconceptualized roles for stakeholders, and reportage generating mechanisms that enable HB-1 to be judged vis-à-vis its effect on the educational crisis rather than by politics as usual. All this happens because educational stakeholders in her state policy are made contributors and problem-solvers empowered by reportage.

CREATING EMERGENCE: HOW SHIFTS IN THOUGHT CAN TRANSFORM POLICYMAKING

HB-1 is possible because policymakers make the three shifts described above and are informed by the many shifts that occur at other levels of the educational system. The policy-level perspective that HB-1 establishes enable Governor Sue, Chairperson Charles, and other policymakers to respond to the successful practices that emerge at the classroom, school, and district levels and are aggregated at the association level. Let's check in with Governor Sue and Chairperson Charles 2 years after HB-1 is signed into law. Policymaking Example 6.11 presents an exchange between them.

Policymaking Example 6.11: Governor Sue Returns

Governor Sue begins by saying, "Chairperson Charles and committee members, I'm pleased to be here to hear your regular review of the State Performance Array and receive your recommendations for the budget and policy package my office will soon submit."

Chairperson Charles replies, "Thank you, Governor Sue. We use the Array to monitor the feedback we get from classrooms, schools, and districts. It helps us identify performance trends, opportunities for improvements, and areas of concern. We also have a standing meeting with Herb and members of Association-B for reviewing the reportage that each of us is seeing via the Array. As the chart on the video screen shows, preliminary data indicates that overall performance, as measured by TIPS-R, has increased year over year. So have the number of schools and districts achieving 1:X. Needless to say, we unanimously recommend continuance of the priority practices that are part of our shared schema. There is one area of the law that's problematic—professional development. Please watch this video. It'll help you to see why we think a couple of amendments to HB-1 are needed."

Governor Sue answers, "Thanks for getting Bruce and Sarah to put that video clip together. Please tell them well done. Our review of the data that Array surfaced led me to make the same conclusion about professional development. In response, I recently met with James and Herb to discuss this matter. We agreed that a change is needed. Are you available to meet with counsel later today? If so, we could get an amendment drafted and introduced so we could solve this problem by end of business tomorrow."

The collectivized stakeholder action that plays out across the network leads to proximal amending of HB-1. This is possible because all stakeholders, including Governor Sue and Representative Charles, use tools derived from the schema they share. The embedded design of the overall educational system in their state produces self-similarity across stakeholders and levels of the system. The causal relationships that HB-1 establishes and the feedback it requires drive interactions among stakeholders that produce new and evolving patterns of behavior and quantifiable growth (e.g., the number of 1:X schools). The interactions among stakeholders generate more feedback, which results in more interconnectivity among levels of the system, and produce more reportage that is used to further refine HB-1. Stakeholders become contributors and policymakers become problem-solvers. Policymaking is proximal, a manifest expression of classroom-level practice.

HB-1 is a scaled and dynamic extension of the behavior patterns that occur throughout the state's educational system. This includes District-B's PBCL, School-B's advanced professional development for mastery teachers, and Association-B's annual conference. Each level benefits from the shifting conditions at all levels. Each is a discrete, emergent, and adaptive act of self-organization. Each solves a discrete problem. Collectively the stakeholders, including Governor Sue and Representative Charles, are a multilevel, self-organizing educational system driven by the constant revision, adaptation, and emergence of its schema (Johnson, 2001). HB-1 arises from the processes, causes, and effects of various levels of that system. It is the embodiment of emergence. The system reaches the point of emergence because of the cumulative interactions of all its levels. The chain of events Governor Sue sets in motion (and those that set her in motion) lead to greater order within the system. As order increases, new structures emerge. Some are simple (e.g., cooperative teaching), others complicated (e.g., Association-B). One informal structure that emerges is a professional relationship between Governor Sue and Chairperson Charles. Even though they belong to different political parties they are united by HB-1. Policymaking Example 6.12 presents an exchange between Chairperson Charles and Governor Sue.

Policymaking Example 6.12:
Chairperson Charles and Governor Sue Chat

Chairperson Charles begins by saying, "Governor, glad I could catch you before you left the chamber. I wanted to tell you that I can't believe what a difference two years make. Two years ago, you and I couldn't agree on anything. Now we're solving problems and improving classrooms and schools with nary a disagreement."

Governor Sue replies, "So true. And the reportage about our efforts is quite impressive. Test scores and graduation rates are up, disciplinary incidents are down, the number of 2-Sigma schools is increasing, and our poll numbers remain high."

Representative Charles tells her, "The most amazing thing for me is how much easier policymaking has become. I used to chase problems; now solutions find me. It's as if they emerge. I hope things will continue to emerge so that the short-term gains we've achieved will be exceeded many times over."

Governor Sue answers, "I agree. James told me that when we are truly leading, genuine change will emerge constantly. I think we've reached that point. As HB-1 interacts with what is going on in the classrooms, schools, and districts, an entirely new system is emerging. James said I was strange attractor. I was offended until he told me that the term refers to a force that emerges from chaos to disrupt the equilibrium of a system. I think you're one, too!"

Governor Sue, chairperson Charles, superintendent James, and executive director Herb have indeed emerged as forces that disrupt the status quo of the educational system of which they are a part. Such emergence is a quality "arising from a system's structures, patterns, and properties" (Corning, 2002). It is not a product of a system's component parts. Rather, it's a consequence of how those components interact (Laughlin, 2005) and the context in which those interactions take place (Corning, 2002). Such interactions connect patterns of behavior that are interconnected and complex (Koestler & Smythies, 1969). The "whole becomes not merely more, but very different from the sum of its parts" (Anderson, 1972). This is what Governor Sue and Chairperson Charles are experiencing.

HOW SHIFTS IN THOUGHT CHANGE
THE PRACTICE OF POLICYMAKING

Conditions for emergent policymaking come from the contributions, problem-solving, and reportage that are genereated by the network of Type-B stakeholders in the educational system. Representative Charles and Governor Sue confirm that their policymaking is an emergent phenomena—a scaled-up iteration of the schema, design, and tools that they share with stakeholders at various levels of the system. Thanks to HB-1, they are external mediating forces that match the work done by the stakeholders at the many levels of the system with the resources and support provided by policies and programs. The roles Chairperson Charles and Govenor Sue play are similar to the roles played by James at the district level, Sarah at the school level, and Herb at the association level. The normal work they do disturbs the equilibrium of the entire network in positive, productive, and self-organizing ways. The Performance Arrays and A to B Toolkits they use enable that work. In this way, edge technology is an emergent driver for the policies and policymaking that evolves as stakeholders evolve.

THE TOOLS POLICYMAKERS NEED
TO SUPPORT EDUCATION

Edge technology extends the policymaking processes. Figure 6.1 depicts a layout from the State Performance Array used by Governor Sue, Chairperson Charles, and other policymakers to implement and refine HB-1. It is a scaled-up version of the Array James uses to analyze District-B's performance.

The work of the committee members and Governor Sue is extended by the statewide trends (e.g., professional development) that the State Performance Array helps them identify and report. On the Array in Figure 6.1, the districts' professional development priorities are reflected on the left side of the layout. The priorities that require problem-solving are reflected in the center field. The summary fields show emerging issues and challenges and the right side shows teacher and student performance. From this view, committee members and Governor Sue can drill down to classroom or school views. They can examine the effects of a policy,

Figure 6.1. State Performance Array

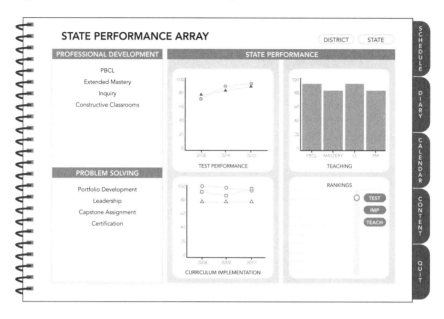

such as HB-1, on teacher performance, professional development, and emerging issues. The views reveal whether policies are proximal or distal expressions of the performance and needs of the stakeholders in the state's educational system.

The policy development components of the A to B Toolkit are depicted in Figure 6.2. It represents the regulation of professional development in Type-B schools and serves as a Type-B corollary to the state education department's Type-A effort to regulate continuing teacher education as described in Chapter 4.

The left side of the layout contains a summary of research on high-power professional development. Specific empirical studies are called out. The center contains guidelines and forms for districts to apply for professional development funds. The right side shows current policies. This view is particularly relevant to Chairperson Charles since his committee oversees HB-1 and the high-power proximal solutions and current activities that HB-1 makes possible at districts and Association-B. The view could help committee members identify gaps in services and emerging needs that stakeholders might be experiencing. The field at the bottom gives the committee members a space to make recommendations.

Committee members use reportage from the State Performance Array and A to B Toolkit: Policy Development Topic to evolve HB-1's professional development provisions. These tools make HB-1 more proximal and higher-power for the teachers and students. Committee members' use of the tools made amending HB-1a simple

Figure 6.2. A to B Toolkit: Policy Development Topic

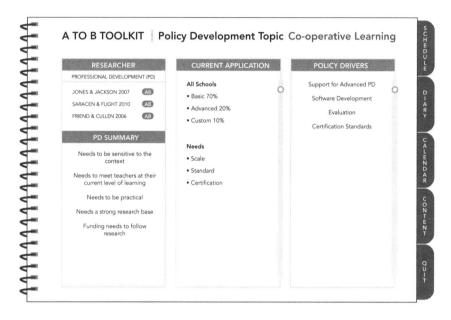

response to the stakeholders' needs. The committee members are positioned to identify the stakeholders' needs because the tools afforded the members a helicopter perspective of the overall educational system. From that perspective they can be sources of strange attraction that disturb the equilibrium of the entire system. The committee members use their tools to capture the actions of the stakeholders' and translate the data about the transactions into reportage that contribute to proximal and high-power refinements of HB-1. Those refinements further bring down the cognitive load of the stakeholders. All this is possible when policymakers can see the performance of schools and classrooms at scale which they can do because of edge technology.

HOW A SHARED SCHEMA HELPS POLICYMAKERS
SUPPORT EDUCATION AT ALL LEVELS

Governor Sue and Chairperson Charles develop and refine HB-1 using the same three-step framework that stakeholders at other levels of the educational system used to move from a Type-A to a Type-B approach. The framework helped Governor Sue and Chairperson Charles examine the key propositions of their policymaking, the role edge technology played in them, and the benefits for their policymaking that might be accrued if the role for edge technology was increased.

New Assumptions

Type-B policymaking embeds explicit processes (e.g., feedback, self-reporting) in policies to foster emergent behavior among stakeholders. In turn, those behaviors, when combined with the Arrays and Toolkits that all stakeholders commonly use, assert collective effects on all levels of the educational system.

Assumption one: Since Type-B policymaking places additional (e.g., increased responsiveness) and complex (e.g., dependency on reportage) demands on policymakers and stakeholders, Type-B policymaking is only achievable through edge technology. The effect of edge technology on policymaking derives from the cognitive load reducing intelligence that is located in the State Performance Array and A to B Toolkit. Those tools collectivize certain behaviors (e.g., feedback) of stakeholders across the system and generate data about the quality of the actions that stakeholders take. The value of edge technology in the making of educational policy is obvious when Herb preps Governor Sue for her visit to District-B, when James and team debrief her afterward, when she directs the bill drafter, and when Chairperson Charles and the committee members appraise the value of HB-1 vis-à-vis the crisis one year after the bill is enacted into law.

Assumption two: Research about educational practice at scale defines Type-B policymaking and the role that edge technology plays in policymaking. The earlier bill, HB-471, was not informed by research-based practice because the field of education, as represented by the task force, had no consensus about what worked at scale so could not provide proximal guidance to policymakers. As a result, Jose and the other policymakers, who championed HB-471 equate educational change with more-of-the-same, and produce a policy that only distally connects to research about best practice, some stakeholders whom the educational crisis is effecting, and ICT. In contrast, the new bill, HB-1, uses edge technology to proximally connect policymakers to all stakeholders throughout the system and to generate reportage that is used to refine the schema that policymakers and stakeholders share.

Assumption three: As Governor Sue and Chairperson Charles demonstrate, policymaking through edge technology and policymaking about edge technology are indistinguishable because it properly addresses the 1:X challenge. They use HB-1 to create the conditions for extending edge technology across the system. Specifically, HB-1 enables policymakers to interact with the contributions that stakeholders make in classrooms and schools and to engage with the feedback that edge technology produce. Governor Sue and Chairperson

Charles come to rely upon the feedback, reportage, and contributions that the State Performance Array and A to B Toolkit provide. These tools, by representing the design and implementation of the system's schema, become drivers of policy change. Although both HB-1 and HB-471 seek to change education and both seek to manage the associated "change and transitions" (Luecke, 2003), only HB-1 assigns proximal responsibility to edge technology by placing it at the center of the effort to end the state's educational crisis.

Assumption four: Access to edge technology is a simple yet fundamental requirement for Type-B policymaking. HB-1 is a result of all stakeholders doing their normal work through edge technology. The commonality and awareness that use fosters are an everyday reality for stakeholders. Chairperson Charles makes this point clear when he reflects about how his policymaking has changed since he began using the Array and toolkit. The dispersed control and feedback that edge technology enables are how policymaking gets done. The dynamic Type-B solution is proximal to the state's crisis and high-power and low-load for its stakeholders.

Assumption five: Making HB-1 through edge technology improves the overall quality of the policymaking, the quality of education in Governor Sue's state, and subsequently ends its educational crisis. HB-1, by placing edge technology in a powerful mediating context for policy development and refinement, leverages well-researched professional practice in ways that are proximal to stakeholders and make the practices in their classrooms and schools high power. Thanks to HB-1 and edge technology Governor Sue makes 1:X attainable for all stakeholders, a reality to which Herb and James attest in the testimony they provide in support of HB-1.

New Design

During the past 3 decades, policymaking efforts to innovate, reform, and change education have yielded few wide-scale performance gains (OECD, 2008; UNESCO, 2008). This is not because policies are scarce. In fact, the number of policies was staggering. It was also not because the policies that are enacted lack aspiration. There was no ambiguity about their intents. Nor are funds lacking. Trillions of dollars are provided (NCES, 2008; OECD, 2008; UNESCO, 2008). Performance gains do not result because Type-A policymaking lacks the capacity to alter the multi-faceted, complexly organized and deeply resistant to change Type-A educational system. Governor Sue takes three steps—solution mapping, component building, and design integration—to design HB-1. Through them, she links crisis resolution, funding, research, processes, and tools in ways that put the state on a trajectory for statewide and sustainable attainment of 1:X and 2-Sigma. Such attainment is reflected in the state's improved test scores, graduation rates, economic indicators, and view of Governor Sue and Chairperson Charles.

Policymakers seldom apply organizational principles such as productivity and conflict resolution to their work. Governor Sue changes this by using Type-B policymaking to engage all stakeholders in *solution mapping.* Together, they (a) consider the state's crisis from the viewpoint of each level of the network, (b) develop a research-based understanding of the key aspects of the crisis and possible level-specific and system-wide solutions, (c) identify obstacles that might impede implementation of the solutions, and (d) develop specific ways to diminish those obstacles.

Governor Sue takes these solution-mapping steps when she realizes the limitations of what the task force has recommended in the first bill, HB-471. In the new bill, HB-1, she incorporates what was already under way at District-B and Association-B, and uses their *edge* technology in a way that makes the Type-B approaches that are in place there occur more readily and rapidly at all levels. When Governor Sue, James, Herb, and others engage in *component building,* they define the resolution of the educational crisis in 1:X terms, clarify the roles for stakeholders at various levels, and articulate specific commitments to attaining 2-Sigma at every school in the state and provide support for the schools agreeing to share the schema, design, and tools that District-B and Association-B share. Stakeholders become contributors, policymakers became problem-solvers, and reportage supports both. When Governor Sue steps up to *design integration,* she enlists the help of Herb, James, and Chairperson Charles to determine which stakeholders would be assigned what responsibilities under HB-1.

New Trajectory

The steps that Governor Sue takes help integrate *edge* technology tightly in HB-1. Since HB-1 is conceived and birthed in an emergent place, it can expand from there. As HB-1 expands, policymaking and all activities at all levels of the state's educational system are on a trajectory to solve the education crisis by meeting the 1:X challenge and attaining 2-Sigma in every school. On that trajectory the circumstances (e.g., election, poor performing schools, and ineffective task force) that drives Governor Sue and Chairperson Charles to change from Type-A to Type-B policymaking become the measures by which HB-1 is appraised—more students completing school, better test scores, and a stronger economy. This is quite an accomplishment given that Type-A policymaking rarely intersects with classrooms, schools, districts, and associations. Greater still, Governor Sue and her colleagues figure out why education fails technology and what policymaking could do about this circumstance.

SUMMARY

- Type-A policymaking is characterized by a more-of-the-same conversation between policymakers and stakeholders that equates more stuff with better education.
- The field of education's lack of consensus about successful practice at scale fosters ambiguous policies that are more politically than educationally created and more distal than proximal to educational stakeholders and their needs.
- In this way Type-A policymaking sustains more-of-the-same in education and inhibits efforts to meet the 1:X challenge.
- Attaining 1:X at scale requires Type-B policymaking in which stakeholders are contributors and problem-solvers who generate real-time reportage about what is happening in the classrooms, schools, districts, and associations in which the stakeholders work.
- Type-B policymaking collectivizes stakeholder interactions in ways that foster self-organizing behaviors across the network levels of the educational system.
- Self-organization makes emergent change possible. Such change is a natural consequence of the capacities present at the various levels of the network that inform, guide, and refine Type-B policymaking.
- Edge technology makes possible the rigorous feedback, analysis, and action that the Type-B approach uses in both the statehouse and the schoolhouse.

CHAPTER 7

The Role of Industry

The customer is never wrong.
—Cesar Ritz

Why don't ICT companies and their education customers pursuing 2-Sigma benefit each other? In this chapter, we draw from our real-world experiences to show (a) a Type-B company that sells hardware, software, and services benefiting various levels of an educational system and vice versa, (b) the company-level shifts that make such benefits possible, and (c) the edge technology that plays an essential role in such shifts and benefits occurring at scale.

THE PROBLEM OF BRINGING EFFECTIVE ICT INTO EDUCATION

Although it is rarely acknowledged, one significant way the field of education fails technology is by not using educational research to inform ICT use in classrooms, schools, districts, and associations (Impagliazzo & Lee, 2010; Palfrey & Gasser, 2008). A consequence of the education field's failure to inform the use of ICT by educational stakeholders is a pervasive inability of the field to provide direction to the ICT industry (Christensen, Horn, & Johnson, 2010; Collins & Halverson, 2009). In turn, the industry is incapable of helping educational stakeholders meet the 1:X challenge because, in the absence of direction from the field of education, the industry can only offer up products that are designed for business and repurposed for education (Campbell-Kelly & Aspray, 2004; Darr, 2006). In this way, the failure of the field of education to inform the ICT use of educational stakeholders results in industry offerings for education that are distal, low-power, and high-load for stakeholders and the work they do.

Four circumstances contribute to this situation. First, the field of education, stuck in the Type-A approach, generally views ICT as something stakeholders access. A case in point is how the field of education focuses on 1:1 computing initiatives (Greaves & Hayes, 2008) rather than on 1:X. Although the field gives lip service to computing initiatives being about teaching and learning, initiatives

159

focus on student-to-computer ratios and automation of activities (e.g., attendance-taking, grade reporting), not learning processes (e.g., instructional management, task structure) and outcomes (e.g., test scores, graduation rates, instructional quality). Second, stemming from its view of ICT as something stakeholders access to automate their activities, the field of education inherently resists innovation, change, and reform in its educational thought and practice (Cuban, 1984; Fuhrman, Clune, & Elmore, 1991; Ravitch, 2000, 2010). This fact is apparent in the field's general ambivalence (Fullan, 2007) about so many students dropping out of school, scoring poorly on tests, and being unprepared for the world of work. It is also apparent in the field's failure to recognize that tinkering with its Type-A approach makes little difference for students overall (Tyack & Cuban, 1995). Third, the field lacks the collective capacity and desire for building consensus (Tyack, 2003) about Type-A and Type-B educational approaches. So the fieled remains trapped in the backward-looking Type-A paradigm that reports about what has happened but not what could happen (Donmeyer, 2006; Fischetti, 1996; Glanz & Behar-Horenstein, 2000), and constructs its future with a view to the past performance of some students rather than an eye on what is possible for all of them (Boyd, 1992; Edge & Richards, 1998; Holdzkom & Kuligowski, 1993). A possibility that requires the field to realize the educational promise of ICT (Ashburn & Floden, 2006). Fourth, the field of education's uninformed-by-research (Fullan, 1993) and autonomously constructed practices (Fischetti, 1996) industry with a fragmented market in which the only option is to sell not design for education low-power distal solutions.

These circumstances serve both the field and industry poorly. Financial (e.g., discounts, donations), not educational (e.g., learning, teaching), considerations dominate the field-industry relationship (Rivero, 2009). The field's fragmentation only affords the industry small and mid-sized sales opportunities. Such limited sales opportunities constrain the types and numbers of products that the ICT industry develops for education (Bennett & Wei, 2006). The industry need not develop sophisticated, proximally focused, education-specific products because the field of education has no consensus about the use of ICT in educational settings and leaves teachers to individually construct their use of ICT the best they can (Johanningmeier & Richardson, 2008). Since the field's ICT use is so fragmented, industry cannot project enough large sales opportunities to make the development of specific products for education a "low-risk" proposition (McGrath, 1995). Scalable business models are simply not feasible (Greaves & Hayes, 2008).

Predictably, when the field does purchases and deploys ICT, its fragmented state contributes to a dysfunctionally and piecemeal, low-volume deployments (Pooler, Pooler, & Farney, 2004). Although the deployments appear to respond to Type-A drivers—doubts about efficacy of the education system, need for technologically literate workers, and new technologies—in reality the deployments do not link the purchase of ICT, the drivers, and educational practice at scale. Moreover, when large-scale and complex deployments are undertaken in the name of

Type-A education they are often too inefficient and incomplete to produce few measureable educational gains in graduation rates and tests scores (Bonifaz & Zucker, 2004; Shapley et al., 2009; Silvernail, 2007). Given this state of affairs, the ICT industry, not surprisingly, limits its investments in education-related product development, research, and dedicated personnel (InfoTrends, 2010).

TYPE-A COMPANIES: THE PROBLEM WITH WHAT WE DO NOW

To understand why this occurs, we need to know how ICT companies view the education field, what drives some of those companies to engage with the field of education, and why the companies engage with it the way they do. Generally, short-term capitalistic desires (Friedman, 1962) for growing business (Hawken, 1987), making money (Smith, 1976), and building brand recognition (Miller & Muir, 2004) drive companies to engage the education field (Milgate, 2004). Companies view education as a potentially large market (Wedel & Kamakura, 1998) in which to sell goods and services, meet potential buyers, and transact business (Owens, 2002). However for the market potential to be realized, opportunities and products have to be brought to the marketplace in large volumes (Ghauri, Hadjik-hani, & Johanson, 2005). To attain large volumes, companies must offer products that educational stakeholders need and want (Cagan, 2008). Unfortunately, since educational stakeholders cannot agree about what they need, education, unlike other fields—such as insurance (de Weert, 2011), manufacturing (Jovane, West-kamper, & Williams, 2009), and medicine (Rovin, 2001)—can neither inform nor support a scalable business model for ICT companies (Hunger & Wheelen, 2007).

   To understand why ICT companies go to the marketplace the way they do involves understanding five questions that leaders of educationally engaged companies ask of themselves (Duncan, 2008). One question concerns opportunity: What products or services will educational stakeholders buy (Geldhof, 1931)? A second question involves evaluating opportunities against their cost of business. Is there a direct pathway from the opportunity to short-term profits? In order to be good, an opportunity must have fewer costs than revenues and a rapid rate of conversion into sales. A third question involves whether the persons responsible for making purchasing decisions are actively engaged in the sales process (Acuff & Wood, 2007). Are company representatives engaged with the right persons, who have the funds to purchase products, at the right moment? The fourth question asks: Is the company capable of pursuing and realizing profitable opportunities (Leonard-Barton, 1992)? To answer this question affirmatively, a company must have skilled and knowledgeable employees (Bach & Sisson, 2000). The fifth question considers the ways societal, technological, regulatory, and/or economic developments defined their actions and opportunities (Murdock, 2006). What effects might such developments have on sales?

Most companies have internal methodologies that help their leaders answer the five questions (Hunger & Wheelen, 2007). The methodologies often include weekly forecast calls, quarterly planning meetings, and annual sales conferences (Holmes, 2007). The methodologies sometimes include software applications for discovering, qualifying, pursuing, on-boarding, and retaining customers (Buttle, 2008). Such software tools help company leaders monitor what products are sold, by whom, and to whom (Eckerson, 2006). Some companies use software that has special analytic functions that help company leaders scrutinize, interpret, and forecast customer actions and preferences. Such analytics can enable market segmentation, targeting, and measurement of product appeal, sales maker productivity, and measurement of marketing program effectiveness (Davenport & Harris, 2007). Companies often find it challenging to manage their methodologies, processes, and systems. The challenges that companies face are exacerbated by having software applications that are limited to a singular function such as the management of sales contacts (e.g., records of interactions with customers), sales pipelines (e.g., deal tracking), client-interface functions (e.g., online purchasing), and/or performance cycles that are measured in 90-day increments when the true cycle is a year or longer (Eades & Kear, 2006). This is the case because the software tools that companies use often just automate the distal low-power processes they use and products they sell.

Every day, thousands of company leaders grapple with the five questions described above (Kotter & Cohen, 2002). Their successes at making their respective companies profitable depend on the answers they generate. One such leader is Félix, the CEO, president, and founder of Company-A. The company incorporated 17 years ago at the beginning of the worldwide expansion of the ICT industry. Two years later, it was publicly traded. It sells hardware, software, networking, and services such as installation, imaging, and training. *Best Products, Best Prices* is the company motto. Last year, 40% of its revenue came from education-related sales. Industry Example 7.1 describes Félix's activity during a late-night work session.

Industry Example 7.1: Félix Works Late

Félix looks at the stack of reports and spreadsheets his assistant printed for him. One report contains a detailed, 5-year summary of the company's major accounts: what each account bought, when they bought it, at what price, and so on. Another report ranks each salesperson by cumulative and quarterly revenues produced, margin, and goal attainment. Yet another report indicates which product was the most profitable relative to cost of doing business, had the greatest drag for sales of other products, and engaged the fewest personnel in the sales cycle. As Félix looks through the reports, he hopes to find a way to return Company-A to profitability; six quarters have passed since the company last turned a profit. He recalls that the last meeting of the board of directors had turned ugly. They told Félix—in no uncertain terms—to turn things around this quarter. Failing do so will result in a 34% reduction in force. After 2 hours of digging through data, Félix clears his desk, empties his coffee mug, and turns off the lights.

The tools and reports Félix uses during his after-hours work session do not give him what he seeks. He hopes to identify an educational product that will save Company-A from financial ruin. But the reports and spreadsheets he has access to only provide him with information that is distal to the problem he faces. The information is low-power and gives him no value-added intelligence with which to work. What Felix sees in the columns and rows of the reports is forensically backward-looking and insufficient for his needs. Moreover, the company's sales tools require him to do more work, not less, hence, they are high-load. Félix is not the only employee who is worried about Company-B's bottom line. Industry Example 7.2 presents a not-so-typical meeting of regional salespersons.

Industry Example 7.2: Bud Leads Meeting

Bud is the regional director for education sales at Company-A. He sits with his team. After clearing his throat, he says, "I didn't bring you here to celebrate making our quarterly goal. We're here because based on our data in SalesForce.com our pipeline for the next 2 quarters is empty. We have to fill it or else."

When Bud asks why this is the case, his team tells him that the economy is bad, districts lack money, school boards aren't convinced that ICT improves learning, computers are sporadically used in class, and money is being used to keep teachers employed. One team member complained about a principal who said teachers at his school rarely use the computers they have, so there was no need to buy more. Another one reported about three superintendents who were fired because their district's test scores declined.

Bud replies, "I get it; times are tough. Tough times, however, will not cut it with Félix and our shareholders. Félix is all over my case, asking about how we prioritize our work, what sales cycle choke points we have that make our processes ineffective, and which of you need coaching. We must fill the pipeline or heads will roll. Tell me what you need." Bud makes notes as members tell him: more discounts, seed units, sponsorships, marketing materials, travel money, and free tech support for customers. Bud answers, "Thanks. I'm meeting with Félix next week; let me see what I can do. In the meantime, please double down your efforts to close business."

Let us examine Félix's late-night work session and Bud's sales meeting using the five questions that company leaders ask of themselves when considering bringing products to market. First, from an opportunity perspective (what will customers buy), Bud and team are living the reality that Company-A's current products are not saleable. Customers are using their limited funds for things they believe to be more essential (e.g., salaries) than the products Company-A sells. For Bud and his team's customers, ICT is a luxury, not mission critical, and only distally connected to teaching and learning. The reality of this distal connection becomes strikingly clear when finances are tight. What Bud and his team offer are low-power solutions to their customer's real needs and problems, so diverting funding from ICT is a viable option for customers. Félix seeks to solve the problem that Bud and team are facing by seeking another product in the company's inventory that might be repurposed in a way that will make it appealing enough so that education customers will buy lots of it. Second, when weighing opportunity (i.e., the pipeline of sales deals that Félix's sales makers have identified) against cost of business, Félix and Company-A would rather reduce its workforce than lose money. Bud made this point painfully clear to his team. Third, Bud's team is not engaged with the persons such as superintendents and technology directors who control the purse strings for school districts. Fourth, when Bud asks his team what they need, "more of the same" characterized the answer they give him. They lacked the capacity to answer the question any other way. They had no meaningful way to engage with customers to determine what the customer needs and will buy. Fifth, Bud and his team are oblivious to the trends, developments, regulations, and tendencies affecting their business and paychecks. They are guilty of looking at their feet when they should be looking at the horizon.

For over 10 years, Bud has sold ICT to school districts. This quarter is the first time he faces not making his quota of sales. He knows that according to longstanding company practice, missing a quarterly sales goal will automatically put him on a corrective action plan, one step away from termination. Bud, with great foreboding, enters the room where Félix has convened an emergency meeting of Company-A's senior managers. Industry Example 7.3 presents highlights from that meeting.

Industry Example 7.3: Félix Presents a Way Forward

"Thanks for coming on short notice. Let's cut to the chase. Our sales have fallen short of goal for 6 straight quarters. Our pipeline is unfilled. We're in trouble! This is happening even though we eliminated sales cycle choke points, provided a better pipeline view, started a sales-coaching program, improved forecasting accuracy by 87%, and prioritized the weekly tasks of every salesperson. I hope you agree with me that business as usual won't produce the necessary revenues.

"Last week, I attended a conference at my daughter's middle school. The principal told me the school did not make AYP this past year and the year before. She said teachers were trying everything possible to get test scores up. When I asked about ICT, she said, 'I wish we had more laptop computers. It would be cool if our school could go 1:1. Would Company-A donate computers to us?' She then offered that if we'd step up with computers the school would be our reference site and she and the teachers would provide testimonials.

"I talked with my daughter. She really likes the principal. I'm thinking the principal's offer has merit, but instead of just doing one school, we should donate computers to 10 schools—one in each sales region. The principal also said we should sign up to sponsor the National Academy of Middle School Principals, of which she is a board member. I accepted her offer. These steps will cost us money upfront but if we increase sales quotas by 7% year over year, and our sales increase, it would be worth it."

Unless things change, a crisis awaits Company-A (and the school that Félix's daughter attends). Trying to avert disaster, Félix seeks direction from three people—his employee Bud, the principal at Félix's daughter's school, and Félix's daughter. The direction that each person provides Félix is distal to the company's problem (but consistent with the direction that the field of education typically provides industry).

The problems that Company-A's customers face—declining tests scores and failure to make annual yearly progress—are obvious. Yet the guidance that Félix receives from his customers pertains to the people giving the guidance not the educational problems they face. The guidance gives Félix no insight into solving Company-A's profitability problem. Hence, the guidance is low-power for Félix. For instance, Bud's sales team, not knowing anything different, requests more of the things they undoubtedly have asked of Félix many times. The guidance Bud's team provides Félix is not actionable. It does not link the school and Company-A's products in ways that will lead the school to having better test scores or the company to having a better sales performance. The guidance that Bud's team and the principal provides Félix is so low power that it even make Félix's daughter's anecdotal views credible. Moreover, since Félix's proposal requires raising the sales quota, it increases the load of his employees.

Many companies use advisory groups and/or executive councils for the purpose of gaining insight into the education market. Companies appoint customers to such entities, and then engage them in discussions about products, messaging, and so on. Industry Example 7.4 presents an excerpt from a conference call that Félix has with members of his advisory group.

Industry Example 7.4: Félix Talks to Advisors

"Glad you could join the call. I want you to be the first to know about the program we're rolling out. It involves us outfitting 10 schools with laptop computers—loaded with cool software—and providing teachers there with several days of professional development. We'll call them *Transformation Schools* and use them as reference sites for driving our sales. This is going to be fun. By the time our PR team is done with this, several teachers will be famous and our bottom line will be in the black again." [Note: Before finishing the call and hanging up the phone, Félix receives emails from all nine members of the advisory council, offering suggestions for schools.]

Not surprisingly, every customer advisor of Company-A wants what Félix offers. However, neither they nor Félix bothers to consider whether Company-A's offer of laptop computers and software can possibly represent an opportunity for either the company or the schools. His Transformation Schools solution, while exactly what the school principal asked for, is too distal, low-power, and high-load to change the fortunes of Company-A. Many of Félix's employees, including Bud, have figured this out.

HOW TYPE-B COMPANIES CAN CHANGE EDUCATION

Isabella formed Company-B 4 years ago. Its employees sell ICT and related services into the education market and advance the Type-B educational approach. The company's motto is *Ex Processus Adveho Uber* (out of process comes product). It is publicly owned; stock prices have doubled since the company's formation. Annual revenues have increased year over year for the past 16 quarters. Education sales account for nearly half of the company's annual revenues. Industry Example 7.5 presents a snippet from a meeting between Isabella and Bud.

Industry Example 7.5: Isabella Welcomes Buds

"Welcome, Bud! We're delighted you accepted our offer to be our Global Vice President of Educational Sales at Company-B. We knew you were the right person for the job when you said during your interview, 'The needs of the customer and the needs of the company are one and the same.' That idea, as you'll find out today, is central to how we do business here.

"Opportunity waits for no one. We must get you oriented as quickly as possible. To do that, we've arranged for you to meet with your regional sales team leaders, have a video conference with our customer advisory partners, and visit three customer sites. Three exciting and informative days await you."

After working for Company-A that provided him with limited knowledge of customers, expected him to meet an unrealistic quota, and gave him few tools for doing either, Bud is about to experience why working at Company-B will indelibly alter his understanding of sales. Industry Example 7.6 reports an exchange between Bud and his new team.

Industry Example 7.6: Bud Meets New Team (Second Day Morning)

Bud says, "Thanks for making time to meet. Isabella said I'm inheriting a top-notch sales team and that you'd show me how we do business here." Forty-five minutes after the briefing begins, Bud tells them, "Wow! I am deeply impressed with what you're doing. Let me summarize what I just saw and heard. Briefly, we share the commitments and schema of our customers. They drive our business. The schema guides what they do at every level of the overall network while the feedback they generate and share informs us about what they need and will buy now and in the future. The information helps us develop a research and development strategy, forecast our opportunities, assign resources, develop products, and provide services. So the schema we share with our customers shapes our sales practices and the tools we use to monitor change in their schema so we can predict the future trajectory of the tools they need and our sales. It also helps us assign sales quotas. And we do our business through private cloud networks—also known as wireless, anytime, anywhere computing—that we create and manage. Did I miss anything? If not, Isabella arranged for me to have a one-on-one session with each of you. I can't wait to get started. What I just heard is so different from the way we did things at Company-A. I have bunches of questions to ask you."

Bud's new colleagues are good instructors and he is a quick study so he grasps the general differences between Company-A and Company-B immediately. Those differences are simple, yet profound. At Company-B customers are proximal; at Company-A customers are distal. His work at Company-B, how he does it, and the tools he uses are similar to those of his customers. Unlike the sales tools (e.g., contact management, sales cycle tracking) he used at Company-A that were complicated and not that useful for meeting his sales quota, the edge technology tools that Bud uses at Company-B directly impact his sales (and thus are high-power) and they make his life and his customers' lives easier (they are low-load). Industry Example 7.7 presents highlights of a meeting that Isabella and Bud have with Company-B's advisory council.

Industry Example 7.7:
Bud Meets Advisory Team (Second Day Afternoon)

Isabella starts the meeting by saying, "Bud, I'm pleased to introduce you to teacher Bruce, principal Sarah, superintendent James, executive director Herb, and Carley from Governor Sue's staff. Each week, we meet virtually to discuss our mutual efforts and problem-solve. This is our regular meeting. You're the answer to one of the customer service problems we've been working on. Let's check in. How are we progressing against our goal of getting all schools to 2-Sigma? What does the data indicate?"

Herb replies, "This morning, the Member School Performance Array sent me an email with an e-report attached about the performance of our members overall. Of those who attained 1:X status last year, 93% remain on track to do so this year, and those who attained 1:X in previous years all maintained status year over year. Of the 7% who are still challenged by 1:X, turnover seems to be a common problem. Most of this is solvable through changes we're making in how teachers progress to Master Teacher status. And, of course, the changes Governor Sue made in requirements for professional development funds will help, too. Oops—in my enthusiasm to make my report, I forgot to say 'Welcome, Bud.'"

Carley speaks next, saying, "The governor's analysts reported similar priorities from their use of the State Performance Array. However, the governor is also concerned about interruptions to service. What is up with this?"

James answers, "The governor is quite astute to notice this recent development. She's become quite savvy with the Array. Bottom line, we have a good news/bad news situation. Unlike our 1:1 program in which computers were sparingly used, in our Type-B approach, students and teachers use their computers to do real work. However, the more work they do, and the more dependent they become on the technology for achieving and maintaining 1:X, the more demands for bandwidth get placed on the network that connects all our computers and servers. The demands are outstripping our districts infrastructure and support capabilities. There is also a lot of unnecessary duplication in staff and back-room equipment."

Sarah replies, "The cooperative teaching work Anne and her colleagues are doing is a good example. They have students teaching lessons to other students. In preparation for doing their teaching, students must access, adapt, and create curriculum using research tools from the A to B Toolkit. Some of the preparation for teaching other students they do during class time, but most they do outside it. At first, there were no problems, but now that students are getting into their expanded role, we've had the system go down several times due to usage that is higher than the system can handle."

Bruce adds, "Also, the type of cooperative teaching my students do involves lots of digital content such as videos, podcasts, and PowerPoints. It puts big demands on the computers, network, and tech support. For instance, 3 nights ago, when Jane, a student of mine, was preparing for teaching her lesson her laptop crashed. She had no tech support available, so the next day I had to adapt my lesson to accommodate her tech problems."

Isabella says, "Yikes! Sorry you're having the tech challenges. The incidents showed up on our reports, too. Rest assured that our team is all over this. Your success is our success. Bud, this is where you come in."

Isabella, Bud, and the advisors to Company-B view edge technology as essential to the dispersal of control for learning to students. They understand that the network problems that James and his district face results from students using computers and the A to B Toolkit away from school. Isabella and Bud know this because they use the same tools that that students and teachers use at District-B. Isabella and Bud are also informed by the technical data that the servers in the district's data-center generate about outages. Isabella assigns Bud to solve the problem. Industry Example 7.8 presents highlights from the follow-up meeting that Bud has at District-B.

Industry Example 7.8:
Bud Meets with James at District-B (Third Day Morning)

James begins, "Welcome, Bud. Our ICT Leadership Team has some additional data about the network." Bud replies, "Great! I have an exciting proposal for them."

James continues, "Let's check in. What does the data show?" One technologist reports that 29 incidents occurred last night, all but four traceable to three sources—a faulty server, bandwidth overload, and user error. Another technologist explains, "We need to fix the problems quickly, not break the momentum of the cooperative teaching program, and keep our 1:X attainment high. We also must swap out the faulty server that is under warranty, get on top of the bandwidth issue, and expand the help desk."

Bud answers, "Our data indicate network failures are recurring across the district's network. We are working on new tools to monitor the pressure points that come from increased student use of the A to B Toolkit, especially at home and elsewhere. Also, given our shared responsibilities, we recommend you consider a cloud approach for the district. Then we could manage your backroom and network services offsite and remove the burden from your tech team. James, our question is, in addition to buying laptops, servers, and services from us, would you consider migrating your data center to us, too? We can provide you with better information about network performance, a help-desk, and more reliable performance overall. This will make it better when students access the network from all over the place." James and his team immediately recognize the value of the cloud approach. James says, "This is a board-level decision, but I understand the value of what you're proposing so let's keep talking. Let's put a proposal together for the board to consider."

At District-B, there is no resistance to Bud's offer because James and his colleagues know that Bud has a helicopter view of their data network. Bud can see issues recurring district-wide. The increased demand on the network is caused by dispersing control to students. The amount of dispersed control to students is increasing at all the schools in the district. That means that students more frequently use their version of the A to B Toolkit outside of school to plan lessons and compile resources for use inside school. Since the network failure came from the proximal, high-power teaching approach that disperses control from teachers to students, James knows the problem will not go away. He views Bud's offer of a cloud solution as a way to evolve the district-wide schema. He also knows that an unstable network will dampen such teaching approaches. His responsiveness to the problem is consistent with how teacher Anne problem-solves with her students about their homework and principal Sarah with her colleagues about their professional development. Each focuses on 1:X, their schema, and what is required to progress both 1:X and the schema. In recent months Herb, the executive director of Association-B, has had separate problem solving sessions with James, Anne, and Sarah. He is about to have a session with Bud. Industry Example 7.9 presents an exchange between Bud and Herb

---

Industry Example 7.9: Bud Meets with Herb (Third Day Afternoon)

Bud and Herb sit in front of a computer in the Association-B office. Herb walks Bud through the Member School Performance Array and A to B Toolkit. Then he briefs him about Governor Sue and HB-1. Herb explains, "As you can see, we're in the midst of a statewide bottom-up educational transformation. Research informs the work that teachers do in classrooms, and that work informs the work done at the school, district, and association levels."

Herb continues, "We share a common schema, are part of a common design that embeds the schema, and use the same tools. The proximal relationship between research, similarity of design, and operation makes 1:X possible at scale. It forms a high-power, low-load environment for teaching and learning. The approach certainly changed this association. And from the beginning, Company-B has been part of the transformation. It's been the yin to our yang. When we have time, remind me to tell you how we used to do our annual meeting."

Bud replies, "It is all is very impressive. I never believed anything like this was possible. Now that I see it, everything makes sense."

Herb tells him, "Now for the good part. We need your help to deliver new versions of our Member School Performance Array and A to B Toolkit. These tools are mission critical to all stakeholders and me. Teachers and students cannot function without them. Because the tools reflect a schema and embedded design, future needs can be predicted in a rational way based upon the feedback generated within the system. The Member School Performance Array helps us identify educational needs, drivers, and problems. We also use it to predict future software and infrastructure needs and manage our hardware refresh cycle so that our equipment is always up-to-date and stable. In this way, the system is dynamic yet much more predictable than the capricious Type-A system where ICT use is idiosyncratic and unpredictable because everyone is doing their own thing and autonomously constructing their practice The good news for you is that we can predict the demand and the purchase cycle in return for you doing the development work necessary to meet our 1:X needs and bringing us new versions of our tools at an agreed-upon price point."

The exchange between Herb and Bud exemplifies what happens when the field of education has a forward-looking paradigm that makes realizing the educational promise of ICT an everyday occurrence for every stakeholder. Realizing such educational promise in turn makes the field more capable of informing the ICT industry, and makes the field a unified sales market that benefits Company-B. Industry Example 7.10 presents a highlight from the closing session of the 24th Annual Conference of Association-B.

Industry Example 7.10: Governor Sue Salutes Isabella and Bud

Governor Sue stands on the dais with James, Sarah, Anne, Bruce, and Herb. She says, "Many persons have contributed to the successful implementation of HB-1, The Educational Reconceptualization Act of 2011. Most have previously been recognized for their efforts in putting us on a path to statewide 1:X. Many are on the stage with me tonight. One mostly overlooked but essential role in the entire Type-B system of education that we've created is played by technology. It is essential to the work that each of us does every day. Can you imagine doing what you do without a computer, or software? Company-B is our primary technology provider. That is the case for one reason, and one reason only. The leaders of the company listen to you, listen to students and parents, and they deliver what we need when we need it. They developed the technology that supports our schema, enables our embedded design, and connects us all. There would be no 1:X today if there was no Company-B. Please give a big hand for Isabella and Bud."

As Bud walks across the stage toward Governor Sue, who holds a special recognition award for him, he thinks to himself, "This sure doesn't feel like a sales job, but I sure do like getting my quarterly commission checks."

Earlier in this chapter five questions were used to examine the circumstances that Félix and Bud faced at Company-A. Let us use the same five questions to unpack the circumstances that Isabella and Bud face at Company-B. First, from an opportunity perspective, Bud has products—improved quality, reduced cost, and better feedback through cloud computing—to offer James that are critical to District-B's success. Although the cloud computing solution is a service that could be offered in a Type-A educational model, Bud's service is distinguished by Company-B's deep and shared understanding of the resources, tools, and transactions that will occur in the cloud if District-B purchases it from Bud. Moreover, Company-B's knowledge of Type-B education makes it possible to offer Type-B services and products to District-B via intelligent Type-B cloud computing. Second, for Company-B, opportunity against cost of business does not include the risk of losing money or reducing workforce. Isabella designed Company-B so this would never be the case. Her company co-evolves with its customers. Third, District-B's areas of greatest pain—strain on the network from dispersal of control to students for the purpose of achieving 1:X district-wide—are areas that Isabella and Bud can readily address with the products and expertise they have. This is the case when Bud steps up with the offer of intelligent cloud computing. Fourth, Isabella knows she had mission critical employees who are skilled and knowledgeable about the Type-B approach and 1:X. This is evident in the way the sales team explains to Bud how things are done at Company-B. Their knowledge helps Bud quickly get up to speed at Company-B. It's is also eveident in how Bud's talents and the business opportunity at District-B are nicely matched by Company-B. Fifth, Company-B is designed so Isabella keeps an eye on the horizon and an ear to the ground. The trends, developments, regulations, and tendencies that might potentially affect Isabella's business (and paycheck) guide the actions that she and her employees take and the products they offer to the company's customers. The trends and so on are visible via the Corporate Performance Array and A to B Toolkit that Company-B's employees use to do their work. Through these tools Isabella, the company's customers, and all other stakeholders have the same view of what is happening at every level of the educational system. This is how Isabella knows that an interruption of service affected James's schools and that her company has a plan for resolving the interruptions before Bud attends the meeting that is being convened to discuss the matter. Bud's timely offer of a cloud computing solution is another example of how Company-B's use of the Corporate Performance Array and A to B Toolkit benefits its customers and itself.

Company-B's operation stands in contrast to the way Company-A functions. It acts proximally in high-power, low-load ways. Company-A does not. Why is this the case?

SHIFTS IN THOUGHT NEEDED TO IMPROVE THE INDUSTRY

Why is Bud able to exceed his sales quota at Company-B, but not at Company-A? Bud's success is enabled by three shifts that Isabella made when she created Company-B. One involved shifting from product to process by focusing on what customers want to do rather than the products they want to buy. This shift makes it possible for Bud to propose an intelligent cloud solution to the district's systemic network problem. A second shift involves Company-B playing an expansive rather than a bounded role with its customers. This means that at District-B Bud is a team member and problem-solver, not a salesperson and that Company-B is a stakeholder, not a vendor. A third shift involves Company-B moving from risk avoidance to risk sharing. Doing so creates the conditions which inform the company and vice versa.

Shift one: Focusing on the process not the product. The design and operation of modern education reflects a deep commitment to the transfer of knowledge from teacher to student (Dewey, 1938). This commitment has long defined education in unidirectional (Michelau & Shreve, 2002) and product-centric ways (Christensen, Horn, & Johnson, 2008). For instance, the product of teaching (i.e., student knowledge) is transferred hierarchically, linearly, and downward to students by their teachers. In this way the "structure of knowledge" (Bruner, 1960) is "fitted to students" (Glatthorn, 1990) through the application of curriculum standards (Spalding, Garcia, & Braun, 2010) and essential learnings (Hirsch, 1987) with scant attention given to the instructional processes through which knowledge is transferred from teacher to student.

Similarly, companies doing business in education seek to transfer their products and services downwardly to customers (Acuff & Wood, 2007). Specific inputs (e.g., sales calls) are correlated to desired outcomes (e.g., sales revenue). Such inputs receive undue attention, yet little attention is given to the core work of customers (Eades & Kear, 2006). This is the case with Company-A whose business approach ignores teaching and learning. Not surprisingly, the company fails financially. The predictable sales model that Félix desperately seeks through the Type-A paradigm is unrealistic.

In contrast, Isabella focuses Company-B on educational processes: how learning happens (e.g., dispersal of control), the practices that the research indicates enable learning to occur more readily (e.g., self-reporting, feedback), and how resources can best be applied to ensure that learning occurs for all students, not just a fortunate few. She and the employees at Company-B view customers via the schema and embedded design they share with customers such as District-B and Association-B. The company's informational interplay with customers defines the *way* and *what* it sells. James, superintendent of District-B has purchased products and services from Company-A and Company-B. He knows Félix and Isabella. Industry Example 7.11 presents James's thoughts doing business with each.

Industry Example 7.11: James Reflects

"Recently, when I was straightening up my office, I found Félix's business card. It has been nearly 3 years since he and I last talked. I like Félix. He gave the district a competitive price. Unfortunately for Félix, in the Type-B approach we now use, there is not much reason for Félix and me to talk.

"When we need something on time, Company-B knows what we need at the same time we do . . . sometimes even before we do. Last week, after Bud and I met with the district's ICT Leadership Team, he shared a report he'd generated from the Corporate Performance Array. The report supported the intelligent cloud approach he'd proposed in the meeting. The argument he made for that solution was compelling—better service, better price, and the opportunity to proximally deploy ICT staff in service to teaching and learning. Bud explained how new compression software could address some of the issues with high bandwidth resources. He also suggested a better way to manage the resources in the tools that would be more bandwidth efficient. Bud's acumen with the tools and process impressed me and built my confidence that the cloud solution really would be intelligent. It also showed why Félix and I seldom talk."

The example shows that Bud and Company-B are quite capable of supporting and responding to the processes (e.g., dispersed control) of District-B by delivering the right product (e.g., cloud computing) to the right stakeholder at the right time. Company-B leverages information it gets via edge technology to improve its services, sales, and productivity. By focusing on process, Company-B creates and seizes unique and profitable opportunities (e.g., HB-1, dispersed control at District-B, and software development at Association-B) for itself. The flexibility and collaboration that characterize its customer relationships distinguishes it within the education market. Similarly, by sharing a schema, design, and tools with Company-B, customers such as District-B, Association-B, and Governor Sue's state can inform the products that they will receive in the future. In comparison, Company-A is prone to critical gaps in product capabilities as evidenced by the company's inability to meet the teaching and learning needs of its customers and subsequent financial decline. At Company-B, edge technology enables information to flow from customer to company and vice versa in a manner that is impossible at Company-A.

Shift two: Customers and companies moving beyond bounded roles. Company-B's product-to-process orientation leads it to play a different, more unbounded role with its customers than its Type-A competitors play. In the Type-A approach, the border between customer and vendor is clearly demarcated. The border forms a bounded space within which customers and vendors interact. The resulting exchanges—meetings, briefings, proposal submissions, oral arguments, best and final offers—play out in a fair, proper, and ethical, yet kabuki-like manner in that bound space (Kubasek, Brennan, & Browne, 2009). Although bounding provides proprietary and ethical protections, it also precludes co-evolution, schema and design sharing, reconciliation of problem and products, and strange attraction. Without such conditions being present, the creation of high-power proximal solutions is prevented because collaboration is limited between stakeholders who might otherwise bring value-added aspects to the respective efforts of the other (Slywotsky, Morrison, & Andelman, 1997).

When Isabella designs Company-B, she seeks to reconcile the benefits of bounded customer relationships and the revenue potential of playing an expanded role. Bud has worked at Company-A whose role with its customers was bounded. He now works at Company-B that has an expanded role with its customers. Industry Example 7.12 presents Bud's thoughts on both companies.

Industry Example 7.12: Bud Reflects

"I could not see how Company-A would remain profitable. So I quit. I didn't believe what Félix wanted to do with the Transformation Schools would make any difference for the company or for that matter the schools. He hadn't genuinely vetted his idea—no research, no data, no nothing. He certainly didn't care what I or anyone else thought.

"A customer with whom I had a good relationship told me Company-B was looking for a a vice president of sales. She put me in touch with Isabella. When I got the job, I was surprised at my good fortune. It was so easy for me to get started here. Sharing a schema, design, and tools with the sales team and our customers makes a huge difference.

"What we provide at Company-B and what customers need are the same, as are our cost of business and opportunities. Most days, it doesn't feel like I'm selling. Customers such as Bruce, Sarah, and Herb help me make my sales quota and I help them achieve 1:X. Our work is important. Everything we do informs everything we do next.

"I know our work makes a difference. I see the impact every day when I check into the Corporate Performance Array and when I look at the number of 1:X schools in the state. All this makes me feel valued and appreciated by the company and its customers. At times, I even feel mission critical to them. During the 10 years I worked for Company-A, I never once felt that way. I don't miss being told "sell something or else" and "go find somebody with money to buy something."

Bud's reflection demonstrates how the unseen aspects (e.g., schema, design, and tools) of Company-B blur the borders between it and its customers. In the common space that the blurring creates, Bud, Company-B, and their customers co-evolve. As Company-B co-evolves with its customers, the understanding of each about what it means to take business risks changes.

Shift three: Stakeholders sharing rather than avoiding risk. A climate of accountability pervades Type-A classrooms, schools, and districts (Fuhrman & Elmore, 2004; Ravitch, 2010). Stakeholders there are under immense pressure to produce specific and measurable outcomes such as improved test scores and graduation rates (Dunham & Varma, 1998). Stakeholders who work in such settings are acutely aware of the risks—budgetary, legal, and public opinion—associated with not producing expected outcomes and the external (e.g., economic, demographic) and internal (e.g., courses assigned to teach) factors that contribute to their inability to do so (Fullan, 2007; Sarason, 1990, 1998). How stakeholders respond to such risks is a much different story.

In Type-A education, the choice for stakeholders is simple. Either they address a source of risk or avoid it. Because most lack the capacity to address it, they opt for avoidance. They do so by containing risk through special programs and projects, accepting risk as a normal aspect of their work, or transferring responsibility for risk to another person or program (Hampton, 2009). By avoiding risk, stakeholders instantiate low-power, high-load distal solutions at all levels of the system because the risk factors that make stakeholders unable to produce positive teaching and learning outcomes never get addressed. Such risk avoidance characterizes the 3-decades-long, more-of-the-same policy-driven efforts to reform schools in the United States (Hess, 2010; Ravitch, 2010; Tyack & Cuban, 1995). Risk avoidance is not unique to the field of education. It is common in business too. In Industry Example 7.13 Isabella describes her impetus for forming Company-B.

Industry Example 7.13: Isabella Reflects

Seven years ago, my daughter took a physics class taught by Bruce. She's not a particularly strong physics student but did quite well in his class. She frequently worked late to prep for teaching a class to her peers. I was curious how this could be, so I arranged to meet with Bruce.

In our meeting, Bruce pulled up the A to B Toolkit on his laptop computer. He showed me the curriculum and cooperative learning tools my daughter used for her assignments. Then he showed me a video of my daughter teaching—teaching a physics lesson, no less. He explained that this was a normal occurrence in his class. I was quite impressed with what Bruce showed me—toolkits, arrays, collaboration tools—and his informative explanation of what was going on in the school and district. I was particularly impressed with their schema, embedded design, and risk sharing.

When I asked Bruce who the industry partners were for the effort, he said, "There aren't any." At that moment, a light went on in my head. I'd been working in the ICT industry for 20 years and had been looking to start my own business. I believed this could be what I'd been looking for.

Bruce recommended that I meet with Governor Sue and Herb. When I did, both told me that they chose to build capacity within and across the various levels of the educational system for addressing risk rather than avoiding it. The information and examples about HB-1 and Association-B that they shared helped me create a company that would share risk with them.

When stakeholders avoid risks, they must make tradeoffs (Peterson, 2009), ignore potential gains (Mandel, 1996), and often take actions that end up being riskier than the actions they seek to avoid (Wakker, 2010). Ignoring potential gains would have occurred if principal Sarah had chosen to stay with the professional development plan that she had in place at her school rather than risk adapting it to better meet the needs of her teachers for learning about mastery teaching. Missing potential gains would have occurred if Herb had opted to ignore the needs of the association's members and made the association more dependent on corporate funding or if Governor Sue had proposed yet another more-more-more policy like HB-471. Although risk avoidance might have been an expeditious approach for Sarah, Herb, and Governor Sue, risk avoidance would have meant that each (and their respective colleagues) missed the benefits (e.g., relevant professional development, member-centric association, and HB-1, a policy that ended the state's education crisis) that risk acceptance ultimately affords them. Sarah, Herb, and Governor Sue can take calculated risks because they share schema, design, and tools disperses responsibility and consequences across stakeholders and proximally include stakeholders in the decisions about how to best address the risk. This means Sarah, Herb, and Governor Sue can confidently open the Pandora's box of education reform issues. They can acknowledge the elephant in the room by calling out that all students are not being well educated and never will be until fundamental changes are made in the overall educational system and the 1:X challenge is met and 2-Sigma attained. Informed risk sharing is a fundamental aspect of Type-B education that helps stakeholders move forward.

HOW SHIFTING THOUGHTS CHANGE COMPANIES IN PRACTICE

By shifting to process, expanding its role, and sharing risk, Company-B builds the sales and service capacities it needs for realizing its business growth targets and helping its customers attain 1:X. With the three shifts in place Isabella's company takes up its customers' schema, design, and tools, and by doing so become an extension of them and them of it. Their systems and processes are self-similar. So are the problems they seek to solve.

Isabella and Bud's successes with District-B, Association-B, and Governor Sue's state are consistent with the research about businesses that shows customers often get more value from purchasing an experience than a product (Slywotzky, Morrison, & Andelman, 1997). In highly commoditized markets such as technology sales, the experiences companies create for customers matter more than the actual product (Pine & Gilmore, 1998). Because Isabella understands this point, she makes the purchasing and using of Company-B's products an experience. Her company's focus on the experience of the customer blurs the lines between process and product, making both a total package. She places the customer at the "center" (Kotler, 2009) of her business's design. So, rather than manage discrete and disparate products, Company-B manages itself to "what customers actually want" (Pine & Gilmore, 2000). Not surprisingly, Company-B grows, while Company-A does not.

THE TOOLS COMPANIES NEED TO HELP REFORM EDUCATION

Isabella forms Company-B because she recognizes the potential of the self-organizing education system scaling to the level of businesses. She sees that potential as an unprecedented opportunity to provide software and services that benefit education and help her make money. The corporate design she puts in place employs the same principles of self-organization (e.g., shared schema, common tools, frequent feedback) that are evident at all levels the Type-B system (e.g., District-B, Association-B, and HB-1). The design enables her company to co-evolve with the whole educational system and to produce software and services that are commercially viable at scale.

The difference between Isabella's company and others in the education marketplace is that hers produces and delivers proximal, high-power solutions. Although some of her competitors have achieved similar scale in terms of overall sales, none do so with services and software that is so proximal to the learning and teaching needs of teachers and students. In fact, her company's strategy is based on the educational system as a whole and its various levels co-developing with businesses. Edge technology makes such co-development and co-evolution possible through the sharing of critical information. The reportage that edge technology helps generate is used by customers and businesses to plan for future products.

Figure 7.1 depicts the Corporate Performance Array that enables Isabella and her staff to view key performance dimensions of its customers. The field at the top left contains key data from the recent annual conference of Association-B. It includes information about overall attendance and attendance at specific sessions. The field at the bottom left contains policy initiatives recently enacted or pending

Figure 7.1. Corporate Performance Array

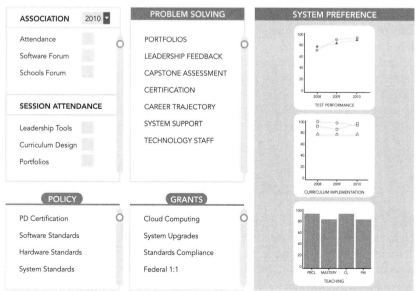

at the state level. The fields in the center contain information about the current needs of schools and grant funding opportunities for them. The fields on the right show the performance of Isabella's customers. Her view is similar to that of all other stakeholders in the system.

Company-B offers to manage the ICT infrastructure of District-B via an intelligent cloud computing strategy that Isabella builds into the company's design. The design gives the company capacity to manage school-level edge technology, personnel systems, and data-centers. The cloud improves efficiency and lower ICT costs overall for District-B. By delivering such results for District-B, the design that Isabella has in place in Company-B serves as a model that can be replicated at districts across the state's education system. The data that District-B and the system generate will enable Company-B to bring cloud-based products to customers that will respond to stakeholders' needs in timely ways.

A HB-1 expanding amendment that is forthcoming from Governor Sue and Chairperson Charles—system-wide standards for school and district software—will create further demand for Company-B's cloud-based products. The amendment will broaden existing standards to make cloud-based products compliant with the standards. The amendment will also provide funding to districts to move their software to the cloud. Isabella will use the expansion of HB-1 to expand the offerings of Company-B, making the company even more responsive to the needs of its customers. The confluence of circumstances, attendance and feedback at the forum, impending changes to HB-1, and new funding for districts to move to the cloud, all described on the Corporate Array, are indications that Isabella's intelligent cloud computing strategy is appropriate and timely.

Company-B is thriving because Isabella has it tapped into the multidirectional information supply chain that begins with the teaching and learning transactions occurring in thousands of classrooms scale up through HB-1 to Company-B. Her company uses the edge technology that manages the feedback that the entire educational system produces to co-evolve with the system and its many levels. The company translates that information into products. Isabella's research efforts, product development, and implementation strategy are shared with system wide stakeholders early and often. The feedback from stakeholders ensures that future products will contain no surprises and meet the evolving needs of the system.

HOW A SHARED SCHEMA CAN
UNITE INDUSTRY AND EDUCATION

When Isabella forms Company-B, she uses the same three-step framework that Herb uses at the association level and governor Sue uses at the policy level to create Association-B and HB-1 respectively. The framework aids her efforts to establish a business that benefits from the role edge technology plays at those and other levels of the educational system.

New Assumptions

Type-A and Type-B companies hold opposing views on most matters of business design and operation. The differing views come from the assumptions about process, customers, and risk that underlay the Type-A and Type-B approaches. The assumptions assert fundamental effects on what companies do, how they do it, who they do it with, and the impact the companies have on the field of education.

Assumption one: The goals of a Type-B approach place additional and complex demands on company employees and customers, and can only be achieved through edge technology. The importance of this assumption is apparent in how Bud performs at Company-A and Company-B. At Company-A, he does not make his sales goal despite that company providing high performers to serve as his sales-coaches, new processes for improving his sales forecasting, prioritization of his work, elimination of sales cycle choke points, and a better pipeline view for him. When such efforts do not help Bud and other sales makers meet their sales quotas and makes CompanyA profitable, Félix funds 10 Transformation School reference sites (and increased the sales quota by 7%). Believing the steps Félix takes places demands on him that he could not meet, Bud (and other employees) quit Company-A. In his first year at Company-B, Bud exceeds his sales goals, receives acclaim from customers, and gets an award from Governor Sue. The edge technology that Isabella builds into the design and operation of Company-B creates the conditions that enables Bud to have such success.

Assumption two: Research on successful business and educational practices define the role for edge technology in Type-B companies. Because their design, operation, and tools seek to optimize the experience of customers, Type-B companies assume some responsibility for customer success by making the experience, not the product, what the customer purchases. The capacity of Type-B companies to offer an experience to their customers comes from the field of education using its research to guide the the companies. The alignment of Company-B with that research and its customers is what Governor Sue calls out at Association-B's annual conference. It is why James and his ICT Leadership Team can present a novel idea to Bud about using students to provide tech-support for other students. Isabella creates Company-B to provide such experiences. Edge technology enables those experiences to happen proximally to stakeholders, in ways that do not increase their cognitive load yet make the work they do have powerful effects. In contrast, the design, operation, and technology of Type-A companies distally connects profitability, products, and customer success. The way Type-A companies' use ICT is low-power: a static support for methodologies and processes that segment, measure, and target customers in ways that move products and generate revenue but do not solve the core problems that their customers face. This is the case with Company-A, where profitability is measured by products, opportunity depends on having a product that customers will buy, and customers want products that Company-A does not offer.

Assumption three: Conducting business through edge technology and business about edge technology are indistinguishable at Type-B companies. For instance, at Company-B, the pursuit and realization of revenue opportunities is synonymous with District-B's, Association-B, and HB-1's pursuit and realization of 1:X. The work Isabella and Bud do is interchangeable with much of the work Governor Sue, Herb, James, and other stakeholders do elsewhere. Each, however, operates at a different level of the overal educational network. Each depends on edge technology serving different yet similar needs. However, edge technology use is not optional for any of them. It is a necesssity. It is the glue that connects them, helps inform their overall network, and drives their pursuit of common and individual goals. Bud conducts his business of selling in much the same way that Bruce teaches, Governor Sue makes policy, and Herb organizes conferencs. The normal work each does contributes to the systemic meeting of the 1:X challenge and the attainment of 2-Sigma.

Assumption four: For Type-B businesses access to edge technology is a simple, yet fundamental, requirement for working with the customers. Such access makes it possible for Isabella and Bud to genuinely serve District-B and Association-B. Their capacity to do so comes from every stakeholder in the educational system—including Governor Sue, Herb, James, Sarah, and Bruce— having access to edge technology. Access to edge technology is not a fundamental requirement for Type-A companies to work with their customers.

Assumption five: Type-B businesses use edge technology to support the overall improvement of education, the increased achievement of all students, and the meeting of the 1:X challenge at scale. Type B companies use edge technology to mediate well-researched professional practice in ways that inform their product development and delivery. Isabella founds Company-B on the assumption that edge technology will help the company serve the entire educational system. That assumption is what binds Company-B and its customers together. It was why Bud succeeded at Company-B and not at Company-A.

New Design

Over the past 3 decades, the revenues generated from companies selling ICT into the field of education increased year over year (O'Brien, 2008). However, education's purchase of ICT failed—despite much good intention—to transfer significant effects to teacher and student performance (Abrami et al., 2006; Weston & Bain, 2009). This should be a stunning state of affairs for the fields of education and ICT. Conditions in education seemed conducive for education to innovate, reform, and improve itself. Educational aspirations were high, goals for improvement of performance unambiguous, funds plentiful, and ICT abundant (Cuban, 2003; Ravitch, 2010). In retrospect, the conditions were, however, lacking in two ways. First, the field of education did not use its knowledge about improving learning and teaching to systematically guide and inform the use of ICT in classrooms, schools, and districts (Kolderie & MacDonald, 2009). Second, in the absence of its systematic guiding and informing of the use of ICT in educational settings, the field of education was unable to "inform the industry" (Jovane, Westkamper, & Williams, 2009) about the ICT tools that the field's educational stakeholders required to achieve 1:X. Hence, the products the industry offered up were distal to the challenges that educational stakeholders faced. The impact of these two circumstances was visible to those who cared to see it. Isabella was one person who did. What she saw led her to step up by creating Company-B. She used the three-step process—solution mapping, component building, and design integration—that had been applied to other levels of the network to design Company-B in a way that made it capable of interacting its customers and by doing so contributing to the customer's capacity for educating all children well through the Type-B approach.

When leaders form companies, they often consider various organizational principles such as allocation of capital, governance of processes, and assignment of responsibility (Cameron & Green, 2009). Isabella experienced such principles when working for previous employers. She found most of the principles hollow and unproductive. The principles lacked the power to do what she now wanted to do: make a profit and contribute to large-scale educational improvement. Isabella took the unprecedented step of engaging customers and employees in a *solution mapping* process. Over a 2-month period, they formally and diligently (a) examined the educational challenges stakeholders faced, (b) developed deep knowledge of those challenges, (c) considered business solutions such as intelligent cloud computing that might aid the efforts of stakeholders at various levels of the educational system, (d) identified impediments such as funding and laws to the implementation of such solutions, and (e) identified specific ways for negating those impediments. Herb, James, and Carley from Governor Sue's staff participated in the solution mapping effort. Afterward, they reported that the effort helped them clarify the work they were already doing with Association-B, District-B, and HB-1. It also led them to conclude, much as Isabella had, that Company-B could play an instrumental role in resolving the state's educational crisis.

When Isabella and team moved on to the *component building* phase, they decided that Company-B would focus on process rather than content, play an unbounded role with customers, and share rather than avoid risk with customers.

They used that new found focus to define outcomes, clarify roles, articulate commitments, and assign support. They found component building to be much easier than the solution mapping that had preceded it.

Next, they *integrated* the components that they had identified into the design (e.g., mission statement, organizational structure, job descriptions, and tools) of Company-B. To no one's surprise, this proved to be an easy task. They simply adapted the schema, embedded design, and edge technology that every stakeholder in the state used. Herb, James, and Carley helped Isabella determine which levels of the state's educational system (e.g., school, district) would inform what portion of the work that Company-B would do, the frequency at which such informing would occur, and so on.

New Trajectory

Using edge technology, Isabella executes the plan of action for Company-B and achieves the revenue and educational goals she sets for the company (and herself). Doing so requires the company to follow the trajectory that classrooms, schools, districts, and associations have followed to meet the 1:X challenge and attain 2-Sigma. Isabella uses the drivers (e.g., profitability and educational impact) that led her to create Company-B as the measures to gauge its progess and success. Few companies ever connect directly with customers to the extent that Company B does. By doing so, Company-B distinguishes itself and realizes an unprecedented and profitable opportunity for making a big difference in the lives of countless students and teachers.

SUMMARY

- The field of education is not benefiting from ICT companies playing proximal, low-load, high-power roles in large scale efforts to innovate, reform, and change education.
- The field of education's lack of consensus about research-informed practice makes it difficult for the ICT industry to build responsive and scalable business models to benefit education.
- The Type-B approach makes it possible for the field of education and ICT companies to reconcile this problem and co-evolve in meeting the 1:X challenge and attaining 2-Sigma at system-wide scale.

CHAPTER 8

Stakeholders Connected

To the timid and hesitating
everything is impossible because it seems so.
—Walter Scott

In this chapter, we reflect upon the key themes of the book, summarize why education has failed technology, and review what to do about it in a big-picture sense. We recap and connect the shifts described in each chapter and show the connections across the levels of a self-organizing education system. Those levels are reconciled as a unified educational paradigm. We employ the schema—assumptions, design, and trajectory—to frame a call for paradigm-shifting educational change in which stakeholders, through the work they do in classrooms, schools, and districts, migrate toward self-organization using the ever-critical *edge* technology we have described.

THE PROBLEM STAKEHOLDERS FACE
AT ALL LEVELS OF THE EDUCATION CRISIS

After 3 decades of failed efforts to improve education, many stakeholders have concluded that educational innovation, reform, and change may not be possible (Berends, Bodilly, & Natarj-Kirby, 2002; Papert, 1997). The evidence supporting the intractable nature of educational reform is multigenerational and compelling (Bain, 2007; McLaughlin & Talbert, 2001; Sarason, 1996; Tyack & Cuban, 1995). The omissions and design flaws of past efforts, and their inability to exert sustainable and scalable effects on student learning, make it easy to armchair quarterback the problem of educational change. One way to address this set of circumstances is to invite a renewed round of efforts to get educational change right by finding better ways to re-engineer, reform, and reinvent schools. We believe that doing more of the same, but in better ways by refining existing methods and models, is unlikely to deliver improved student learning at scale because even the approaches employed in most contemporary change efforts (e.g., charter schools) are too similar to the approaches they seek to change.

One of the best examples of the more-of-the-same problem in education is the way technology is invoked by advocates as an alternative to conventional schooling. Virtual schools and online learning systems, as we described in Chapter 2, are often lauded by technology advocates as sources of profound disruption in the existing educational system and as solutions to 1:X. According to Christensen, Horn, and Johnson (2008), such virtual schools and systems disintermediate and radically alter the modus operandi of schooling. However, the supposedly disruptive approaches they champion build on conventional educational design metaphors and require conventional attitudes, dispositions, and skills of teachers and students. Christensen et al., vest the use of ICT to change the 1:X ratio to 1:1 by varying where, not what and how, learning happens. Students access learning materials on a 1:1 basis, but they do so without a corresponding profound change in the nature of the learning experience. Online and virtual approaches are similar to efforts to provide every student with access to a laptop computer, like those described in Chapter 1, where a distal change in the access ratio was conflated with a proximal effect on learning.

Not surprisingly, the new online and virtual learning approaches produce the same results as the old educational approaches (Smith, Clark, & Blomeyer, 2005). The online and virtual efforts, by not taking up the 1:X challenge in powerful, proximal, and load-reducing ways, are neither disruptive nor paradigm-shifting. They disproportionately invest in access to technology as the primary driver for improved learning.

In contrast, Bruce, Phil, and Eladio, the teachers whose work was described in Chapter 2, each employed genuinely disruptive edge technologies to alter their teaching and differentiate the learning experiences of their students. To date, such deep engagement with differentiated practice has eluded the champions of the virtual and online learning approaches. As history shows, for a paradigm to shift (Kuhn, 1996) to occur, a significantly different and substantially better course of action must be offered. A shift is not an act of re-engineering the prevailing paradigm. By way of illustration, the CD did not emerge from re-engineering the cassette and the car did not emerge from re-engineering the horse. Likewise, the tools of the Type-B educational system described herein will not emerge from attempts to fix the current Type-A system or from automating the Type-A system with technology. Attempting to fix and/or automate the practices of Type-A education creates simplified realities that produce the same underwhelming effects on learning and teaching of the access to ICT agenda that currently pervade classrooms and schools. A new paradigm must resolve the irresolvable or anomalous problems of the old (Kuhn, 1996). Putting forth an educational paradigm that is capable of resolving 1:X and attaining 2-Sigma necessitates shifting the underlying thought, theory, and action of the field of education. This requires recognizing that the paradigmatic challenge facing the field is resolving the 1:X challenge by employing ICT, proving that the resulting paradigm is unequivocally more effective that the Type-A one it supplants, and taking the new paradigm to scale through stakeholder migration.

Rather than pursuing standard uses of ICT—access to the Internet and personal computers, student-to-computer ratios, and creating digitized content—the field of education must engage deeply with the challenge of 1:X and in so doing establish a more genuine role for ICT in a more complex and responsive educational paradigm. This requires the field of education to use its research and practice to inform what it does at scale.

The failure of the field of education to use its research to inform practice was illustrated in the Type-A approach at the classroom, school, and district levels and in the association, policy, and industry arenas. This included Bruce's inability to resolve students' learning needs in his Type-A physics class. The problems in Bruce's classroom scaled up and were reflected in the science department's inability to resolve the TIPS-R problem, which in turn scaled up to became a district-level problem. The same district stumbled into a 1:1 laptop initiative in which a computer company defined the district's curricular vision. Subsequently, Herb's rootless, self-serving Type-A association—lacking a genuine professional practice mandate—was shown bumbling from one annual meeting to another. These circumstances came to a head when Governor Sue ran into the nothing-new, clichéd Type-A policy agenda when she engaged with some of the educational thought leaders in the state during her re-election campaign. Félix, who was focused on a 90-day business cycle, was buffeted by the vagaries of economic downturns, incentives, and customer whims, tried unsuccessfully to establish a compelling need among customers for his company's products.

In each case, the field of education's failure to articulate and implement a body of research-informed professional practice at scale confounded the best efforts of Type-A stakeholders to teach, manage, lead, serve, govern, and sell at their respective levels of the educational system. The field's inability to build and implement a complete scalable model (or even models) of professional practice disadvantaged all stakeholders, contributing to one of the greatest tragedies of our generation—the failure to capture the transformational benefits of technology to resolve the 1:X challenge and realize 2-Sigma for all students.

SHIFTS IN THOUGHT NEEDED TO MAKE
REAL CHANGE IN EDUCATION

The shifts described in each chapter explained how stakeholders at various levels of the educational system support a move from Type-A to Type-B education by using practices informed by the field of education's research. Collectively those shifts comprise a new theory structure for the design of education. For instance, Bruce's shift from a simple Type-A schema that created overwhelming cognitive load and irresolvable problems for him and his students, to a more complex, research informed, and edge technology–driven Type-B schema helped him attain

1:X. Similarly, shifts that Principal Sarah made helped her become more capable of addressing the needs of the students and teachers at her school. She and Superintendent James made the shifts that enabled them and their colleagues to solve District-B's TIPS-R problem. Herb shifted to an association that genuinely reflected the needs of its members. Governor Sue shifted to transformative polices, and Isabella to interdependence and co-evolution among her company's education customers. Individually and collectively, each person made less of more by broadly applying a shared schema. The shifts that affected Bruce's classroom practice affected stakeholders at other levels in the system.

The educational transformation that resulted from the shifts that each of the stakeholders made at their respective levels were not autogenetic or spontaneous. Rather, their shifts emerged from a schema that was shared from classroom to corporation and schoolhouse to statehouse. The shared schema, based upon the theory and principles of self-organization, produced a network of levels within a system that worked interactively to resolve 1: X. Principal Sarah described the way her school was transformed with a new curriculum model and redefined by new roles for teachers and students. She employed a powerful feedback approach, and edge technology, including the A to B Toolkit, Array, and Co-development Tools to create the transformation. The processes and tools were reiterated in James's district, Herb's association, and Isabella's company. Each had their own A to B Toolkit, Array, and Co-Development Tools. The schema and edge technology tools used in classrooms and schools scaled up to all levels of the system (Waldrop, 1992). The tools expressed the theory and principles in action. Superintendent James scaled up the new high power PBCL (Problem-Based Collaborative Learning) teaching approach. Herb's association constructed itself using the same design principles to better represent is members, support and recognize their attainment of 2-Sigma, and attract new schools to the system. Edge technology afforded Herb's association deep, interdependent access to members, their needs, current performance, and problem-solving. Similarly, Principal Sarah looked into Association-B's actions, plans, and processes to inform the work of her school. Governor Sue and other policymakers used tools like those employed by Superintendent James to view the needs of teachers, parents, and students and to produce a powerful, proximal, and load-reducing policy (HB-1) that benefited stakeholders statewide. Common principles in the design of each made it possible for key features to reiterate throughout them and the tools they used.

The Arrays captured the feedback about teaching and learning that became the lifeblood of the overall system. That feedback made it possible for the system to talk to itself (Pascale, Millemann, & Gioja, 2000). From classroom to boardroom, stakeholders used feedback to determine what to do next. Feedback made it possible for Jane to modify her curriculum, for Sarah to develop the mastery-teaching component of the school's professional development program, for James's engagement of parents, for Chairperson Charles's refinement of HB-1, and for Isabella to help fix the district's overload problem. Even though all played different roles and were engaged in original and creative ways within the overall system, their work was nonetheless similar because of the schema, design, and the tools that made sharing feedback possible.

Shared feedback also made it possible for one level of the system to leverage the high-power proximal solutions of other levels. Teachers at District-B piloted the high-power Problem-Based Collaborative Learning (PBCL) to solve their TIPS-R problem, Herb saw the solution and magnified its effect by getting the association to support widespread adoption of PBCL. In turn, PBCL became a design agenda for Isabella's company and a software development initiative that made PBCL more accessible for many teachers. PBCL did not emerge downward in a hierarchical system. Rather, it emerged bottom-up because the system was self-organizing and its design enabled the dispersal of control for innovation across many levels. The self-similar shared schema and tools of the classrooms, schools, districts, associations, and companies empowered the work of all stakeholders in them.

Even though stakeholders were separated in time, space, and level, their combined capacity and action to self-organize brought them together. Their edge technology made such self-organization possible, transferred theory to action, built their capacities, shortened the cognitive distance between them, and produced high-power, low-load proximal solutions for their common problems. The examples of problem-solving—TIPS-R, PBCL, parent involvement, conference planning, policy and product development—showed the dynamic self-organizing nature of the system and the processes required for resolving the 1:X challenge. The system and its schema, design, and capacity for feedback were never static. The problem-solving driven by that feedback made the system subject to constant dynamic change, enabling it to emerge over time in a new more adaptive form.

Strange attraction (Merry, 1995), the force that drives a system away from equilibrium, facilitated this process of dynamic change. Student Jane questioned the design of her curriculum; Principal Sarah questioned her school's professional development model, Superintendent James questioned the role of parents in his district, and Herb questioned the design of the association's national conference. Each of them questioned the educational status quo, identified needs, and then acted to push their organizations away from an equilibrium position.

We described the phenomenon of strange attraction (Merry, 1995) as one way to illustrate the process of dynamic change. Jane questioned the design of her curriculum; Sarah questioned her school's professional development model, James questioned the role of parents in his district, and Herb questioned the design of the association's national conference. Each of them questioned the educational status quo, identified needs, and pushed stakeholders away from an equilibrium position. In a self-organizing system, change emerges bottom-up and control is dispersed, and leaders—with their helicopter perspective—prompt change. When they do, they do more than respond to bottom-up emergent needs.

HOW SHIFTING THOUGHTS CAN IMPROVE
EDUCATION IN PRACTICE

The profound shifts in thought, theory, and action described throughout the book, contributed to a multilevel technology-driven self-organizing educational system. That system emerged at a small scale; co-existing within the systemic context of Type-A schools, districts, states, associations, and companies. James the superintendent negotiated a path through the state's distal, re-regulation of teacher professional development to get funds for District-B's research-driven professional development institutes. He managed to co-opt the old Type-A regulations and resources for Type-B purposes. While his actions exemplified co-existence—whereby stakeholders at all levels of the Type-B system could access, evaluate, and co-opt existing Type-A policies, funding, and infrastructure to attain 1:X—his leadership prevented District-B from reverting to the Type-A approach. We envisage co-existence as a key phase early-on in the stakeholder migration from the Type-A to a Type-B educational paradigm and the need for some of the initial migrants to deftly navigate (as James did) the territory in between.

Simultaneous change in thought, theory, and action at scale in the face of a small, emerging, self-organizing educational system is an unrealistic expectation. For instance, it is unrealistic to expect new state policies to be enacted in response to the existence of a few Type-B schools and districts. Similarly, it is unrealistic to expect associations and companies to offer scalable services or products until Type-B schools and districts reach a point of criticality that makes such services and products profitable. Without ample demand, no service or product will be supplied.

The start-up phase is the emergent challenge of the self-organizing system. It is the reason why co-existence is so important early in the process of changing paradigms. However, co-existence is only a solution if the system that emerges is growing and thriving because it can resolve 1:X, meets the high standards of a new paradigm, and drives the demand for different services and products. A self-organizing system has to co-evolve whereby the viability of one self-organizing school increases the likelihood of another, and an aggregation of schools drives the need for associations, policies, products, and so on. Kauffman (1995) describes the co-evolution phenomenon this way, "With the horse went the buggy, the buggy whip, the smithy, the saddlery, the harness maker. With the car came the oil and gasoline industry, motels, paved roads, traffic courts, suburbs, shopping malls, and fast food restaurants" (p. 240). He makes clear that the ebb and flow of educational innovation must reflect the degrees of fitness possessed by stakeholders as they struggle for survival and success.

For co-evolution to occur successful self-organizing schools must drive the need for association representation, policies, and products at an ever-increasing scale. Association-B epitomized this concept by drawing new members to the system and recognizing those that had 2-Sigma performance. The Type-B system must grow in sufficiently robust ways to resolve the 1:X challenge and thus enable co-evolution. This means schools, districts, associations, policymaking bodies, and companies must grow in a manner analogous to the trajectory of Kauffman's automobile that brought roads, gas stations, and ultimately emergent change to the urban landscape. We envision this kind of emergent change in an education system where classrooms, schools, and districts co-evolve with new associations, policies, and companies.

THE TOOLS NEEDED TO MAKE REAL CHANGE

A challenge in writing a solution-oriented book about education, technology, and change is remaining focused on the theme of technology when technology is not the problem. We echo this frustration in every chapter, showing what could or should be done in terms of technology use while amplifying the educational shifts that would permit it to fulfill its potential in a new paradigm.

A paradigm shift in education is impossible without *e*dge technology. Widespread attainment of 1:X calls for approaches to classroom teaching and learning that make less of more. Bruce's big jump module required a more complex schema. Bruce needed tools to enact that schema and reduce his cognitive load so that he could simultaneously manage multiple groups, different resources, and assessments. Only with *e*dge tools could Bruce, Sarah, James, Herb, and the others we've mentioned make less of more in their new, more sophisticated, and complex roles and levels of the overall educational system.

*E*dge technology shortens the cognitive distance between stakeholders in the system, extends learning opportunities in both form and location, and builds the capacity of all. The lesson formatter described in Chapter 2 enabled a teacher to begin with a non-research-informed lesson and as a result of a process mediated by the tool imbue that lesson with the characteristics of research-based practice. The tool addressed the professional capacity required to deliver 1:X and to learn the unseen teaching and learning approaches required for addressing the 1:X challenge. Curriculum development tools enabled the curriculum development effort undertaken by the science department. The capacity-building role of *e*dge tools is not confined to the classroom. The tools also enabled Principal Sarah to learn about feedback and collaboration, James to learn about the factors that contributed to student success, and Herb and his team to learn how to run an association that exerted a high-power, proximal influence on classrooms, schools, and districts. The tools teach the system's stakeholders how to be better at what they do.

*E*dge technology is antithetical to the technological determinism that currently underpins the use of ICT in schools. Such determinism is characterized by a belief that ICT will spontaneously redress the ills of contemporary education as reflected in the ill-fated Type-A district-level laptop initiative described in chapter four. In such initiatives, there is no possibility for any substantive educational benefit because education is not considered. We believe *e*dge technology will ultimately determine the success of the self-organizing educational system we envision. However, that determination will emerge from a sophisticated interaction between technology and the research-based extant knowledge of the field of education as reflected in the tools described throughout this book.

HOW SHARED SCHEMA UNITES
STAKEHOLDERS FOR REAL REFORM

Our purpose for writing this book is to issue a call for action based on a new theory structure for education that meets the educational needs of all students all the time by meeting the 1:X challenge and attaining 2-Sigma. We frame our call for action using the three-step framework employed in each of the preceding chapters.

Assumptions

We began the book with a critique of the current condition of ICT, focusing on the faulty assumptions that frame ICT use in education. The assumptions characterize educational ICT as a deterministic tool of change capable of exerting autogenic and spontaneous effects on students and teachers. We suggested that there is a need for new assumptions about the role of ICT in which the research-based knowledge of the field mediated its use. We showed how ICT enacted cognitive structures and created cognitive tools that were inseparable from the thinking that underpinned them.

We challenge readers to apply the new assumptions to their day-to-day decision-making about ICT and by doing so move beyond the blunt goals in their district's technology plan, the automating technologies that dominate the educational marketplace, and the associations and policies the keep the status quo in place. Applying new assumptions means asking why not define educational practice in proximal, high-power, and low-load ways that recognize that doing so is key to getting a return on investment from ICT in education. ICT can make less of more, shorten the cognitive distance between stakeholders, build their capacity for 1:X, and create an *edge*. Asking these questions challenges the status quo use of technology, moves stakeholders beyond a tacit acceptance of simplistic ICT solutions, and dispels expectations that autogenic effects will happen within the educational system rom students and teachers merely having access to ICT.

New Design

We challenge the reader to ask questions about how our schools, associations, policymaking bodies, and companies are designed to address the 1:X challenge. Do schools and so on perpetuate the one-size-fits-all Type-A educational approach? Do they share a commitment to research-based practice? Is the design of them an instrumental expression of the Type-A approach? Can they get to Type-B? Does sufficient order exist for dispersal of control? Do they generate the feedback necessary for self-organization? What role do you play in the current design? What contributions do you make? When it comes to 1:X, are you a strange or point attractor? Do you perpetuate or disturb Type-A equilibrium?

We ask these questions of ourselves constantly. The answers we got drove us to write this book. To get answers, we had to step away, sometimes momentarily and sometimes at length, to use a Type-B perspective to examine our location relative to the current condition. We assessed the current reality and future trajectory of our roles as agents in the educational enterprise. We saw windows of co-existence where we could create a foothold for Type-B and an alternative trajectory for ourselves.

New Trajectory

The path ahead for education requires those of us for whom the Type-A paradigm no longer meets our demands and guides our practice to acknowledge our realities. The Type-A approach's inability to realize the benefits of ICT is a symptom of a multigenerational education crisis of unprecedented proportions. Once we acknowledge this—and move away from the status quo by crossing the border—the next step is to embrace an alternate approach that has sufficient power to meet the demands of 1:X and 2-Sigma.

Not everyone is suited for what such a search entails. Those of us who are, however, have a moral obligation to blaze a trail for other border crossers to follow, establishing an outpost with a foundation built on the shifts and a reconceptualized role for ICT that make them possible. If you are up for the challenge, join us. If not, please know that we await your arrival.

References

Abrahams, J. (2007). *101 mission statements from top companies: Plus guidelines for writing your own mission statement*. Berkeley: Ten Speed.

Abrami, P., Bernard, R., Wade, C., Schmid, R., Borokhovski, E., Tamim, R., et al., (2006). *A review of e-learning in Canada: a rough sketch of the evidence, gaps and promising directions*. Montreal: Centre for the Study of Learning and Performance, Concordia University.

Acuff, J., & Wood, W. (2007). *Stop acting like a seller and start thinking like a buyer: improve sales effectiveness by helping customers buy*. Hoboken, NJ: Wiley.

Aladjem, D., & Borman, K. (2005, April 11–15). *The lifecycle of comprehensive school reform*. Paper presented at the American Educational Research Association, Montreal.

Alavi, M., & Leidner, D. (2001). Knowledge management and knowledge management systems: Conceptual foundations and research issues. *MIS Quarterly, 25*(1), 107–136.

American Association of School Administrators. (2010). About AASA. Retrieved from http://www.aasa.org/

American Association of School Administrators Journal of Scholarship & Practice. (2010). AASA publications. Retrieved from http://www.aasa.org/jsp.aspx

American Association of School Administrators. (2010). AASA by-laws, beliefs and position statements. Retrieved from http://www.aasa.org/content.aspx?id=1326

American School Counselor Association. (2010). State certification requirements. Retrieved from http://www.schoolcounselor.org/content.asp?contentid=242

American Speech-Language-Hearing Association. (2010). Certification. Retrieved from http://www.asha.org/certification/

Anderson, P. (1972). More is different: Broken symmetry and the nature of the hierarchical structure of science. *Science, 177*(4047), 393–396.

Anderson, R., Spiro, R., & Montague, W. (1977). *Schooling and the acquisition of knowledge*. Hillsdale, NJ: Erlbaum.

Angrist, J., & Lavy, V. (2002). New evidence on classroom computers and pupil learning. *Economic Journal, Royal Economic Society, 112*(482), 735–765.

Annett, J. (1969). *Feedback and human behaviour: The effects of knowledge of results, incentives, and reinforcement on learning and performance.* Baltimore: Penguin Books.

Antil, L., Jenkins, J., Wayne, S., & Vadasy, P. (1998). Cooperative learning: Prevalence, conceptualizations, and the relation between research and practice. *American Educational Research Journal, 1*(35), 419–454.

Ash, K. (2009). Maine laptop expansion moves forward. *Digital Directions, 2*(4).

Ashburn, E., & Floden, R. (Eds.). (2006). *Meaningful learning using technology: what educators need to know and do.* New York: Teachers College

Avramidis, E., & Norwich, B. (2002). Mainstream teachers' attitudes toward inclusion/integration: a review of the literature. *European Journal of Special Needs Education, 17*(2), 1–19.

Bach, S., & Sisson, K. (2000). *Personnel management: A comprehensive guide to theory and practice.* Malden, MA: Blackwell.

Bain, A. (2007). *The self-organizing school: Next generation comprehensive school reforms.* Lanham, MD: Rowman & Littlefield.

Bain, A. (2010). A longitudinal study of the practice fidelity of a site-based school reform. *Australian Educational Researcher, 37*(1), 107–124.

Bain, A., & Hess, P. (2002) *School reform and faculty culture: A longitudinal case study.* (ERIC Document Reproduction Service No. ED472655).

Bain, A., & Huss, P. (2000). The Curriculum Authoring Tools: Technology enabling school reform. *Learning & Leading with Technology, 28*(4), 14–17.

Bain, A., Huss, P., & Kwong, H. (2000). The evaluation of a hypertext discussion tool for teaching English literature to secondary school students. *Journal of Educational Computing Research, 23*(2), 203–216.

Bain, A., Lancaster, J., & Zundans, L. (2008). Pattern language development in the preparation of inclusive educators. *International Journal of Teaching and Learning in Higher Education, 20*(3), 336–349.

Bain, A., & Parkes, R. (2006). Curriculum Authoring Tools and inclusive classroom teaching practice: A longitudinal study. *British Journal of Educational Technology, 37*(2), 177–189.

Bain, A., & Swan, G. (In review). Tools for reform: Professional growth tools: Knowledge management from feedback.

Bain, A., & Weston, M. E. (2009). One to one computing: Which side of the border are you on? *Independent School, 68*(2), 50–56.

Baines, L. (1997, March). Future schlock: Using fabricated data and politically correct platitudes in the name of education reform. *Phi Delta Kappan, 78,* 493–498.

Bangert, R., Kulik, J., & Kulik, C. (1983). Individualized systems of instruction in secondary schools. *Review of Educational Research, 53*(2), 143–158.

Barab, S., Gresalfi, M., & Arici, A. (2009). Why educators should care about games. *Educational Leadership, 67*(1), 76–80.

Barabási, A.-L. (2003). *Linked: How everything is connected to everything else and what it means.* New York: Plume.

Barbeito, C. (2004). *Human resource policies and procedures for nonprofit organizations.* Hoboken, NJ: Wiley.

Barrow, L., & Rouse, C. (2005). *Causality, causality, causality: The view of education inputs and outputs from economics.* Chicago: Federal Reserve Bank.

Barton, P., & Coley, R. (2009). *Parsing the Achievement Gap II. Policy Information Report.* Princeton, NJ: Educational Testing Service.

Beach, M., & Floyd, E. (1998). *Newsletter sourcebook.* Cincinnati, OH: Writer's Digest Books.

Becker, H. (1999). *Internet use by teachers: Conditions of professional use and teacher-directed student use.* Irvine, CA: University of California, Center for Research on Information Technology and Organizations.

Becker, H. (2001). How are teachers using computers in instruction? [Electronic Version]. *American Educational Research Association.* Retrieved from http://www.crito.uci.edu/tlc/FINDINGS/special3/

Becker, H., & Riel, M. (1999). *Teacher professionalism, school work culture and the emergence of constructivist-compatible pedagogies.* Irvine, CA: University of California.

Beckham, J., & Maiden, J. (2003). The effects of technology inclusion on school bond election success in Oklahoma. *Journal of Education Finance, 28*(4), 557–574.

Bennett, P., & Wei, L. (2006). Market structure, fragmentation, and market quality. *Journal of Financial Markets, 9*(1), 49–78.

Berends, M., Bodilly, S., & Natarj-Kirby, S. (2002). *Facing the challenges of whole-school reform: New American Schools after a decade.* Santa Monica, CA: RAND.

Berners-Lee, T., & Fischetti, M. (1999). *Weaving the Web: The original design and ultimate destiny of the World Wide Web by its inventor.* San Francisco: HarperSanFrancisco.

Bertalanffy, L. (1973). *General system theory: Foundations, development, applications.* Harmondsworth, UK: Penguin.

Berube, M. (1994). *American school reform: Progressive, equity, and excellence movements, 1883–1993.* Westport, CT: Praeger.

Bierlein, L., & Molholland, S. (1993). *A national review of open enrollment and choice: Debates and description.* Tempe: Arizona State University.

Blaz, D. (2008). *Differentiated assessment for middle and high school classrooms.* Larchmont, NY: Eye On Education.

Bloom, B. S. (1976). *Human characteristics and school learning.* New York: McGraw-Hill.

Bloom, B. S. (1977). Favorable learning conditions for all. *Teacher, 95*(3), 22–28.

Bloom, B. S. (1984a). The 2 sigma problem: The search for methods of group instruction as effective as one-to-one tutoring *Educational Researcher, 13*(6), 14–16.

Bloom, B. S. (1984b). The search for methods of group instruction as effective as one-to-one tutoring. *Educational Leadership, 41*(8), 4–17.

Bloom, B. S. (1988). Helping all children learn well in elementary school—and beyond. *Principal, 67*(4), 12–17.

Bolman, L., & Deal, T. (2008). *Reframing organizations: artistry, choice, and leadership.* San Francisco: Jossey-Bass.

Bonifaz, A., & Zucker, A. (2004). *Lessons learned about providing laptops for all students.* Newton, MA: Education Development Center.

Boyd, W. (1992). The power of paradigms: Reconceptualizing educational policy and management. *Educational Administration Quarterly, 28*(4), 504–528.

Brafman, O., & Beckstrom, R. (2006). *The starfish and the spider: The unstoppable power of leaderless organizations.* New York: Portfolio.

Briesch, A., & Chafouleas, S. (2009). Review and analysis of literature on self-management interventions to promote appropriate classroom behaviors 1988–2008. *School Psychology Administrator, 24*(2), 106–111.

Brimly, V., & Garfield, R. (2007). *Financing education in a climate of change.* Boston: Pearson Allyn and Bacon.

Brinko, K. (1993). The practice of giving feedback to improve teaching. What is effective? *Journal of Higher Education, 64*(5), 574–593.

British Quality Foundation. (2001). *Drive continuous improvement . . . using the excellence model.* London: British Quality Foundation.

Brown, J., & Duguid, P. (1998). Knowledge and organization: A social-practice perspective. *Organization Science, 12*(2), 198–213.

Brown, R. (1996). *The strength of a people: The idea of an informed citizenry in America, 1650–1870.* Chapel Hill, NC: University of North Carolina.

Bruk, I. (1961). *Electronic computers in the service of the national economy.* Santa Monica, CA: RAND

Bruner, J. (1960). *The process of education.* Cambridge, MA: Harvard University.

Bunch, G., & Valeo, A. (2009). *Inclusive education: To do or not to do: England, Germany, Croatia, Canada, India, Spain, Malta.* Toronto: Inclusion Press.

Burns, T., & Stalker, G. (1961). *The management of innovation.* London: Tavistock.

Buttle, F. (2008). *Customer relationship management: Concepts and methodologies.* Burlington, MA: Butterworth-Heinemann.

Byrd, J., Drews, C., & Johnson, L. (2006). Factors impacting superintendent turnover: Lessons learned from the field [Electronic Version]. Retrieved from http://cnx.org/content/m14507/latest

C2K. (2010). About C2K. Retrieved from http://www.c2kni.org.uk/

Cagan, M. (2008). *Inspired: How to create products customers love.* San Francisco: Silicon Valley Product Group.

Cameron, E., & Green, M. (2009). *Making sense of change management: A complete guide to the models, tools & techniques of organizational change.* Philadelphia: Kogan Page.

Campbell-Kelly, M., & Aspray, W. (2004). *Computer: a history of the information machine.* Boulder, CO: Westview.

Campuzano, L., Dynarski, M., Agodini, R., & Rall, K. (2009). *Effectiveness of reading and mathematics software products: Findings from two student cohorts.* Jessup, MD: Institute of Education Sciences, National Center for Education Evaluation and Regional Assistance.

Cañas, K., & Sondak, H. (2008). *Opportunities and challenges of workplace diversity: theory, cases, and exercises.* Upper Saddle River, NJ: Pearson/Prentice Hall.

Carroll, J. (1963). A model of school learning. *Teachers College Record, 63,* 723–733.

Carter, N. (1989). Performance indicators: "Backseat driving" or "hands off" control? *Policy & Politics, 17*(2), 131–138.

Cavaney, R., Wasch, K., & Holleyman, R. (2007). *The business of membership organizations: industry leaders on achieving successful stewardship, establishing financial goals, and providing value to members.* Boston: Aspatore Books.

CEO Forum. (1997). *School Technology and Readiness Report: From Pillars to Progress. The CEO Forum on Education and Technology, Year One.* Washington, DC: CEO Forum on Education and Technology.

Cetron, M., & Davies, O. (1997). *Probable tomorrows: How science and technology will transform our lives in the next twenty years.* New York: St. Martin's.

Cheung, C. (2009). Evaluating the benefit from the help of the parent teacher association to child performance. *Evaluation and Program Planning, 32*(3), 247–256.

Christensen, C., Horn, M., & Johnson, C. (2008). *Disrupting class: How disruptive innovation will change the way the world learns.* New York: McGraw-Hill.

Clay, C. (2009). *Great Webinars: How to create interactive learning that is captivating, informative and fun.* New York: Punchy.

Clinchy, E. (1996, December). Reforming American education from the bottom to the top: Escaping academic captivity. *Phi Delta Kappan, 78,* 269–270.

Clotfelter, C., Ladd, H., & Vigdor, J. (2008). Scaling the digital divide: Home computer technology and student achievement [Electronic Version]. Retrieved from http://www.hks.harvard.edu/pepg/PDF/events/colloquia/Vigdor_ScalingtheDigitalDivide.pdf

Cohen, R., & Havlin, S. (2010). *Complex networks: Structure, robustness, and function.* New York: Cambridge University.

Cole, R. (2008). *Educating everybody's children: Diverse teaching strategies for diverse learners.* Alexandria, VA: ASCD.

Collins, A., & Halverson, R. (2009). *Rethinking education in the age of technology: The digital revolution and schooling in America.* New York: Teachers College.

Commission on the Skills of the American Workforce. (1990). *America's choice: High skills or low wages!* Rochester, NY: National Center on Education and the Economy.

Commission on the Skills of the American Workforce. (2007). *Tough choices or tough times: The report of the new commission on the skills of the American workforce.* San Francisco: Wiley.

Connolly, S. (2003). *The Industrial Revolution.* Chicago: Heinemann Library.

Corning, P. (2002). The re-emergence of emergence: A venerable concept in search of a theory. *Complexity, 7*(6), 18–30.

Cortada, J. (2004).The digital hand. How computers changed the work of American manufacturing, transportation, and retail industries. New York: Oxford University.

Cross, V., & Sudkamp, T. (2002). *Similarity and compatibility in fuzzy set theory: Assessment and applications.* New York: Physica-Verlag.

Cuban, L. (1984). *How teachers taught: Constancy and change in American classrooms, 1890–1980.* New York: Longman.

Cuban, L. (1990). Reforming again, again, and again. *Educational Researcher, 19*(1), 3–13.

Cuban, L. (2001). *Oversold and underused: Computers in the classroom.* Cambridge, MA: Harvard University.

Cuban, L. (2003). *Why is it so hard to get good schools?* New York: Teachers College.

Cuban, L., Kirkpatrick, H., & Peck, C. (2001). High access and low use of technologies in high school classrooms: Explaining an apparent paradox. *American Educational Research Journal, 38*(4), 813–834.

Cummings, W., & Williams, J. (2008). *Policy-making for education reform in developing countries.* Lanham, MD: Rowman Littlefield.

Currie, I. (1974). *Fundamental mechanics of fluids.* New York: McGraw-Hill.

Curtis, D. (2003). A computer for every lap: The Maine Learning Technology Initiative [Electronic Version]. *edutopia.* Retrieved from http://www.edutopia.org/computer-every-lap

Daft, R. (2007). *Organization theory and design.* Mason, OH: Thomson South-Western.

Dahlman, C. J., & Aubert, J.-E. (2001). *China and the knowledge economy: Seizing the 21st century.* Washington, DC: World Bank.

Darling-Hammond, L. (2010). *The flat world and education: how America's commitment to equity will determine our future.* New York: Teachers College.

Darling-Hammond, L., Wei, R., Andree, A., Richardson, N., & Orphanos, S. (2009). *Professional learning in the learning profession: A status report on teacher development in the United States and abroad.* Dallas: National Staff Development Council.

Darr, A. (2006). *Selling technology: the changing shape of sales in an information economy.* Ithaca, NY: Cornell University.

Davenport, T., & Harris, J. (2007). *Competing on analytics: the new science of winning.* Boston: Harvard Business School.

Davis, S., & Botkin, J. (1994). *The monster under the bed: How business is mastering the opportunity of knowledge for profit.* New York: Simon & Schuster.

Dawkins, J. (1988). *A changing workforce.* Canberra: Australian Government Publishing.

De Lia, E., & Fredericks, E. (2005). *From cross purposes to cooperation: The ten factors that unify a cross-functional team.* Bloomington, IN: iUniverse.

de Weert, F. (2011). *Bank and insurance capital management* New York: Wiley.

Deal, T. (1985). National commissions: Blueprints for remodeling or ceremonies for revitalizing public schools? *Education and Urban Society 17,* 145–156.

DesChenes, S., Cuban, L., & Tyack, D. (2001). Mismatch: Historical perspectives on schools and students who don't fit them. *Teachers College Record, 103*(4), 127–148.

Dede, C., Honan, J., & Peters, L. (Eds.) (2005). *Scaling up success: Lessons learned from technology-based educational improvement.* San Francisco: Jossey-Bass.

de Groot, S. (1952). *Thermodynamics of irreversible processes.* New York: Inter-science.

Department for Education Employment and Workplace Relations. (2010). Building the education revolution: Overview. Retrieved from http://www.deewr.gov.au/Schooling/BuildingTheEducationRevolution/Pages/BEROverview.aspx

Department of Education and Science. (1985). *Quality in schools: Evaluation and appraisal.* London: HMSO.

Deschenes, S., Cuban, L., & Tyack, D. (2001). Mismatch: Historical perspectives on schools and students who don't fit them. *Teachers College Record, 103*(4), 127–148.

Desimone, L., Porter, A., Garet, M., Yoon, K., & Birman, B. (2002). How can comprehensive school reform models be successfully implemented? *Review of Educational Research, 72*(3), 433–479.

Deubel, P. (2009). Social networking in schools: Incentives for participation [Electronic Version]. *T H E Journal (Technological Horizons In Education).* Retrieved from http://thejournal.com/articles/2009/09/16/social-networking-in-schools-incentives-for-participation.aspx

Dewey, J. (1938). *Logic, the theory of inquiry.* New York: Holt.

Didsbury, H. (2003). *21st century opportunities and challenges: An age of destruction or an age of transformation.* Bethesda, MD: World Future Society.

Dimmock, C., & Hattie, J. (1994). Principals' and teachers' reactions to school restructuring. *Australian Journal of Education, 38*(1), 36–55.

DiSessa, A. (2000). *Changing minds: Computers, learning, and literacy.* Cambridge, MA: MIT.

Dixon, R. (1994). Future schools and how to get there from here. *Phi Delta Kappan, 75*(5), 360–365.

Donmoyer, R. (2006). Take my paradigm . . . please! The legacy of Kuhn's construct in educational research. *International Journal of Qualitative Studies in Education, 19*(1), 11–34.

Drucker, P. (2006). *Managing the nonprofit organization: Principles and practices.* New York: Harper.

Duncan, K. (2008). *So what?: The definitive guide to the only business questions that matter.* Hoboken, NJ: Wiley.

Dunham, J., & Varma, V. (1998). *Stress in teachers: past, present, and future.* London: Whurr.

Durham, W. (1991). *Coevolution: Genes, culture, and human diversity.* Palo Alto, CA: Stanford University.

Dwyer, D. (2000). *Changing the conversation about teaching learning and technology: A report about ten years of ACOT research.* Cupertino, CA: Apple Computer.

Dynarski, M., Agodini, R., Heaviside, S., Novak, T., Carey, N., Campuzano, L., et al. (2007). *Effectiveness of reading and mathematics products: Findings from the first student cohort.* Washington, DC: U.S. Department of Education.

Eades, K., & Kear, R. (2006). *The solution-centric organization.* New York: McGraw-Hill.

Eckerson, W. (2006). *Performance dashboards: Measuring, monitoring, and managing your business.* Hoboken, NJ: Wiley.

Edge, J., & Richards, K. (1998). Why best practice is not good enough. *TESOL Quarterly, 32*(3), 569–575.

Elliot-Ingram, M. (1941). Teaching students to teach. *American Journal of Nursing, 41*(10), 1189–1191.

Elmore, R., & Fuhrman, S. (2001). Holding schools accountable: Is it working? *Phi Delta Kappan, 83.*

Elster, J. (1991). The possibility of rational politics. In D. Held (Ed.), *Political Theory Today* (pp. 115–142).Palo Alto, CA: Stanford University.

Ertmer, P. (2005). Teacher pedagogical beliefs: The final frontier in our quest for technology integration? *Educational Technology Research and Development, 53*(4), 25–40.

Evans, L. (2010). *Social media marketing: strategies for engaging in Facebook, Twitter & other social media.* Indianapolis, IN: Que.

Eyestone, R. (1971). *The threads of public policy: a study in policy leadership.* Indianapolis: Bobbs-Merrill.

Facer, K., & Sandford, R. (2009). The next 25 years? Future scenarios and future directions for education and technology. *Journal of Computer Assisted Learning, 26*(74–93).

Feldon, D. (2007). Cognitive load and classroom teaching: The double-edged sword of automaticity. *Educational Psychologist, 42*(3), 123–137.

Ferdig, R., DiPietro, M., & Papanastasiou, E. (2005). *Teaching and learning in collaborative virtual high schools.* Naperville, IL: Learning Point Associates.

Finn, C. (1991). *We must take charge: Our schools and our future.* New York: Free Press.

Fischetti, J. (1996). Shifting paradigms: Emerging issues for educational policy and practice. *Teacher Educator, 31*(3), 189–201.

Fisher, C., Dwyer, D., & Yocam, K. (1996). *Education and technology: Reflections on computing in classrooms.* San Francisco: Jossey-Bass.

Fitzpatrick, M. (Ed.). (2004). *The Enlightenment world*. New York: Routledge.

Foot, D. (1977). *A discrete time interpretation of negative feedback loops in systems dynamics models*. Toronto: Institute for Policy Analysis.

Fouts, J. (2000). *Research on computers and education: Past, present and future*. Seattle, WA: Gates.

Franceschini, L. (2002, April 1–5). *Memphis, what happened? Notes on the decline and fall of comprehensive school reform models in a flagship district*. Paper presented at the Annual Meeting of the American Educational Research Association, New Orleans.

Fraser, B., Walberg, H., Welch, W., & Hattie, J. (1987). Syntheses of educational productivity research. *International Journal of Educational Research, 11*(2), 147–252.

French, D. (2009). *Model articles of association for companies*. New York: Oxford University.

Friedman, M. (1962). *Capitalism and freedom*. Chicago: University of Chicago.

Friedman, M., & Friedman, R. (1980). *Free to choose: A personal statement*. New York: Harcourt Brace Jovanovich.

Fuchs, D., Fuchs, L., Mathes, P., & Simmons, D. (1997). Peer-assisted learning strategies: making classrooms more responsive to diversity. *American Educational Research Journal, 34*(1), 174–206.

Fuhrman, S., Clune, W., & Elmore, R. (1991). Research on education reform: Lessons on the implementation of policy. In A. Odden (Ed.), *Education Policy Implementation* (pp. 197–218). Albany, NY: State University of New York.

Fuhrman, S., & Elmore, R. (2004). *Redesigning accountability systems for education*. New York: Teachers College.

Fullan, M. G. (2007). *The new meaning of educational change* (4th ed.). New York: Teachers College.

Fullan, M. G. (1993). *Change forces*. London: Falmar.

Gale, J. (2010). *Encyclopedia of associations*. Retrieved from http://library.dialog.com/bluesheets/html/bl0114.html

Garet, M., Porter, A., Desimone, L., Birman, B., & Yoon, K. (2001). What makes professional development effective? Results from a national sample of teachers. *American Educational research Journal, 38*(4), 915–945.

Garnsey, E., & McGlade, J. (2006). *Complexity and co-evolution: continuity and change in socio-economic systems*. Northampton, MA: Elgar.

Geldhof, P. (1931). *How 22 manufacturers built sales appeal through improved design. Methods in engineering the product that resulted in: better appearance, higher production, lighter weight, greater sales, higher speed, greater durability, more style, greater economy*. New York: McGraw-Hill.

Gell-Mann, M. (1994). *The quark and the jaguar: Adventures in the simple and the complex*. New York: W. H. Freeman.

Gettinger, M. (1984). Measuring time needed for learning to predict learning. *Exceptional Children, 51*(3), 244–248.

Ghauri, P., Hadjikhani, A., & Johanson, J. (2005). *Managing opportunity development in business networks*. New York: Palgrave Macmillan.

Ghosh, S. (2007). *History of education in India*. Jaipur, India: Rawat Publications.

Ginsberg, R., & Wimpelberg, R. (1987). Educational change by commission: Attempting "Trickle-down" reform. *Educational Evaluation and Policy Analysis, 10*, 344–360.

Glanz, J., & Behar-Horenstein, L. (Eds.). (2000). *Paradigm debates in curriculum and supervision: Modern and postmodern perspectives*. Westport, CT: Bergin Garvey.

Glaser, W. (1993). *The role of education associations in health and other public policy: Cross-national comparisons*. Washington, DC: National Education Association.

Glatthorn, A. (1990). *Supervisory leadership: Introduction to instructional supervision*. Reading, MA: Addison-Wesley.

Gleick, J. (1987). *Chaos: Making a new science*. New York: Viking.

Glennan, T., & Melmad, A. (1996). *Fostering the use of educational technology: Elements of a national strategy* (No. MR-682-OSTP). Santa Monica, CA: RAND.

Goertz, M., Floden, R., & O'Day, J. (1996). *The bumpy road to education reform*. New Brunswick, NJ: Rutgers University.

Goldin, C., & Katz, L. (Eds.). (2001). *Decreasing (and then increasing) inequality in America: A tale of two half centuries*. Chicago: University of Chicago.

Golon, A. (2008). *Visual-spatial learners: Differentiation strategies for creating a successful classroom*. Waco, TX: Prufrock.

Gonzales, P. (2004). *Highlights from the Trends in International Mathematics and Science Study (TIMSS) 2003*. Washington, DC: National Center for Education Statistics.

Goodlad, J. (1984). *A place called school: Prospects for the future*. New York: McGraw-Hill.

Gordon, D., & Graham, P. (2003). *A nation reformed : American education 20 years after A Nation at Risk*. Cambridge, MA: Harvard Education.

Gorrill, B. (1999). Making authentic assessment real for individual students. In T. Hillman & C. Thorn (Eds.), *Oh What a Web We Weave* (pp. 273–279). Gilman, NH: Avocus.

Graham, J., & Havlick, W. (1994). *Mission statements: a guide to the corporate and nonprofit sectors*. New York: Garland.

Greaves, T., & Hayes, J. (2008). *America's Digital Schools 2008: Six trends to watch*. Shelton, CT: Market Data Retrieval.

Greenwood, C., Maheady, L., & Delquardi, J. (2002). Classwide peer tutoring. In G. Stoner, M. Shinn, & H. Walker (Eds.), *National Association of School Psychologists: Interventions for achievement and behavior Problems* (pp. 611–649). Washington, DC: National Association of School Psychologists.

Gregory, G., & Chapman, C. (2002). *Differentiated instructional strategies*. Alexandria, VA: ASCD.

Guskey, T. (2003). How classroom assessment improves learning. *Educational Leadership, 60*(5), 6–11.

Guskey, T., & Schulz, T. (1996). *Implementing mastery learning.* Belmont, CA: Wadsworth.

Hall, D. (2008). *The technology director's guide to leadership: The power of great questions.* Eugene, OR: International Society for Technology in Education.

Hampton, J. (2009). *Fundamentals of enterprise risk management: how top companies assess risk, manage exposures, and seize opportunities.* New York: American Management Association.

Hannig, U. (2002). *Knowledge management and business intelligence.* New York: Springer.

Hanushek, E., & Lindseth, A. (2009). *Schoolhouses, courthouses, and statehouses: solving the funding-achievement puzzle in America's public schools.* Princeton, NJ: Princeton University.

Hanushek, E., & Woessmann, L. (2010). *Sample selectivity and the validity of international student achievement tests in economic research.* Cambridge, MA: National Bureau of Economic Research.

Hattie, J. (2003, October). *Teachers make a difference: What is the research evidence?* Paper presented at the Australian Council for Educational Research: Annual Conference on Building Teacher Quality. Retrieved from http://research.acer.edu.au/research_conference_2003/4/

Hattie, J. (2009). *Visible learning: A synthesis of over 800 meta-analyses relating to achievement.* New York: Routledge.

Hausknecht, J., Halpert, J., DiPaulo, N., & Gerrard, M. (2007). Retesting in selection: A meta-analysis of coaching and practice effects of tests of cognitive ability. *Journal of Applied Psychology, 92*(2), 373–385.

Hawken, P. (1987). *Growing a business.* New York: Simon & Schuster.

Hayes, W. (2004). *Are we still a nation at risk two decades later?* Lanham, MD: Scarecrow.

Heck, R. (2004). *Studying educational and social policy: Theoretical concepts and research methods.* Mahwah, NJ: Lawrence Erlbaum.

Herring, W., McGrath, D., & Buckley, J. (2007). *Demographic and school characteristics of students receiving special education in the elementary grades.* Jessup, MD: National Center for Education Statistics.

Herrington, J., & Kervin, L. (2007). Authentic learning supported by technology: Ten suggestions and cases of integration in classrooms. *Educational Media International, 44*(3), 219–236.

Hess, F. (2002). *School boards at the dawn of the 21st century: Conditions and challenges of district governance.* Alexandria, VA: National School Boards Association.

Hess, F. (2010). *Education unbound: the promise and practice of greenfield schooling.* Alexandria, VA: Association for Supervision and Curriculum Development.

High School Survey of Student Engagement. (2010). High school survey of student engagement. Retrieved from http://ceep.indiana.edu/hssse/index.htm

Hill, P., Pierce, L., & Guthrie, J. (1997). *Reinventing public education: How contracting can transform America's schools.* Chicago: University of Chicago.

Hirsch, E. (1987). *Cultural literacy.* Boston: Houghton Mifflin.

Holdzkom, D., & Kuligowski, B. (1993, April 12-16). *Shifting paradigms or shifting perspectives: An analysis of fifty years of education reform.* Paper presented at the Annual Meeting of the American Educational Research Association, Atlanta.

Holmes, C. (2007). *The ultimate sales machine: Turbocharge your business with relentless focus on 12 key strategies.* New York: Portfolio.

Hu, W. (2007, May 4). Seeing no progress, some schools drop laptops. *NewYorkTimes.com* Retrieved from http://www.nytimes.com/2007/05/04/education/04laptop.html

Hughes, J., & Salvia, C. (1990). *Curriculum-based assessment: Testing what is taught.* Upper Saddle River, NJ: Prentice Hall.

Hunger, J., & Wheelen, T. (2007). *Essentials of strategic management.* Upper Saddle River, NJ: Pearson.

Hunter, R. (2004). *Madeline Hunter's mastery teaching: Increasing instructional effectiveness in elementary and secondary schools.* Thousand Oaks, CA: Corwin.

Huselid, M., Becker, B., & Beatty, R. (2005). *The workforce scorecard: managing human capital to execute strategy.* Boston: Harvard Business.

Hyams, B., & Bessant, B. (1972). *Schools for the people? An introduction to the history of state education in Australia.* Camberwell, AUS: Longman.

Impagliazzo, J., & Lee, J. (Eds.). (2010). *History of computing in education.* Norwell, MA: Kluwer.

InfoTrends. (2010). *Opportunities in the education market.* Weymouth, MA: InfoTrends.

International Society for Technology in Education. (2010a). About ISTE. Retrieved from http://www.iste.org/

International Society for Technology in Education. (2010b). About ISTE. Retrieved from http://www.iste.org/about-iste/governance/strategic-pla.aspx

International Society for Technology in Education. (2010c). ISTE by-laws. Retrieved from http://www.iste.org/about-iste/governance/bylaws.aspx International Society for Technology in Education Journal of Digital Learning in Teacher Education. (2010d). ISTE Publications. Retrieved from http://www.iste.org/Content/NavigationMenu/Publications/JDLTEJournalofDigitalLearningin-TeacherEducation/Journal_of_Digital_Learning_in_Teacher_E.htm

Jacobs, J., & Glassie, J. (2004). *Certification and accreditation law handbook.* Washington, DC: American Society of Association Executives.

Jaillet, A. (2004). What is happening with portable computers in schools? *Journal of Science Education and Technology, 13*(1), 115–128.

Jenkins, J., & Jenkins, L. (1985). Peer tutoring in elementary and secondary programs. *Focus on Exceptional Children, 17*(6), 1–12.

Johanningmeier, E., & Richardson, T. (2008). *Educational research, the national agenda, and educational reform: A history.* Charlotte, NC: Information Age.

Johnson, D., & Maddux, C. (2003). *Technology in education: A twenty-year retrospective.* New York: Haworth.

Johnson, S. (2001). *Emergence: The connected lives of ants, brains, cities, and software.* New York: Scribner.

Johnstone, B. (2003). *Never mind the laptops: Kids, computers, and the transformation of learning:* iUniverse.

Johnstone, B. (2006). *I have computers in my classroom—now what?* Portsmouth, NH: Heinemann.

Jones, R. (1997). Kids as education customers. *Education Digest, 62*(5), 10–16.

Jones, S. (2003). *Blueprint for student success: A guide to research-based teaching practices, K–12.* Thousand Oaks, CA: Corwin.

Jovane, F., Westkämper, E., & Williams, D. (2009). *The manufuture road: towards competitive and sustainable high-adding-value manufacturing.* Berlin, Germany: Springer-Verlag.

Kamps, D., Greenwood, C., Arreaga-Mayer, C., Veerkamp, M., Utley, C., Tapia, Y., et al. (2008). The efficacy of class-wide peer tutoring in middle schools. *Education and Treatment of Children, 31*(2), 119–115.

Kauffman, S. (1995). *At home in the universe: The search for laws of self-organization and complexity.* New York: Oxford University.

Kearns, D., & Doyle, D. (1988). *Winning the brain race: A bold plan to make our schools competitive.* New York: ICS.

Kearns, D., & Doyle, D. (1989). *Winning the brain race: A bold plan to transform our nation's schools.* San Francisco: ICS.

Kerr, K., Pane, J., & Barney, H. (2003). *Quaker Valley Digital School District: Early effects and plans for future evaluation* (No. Technical Report TR-107-EDU). Santa Monica, CA: RAND.

King, A. (2000). From lunchboxes to laptops: Giving our kids computers will change their future and Maine's [Electronic Version]. Retrieved from *http://www.papert.org/articles/laptops/lunchboxes_laptops.html*

King, J. (1995). *Writing high-tech copy that sells.* New York: J. Wiley.

Kinsella, R., & McBrierty, V. (1998). *Ireland and the knowledge economy: The new techno-academic paradigm.* Dublin: Oak Tree.

Kirst, M. (1984). *Who controls our schools? American values in conflict.* Stanford, CA: Stanford Alumni Association

Kirst, M., & Meister, G. (1985). Turbulences in American secondary schools: What reforms last? *Curriculum Inquiry, 15,* 169–186.

Kirst, M., & Wirt, F. (1969). *Political and social foundations of education.* New York: Little, Brown and Company.

Klopfer, E., Osterweil, S., Groff, J., & Haas, J. (2009). Using the technology of today in the classroom today [Electronic Version]. *The Education Arcade.* Retrieved from http://hub.mspnet.org/index.cfm/18746

Koestler, A., & Smythies, J. (Eds.). (1969). *Beyond reductionism: New perspectives in the life sciences.* London: Hutchinson.

Kolb, L. (2008). *Toys to tools: Connecting student cell phones to education.* Eugene, OR: International Society for Technology in Education.

Kolderie, T., & MacDonald, T. (2009). *How information technology can enable 21st century schools.* Washington, DC: Information Technology and Innovation Foundation.

Kotler, P. (2009). *Marketing management.* New York: Prentice Hall.

Kotter, J., & Cohen, D. (2002). *The heart of change: real-life stories of how people change their organizations.* Boston: Harvard Business.

Kouzes, J., & Posner, B. (1987). *The leadership challenge: how to get extraordinary things done in organizations.* San Francisco: Jossey-Bass.

Kowalski, T. (2005). *The school superintendent: Theory, practice and cases.* Thousand Oaks, CA: Sage.

Kubasek, N., Brennan, B., & Browne, M. (2009). *The legal environment of business: a critical thinking approach.* Upper Saddle River, NJ: Pearson Prentice Hall.

Kuhn, T. (1996). *The structure of scientific revolutions* (3rd ed.). Chicago: University of Chicago.

Kunin, M. (1995). Education reform: Staking out common ground. *Daedalus, 124*(4), 193–197.

Larrivee, B. (2009). *Authentic classroom management: Creating a learning community and building reflective practice.* Boston: Pearson/Allyn and Bacon.

Lathouwers, K., de Moor, J., & Didden, R. (2009). Access to and use of Internet by adolescents who have a physical disability: A comparative study. *Research in Developmental Disabilities: A Multidisciplinary Journal, 30*(4), 702–711.

Laughlin, R. (2005). *A different universe: Reinventing physics from the bottom down.* New York: Basic Books.

Law, N., Pelgrum, W., & Plomp, T. (Eds.). (2008). *Pedagogy and ICT use in schools around the World: Findings from the IEA SITES 2006 Study.* New York: Springer.

Lawr, D., & Gidney, R. (1973). *Educating Canadians: A documentary history of education.* Toronto: Van Nostrand Reinhold.

Leask, M., & Pachler, N. (2005). *Learning to teach using ICT in the secondary school: A companion to school experience.* New York: Routledge.

Leatherman, J., & Niemeyer, J. (2005). Teachers' attitudes toward inclusion: factors influencing classroom practice. *Journal of Early Childhood Education, 26,* 23–36.

Lei, J., Conway, P., & Zhao, Y. (2008). *The digital pencil: One-to-one computing for children.* New York: Erlbaum.

Lei, J., & Zhao, Y. (2006). What does one-to-one computing bring to schools? In C. Crawford, D. A. Willis, R. Carlsen, I. Gibson, K. McFerrin, J. Price & R. Weber (Eds.), *Proceedings of Society for Information Technology and Teacher Education International Conference 2006* (pp. 1690–1694). Chesapeake, VA: AACE.

Lemke, J. (2006). *Toward systemic educational change: Questions from a complex systems perspective.* Cambridge, MA: New England Complex Systems Institute.

Leonard-Barton, D. (1992). Core capabilities and core rigidities: A paradox in managing new product development. *Strategic Management Journal, 13*(S1), 111–125.

Lessem, R., & Palsule, S. (1997). *Managing in four worlds: From competition to co-creation.* Malden, MA: Blackwell.

Leuven, E., Lindahl, M., Oosterbeek, H., & Webbink, D. (2004). *The effect of extra funding for disadvantaged pupils on achievement.* Bonn, Germany: Institute for the Study of Labor.

Lewis, M. (2000). *The new new thing: A Silicon Valley story.* New York: W. W. Norton.

Lieberman, M. (1993). *Public education: An autopsy.* Cambridge, MA: Harvard.

Lindblom, C. (1968). *The policy-making process.* Englewood Cliffs, NJ: Prentice-Hall.

Linn, M. C., & Hsi, S. (2000). *Computers, teachers, peers: Science learning partners.* Mahwah, NJ: Lawrence Erlbaum Associates.

Lippitt, R. (1965). *Feedback process in the community context.* Washington National Training Laboratories, National Education Association.

Loewenstein, A. (2008). *The blogging revolution.* Carlton, Victoria: Melbourne University.

Lortie, D. (1975). *Schoolteacher: A sociological study.* Chicago: University of Chicago.

Luecke, R. (2003). *Managing change and transition.* Boston: Harvard Business School.

MacMillan, D. (2006). A laptop at every desk [Electronic Version]. *Businessweek Online.* Retrieved from http://www.businessweek.com/technology/content/sep2006/tc20060920_029230.htm

Mandel, M. (1996). *The high-risk society: Peril and promise in the new economy.* New York: Times Business.

Mann, D. (2008). *Documenting outcomes from Henrico County Public School's laptop computing initiative: 2005–06 through 2007–08.* Ashland, VA: Interactive Inc.

Marshall, R., & Tucker, M. (1992). *Thinking for a living: Education and the wealth of nations.* New York: Basic Books.

Marshall, S. (1995). *Schemas in problem solving.* Cambridge: University of Cambridge.

Martin, M. (2004). *TIMSS 2003: International science report: Findings from IEA's Trends in International Mathematics and Science Study at the fourth and eighth grades*. Chestnut Hill, MA: International Study Center.

Martin, M., Mullis, I., & Chrostowski, S. (2004). *TIMSS 2003 technical report: Findings from IEA's Trends in International Mathematics and Science Study at the Fourth and Eighth Grades*. Chestnut Hill, MA: International Study Center.

Marzano, R. (1998). *A theory-based meta-analysis of research on instruction*. Aurora, CO: Mid-continent Research for Education and Learning.

Masemann, V., Bray, M., & Manzon, M. (2007). *Common interests, uncommon goals: Histories of the World Council of Comparative Education Societies and its members*. Hong Kong: Comparative Education Research Center.

Mastropieri, M., & Scruggs, T. (2007). *The inclusive classroom: Strategies for effective instruction*. Upper Saddle River, NJ: Merrill Prentice Hall.

McCarthy, P., & Breen, Y. (2001). Teaching and learning for tomorrow: A learning technology plan for Maine's future [Electronic Version], 99. Retrieved from http://maine.gov/mlti/resources/history/mlterpt.pdf

McChesney, R., Wood, E., & Foster, J. (1998). *Capitalism and the information age: The political economy of the global communication revolution*. New York: Monthly Review.

McGrath, C. (2007). *The inclusion-classroom problem solve: Structures and supports to serve all learners*. Portsmouth, NH: Heinemann.

McGrath, M. (1995). *Product strategy for high-technology companies how to achieve growth, competitive advantage, and increased profits*. Burr Ridge, IL: Irwin.

McKenzie, P., Mitchell, P., & Oliver, P. (1995). *Competence and accountability in education*. Aldershot, UK: Arena.

McLaughlin, M. (2009). *Between movement and establishment: organizations advocating for youth*. Palo Alto, CA: Stanford University.

McLaughlin, M., & Talbert, J. (2001). *Professional communities and the work of high school teaching*. Chicago: University of Chicago.

Meier, D., & Wood, G. (2004). *Many children left behind: how the No Child Left Behind Act is damaging our children and our schools*. Boston: Beacon.

Merry, U. (1995). *Coping with uncertainty: Insights from the new sciences of chaos, self-organization, and complexity*. Westport, CT: Praeger.

Michelau, D., & Shreve, D. (2002, December). Education reform from the top down: The Federal government early this year passed the most comprehensive education legislation in recent memory. but there are many questions and few answers about the ramifications for states. *State Legislatures, 28*, 21–26.

Milgate, M. (2004). *Transforming corporate performance: measuring and managing the drivers of business success*. Westport, CT: Praeger.

Miller, D., Sen, A., & Malley, L. (2007). *Comparative indicators of education in the United States and other G-8 Countries: 2006*. Jessup, MD: National Center for Education Statistics.

Miller, J., & Muir, D. (2004). *The business of brands*. Hoboken, NJ: Wiley.

Miller, R. (1996). *Measuring what people know: Human capital accounting for the knowledge economy*. Paris: Organization for Economic Co-operation and Development.

Mina, E. (2000). *The complete handbook of business meetings*. New York: AMACOM.

Mitakidou, C. (2009). *Beyond pedagogies of exclusion in diverse childhood contexts: Transnational challenges*. New York: Palgrave Macmillan.

Mitchell, D. (2005). *Contextualizing inclusive education: Evaluating old and new international perspectives*. London: Routledge.

Moje, E. (2009). Standpoints: A call for new research on new and multi-literacies. *Research in the Teaching of English, 43*(4), 348–362.

Mooney, P., Ryan, J., Uhing, B., Reid, R., & Epstein, M. (2005). A review of self-management interventions targeting academic outcomes for students with emotional and behavioral disorders. *Journal of Behavioral Education, 14*(3), 203–221.

Moreau, R. (1984). *The computer comes of age: The people, the hardware, and the software*. Cambridge, MA: MIT.

Morrison, M. (2000). *Unifying scientific theories: Physical concepts and mathematical structures*. New York: Cambridge University.

Muir, M. (2005). Laptops for learning: The Maine Learning Technology Initiative. University of Maine, Center for Meaningful Engaged Learning.

Murdock, S. (2006). *Demographics: a guide to methods and data sources for media, business, and government*. Boulder, CO: Paradigm.

Naney, C., & Chalkley, M. (2009). *Model T Education: How to Replace Our Assembly Line Instruction and Meet the Challenges of the 21st Century*. Dallas, TX: Grindl Press.

National Center for Education Statistics. (1989). *Analysis report: Dropout rates in the United States: 1988* (No. NCES 89-609). Washington, DC: Office of Educational Research and Improvement, U.S. Department of Education.

National Center for Educational Statistics. (2005). *The nation's report card: fourth-grade students reading aloud: NAEP 2002 special study of oral reading*. Washington, DC: National Center for Education Statistics.

National Center for Education Statistics. (2006). *The nation's report card: science 2005 : assessment of student performance in grades 4, 8, and 12*. Washington, DC: U.S. Department of Education, Institute for Education Sciences.

National Center for Education Statistics. (2008). *Digest of education statistics*. Washington, DC: U.S. Department of Education, Institute for Education Sciences.

National Center for Education Statistics. (2009). *Achievement gaps: How black and white students in public schools perform in mathematics and reading on the National Assessment of Educational Progress*. Washington, DC: U.S. Dept. of Education, National Center for Education Statistics, Institute for Education Sciences.

National Commission on Excellence in Education. (1983). *A nation at risk: The imperative of education reform.* Washington, DC: U.S. Department of Education.

National Education Association of the United States. (1969). *A primer in publicity for education associations.* Washington, DC: National Education Association of the United States, Division of Press Radio and Television Relations.

NationMaster. (2010). Student attitude: Dislike of school. Retrieved from http://www.nationmaster.com/graph/edu_stu_att_wil_not_go_to_sch-education-student-attitude-dislike-school

Natkin, G., Cooper, B., Fusarelli, L., Alborano, J., Padilla, A., & Ghosh, S. (2002). Myth of the revolving door superintendency. *School Administrator, 59*(5), 28–31.

Negroponte, N. (1995). *Being digital.* New York: Knopf.

Nemitz, B. (2000, March 8). Why can't Maine kids be plugged in? *Portland Press Heral.* Retrieved from http://www.papert.org/aticles/laptops/why_cant_maine.html

North Central Regional Educational Laboratory. (2008). enGauge: A framework for effective technology use. Retrieved from http://www.ncrel.org/engauge/

Nusselder, A. (2009). *Interface fantasy: A Lacanian cyborg ontology.* Cambridge, MA: MIT.

O'Brien, A. (2008). *United States Education IT spending 2006–2011 forecast.* Falls Church, VA: Goverment Insights.

O'Melia, M., & Rosenberg, M. (1994). Effects of cooperative homework teams on the acquisition of mathematics skills by secondary students with mild disabilities. *Exceptional Children, 60*(6), 538–548.

Organization for Economic Cooperation and Development. (2008). *Education at a glance 2008: OECD indicators.* Paris: OECD.

Owens, M. (2002). International trade in education programs, goods, and services. Retrieved from http://www.encyclopedia.com/doc/1G2-3403200338.html

Pakroo, P. (2009). *Starting & building a nonprofit: a practical guide.* Berkeley, CA: Nolo.

Palfrey, J., & Gasser, U. (2008). *Born digital: understanding the first generation of digital natives.* New York: Basic Books.

Papert, S. (1993a). *The children's machine: Rethinking school in the age of the computer.* New York: Basic Books.

Papert, S. (1993b). *Mindstorms: Children, computers, and powerful ideas.* New York: Basic Books.

Papert, S. (1997). Why school reform is impossible. *Journal of the Learning Sciences, 6*(4), 417–427.

Partnership for 21st Century Skills. (2002). *Learning for the 21st century: A report and mile guide for 21st century skills.* Washington, DC: Author.

Partnership for Schools. (2010). Building schools for the future. Retrieved from http://www.partnershipsforschools.org.uk/about/aboutbsf.jsp

Pascale, R., Millemann, M., & Gioja, L. (2000). *Surfing the edge of chaos: the laws of nature and the new laws of business.* New York: Crown.

Passow, H. (1984). *Reforming Schools in the 1980s: A Critical Review of the National Reports.* New York: Teachers College.

Pearce, J. (2010). *Status in management and organizations.* New York: Cambridge University.

Pelech, J. (2010). *The comprehensive handbook of constructivist teaching from theory to practice.* Charlotte, NC: Information Age.

Penuel, W. (2006). Implementation and effects of one-to-one computing initiatives: A research synthesis. *Journal of Research on Technology in Education, 38*(3), 329–348.

Penuel, W., Kirn, D., Michalchik, V., Lewis, S., Means, B., & Murphy, B. (2001). *Using technology to enhance connections between home and school: A research synthesis.* Menlo Park, CA: SRI.

Perls, F. (1969). *Gestalt therapy verbatim.* Lafayette, CA: Real People.

Peterson, M. (2009). *An introduction to decision theory.* New York: Cambridge University.

Peterson, P. (1983). Did the educational commissions say anything? *Brookings Review, 1*, 3–11.

Pflaum, W. (2004). *The technology fix: The promise and reality of computers in our schools.* Alexandria, VA: Association for Supervision and Curriculum Development.

Picot, B. (1988). *Administering for excellence: Taskforce to review education administration.* Auckland, NZ.

Pine, J., & Gilmore, J. (1998). Welcome to the experience economy. *Harvard Business Review, 98*, 97–105.

Pine, J., & Gilmore, J. (2000). Satisfaction, sacrifice, surprise: Three small steps create one giant leap into the experience economy. *Strategy and Leadership, 28*(1), 18–23.

Pittas, P., & Gray, K. (2004). *Addressing education: Purposes, plans, and politics.* Philadelphia: Xlibris.

Plank, D., & Ginsberg, R. (1990). Catch the wave: Reform commissions and school reform. In J. Murphy (Ed.), *The Educational Reform Movement of the 1980s.* Berkeley, CA: McCutchan.

Pogrow, S. (1996, June). Reforming the wannabe reformers: Why education reforms almost always end up making things worse. *Phi Delta Kappan, 77*, 656–663.

Polloway, E., Epstein, M., & Foley, R. (1992). A comparison of homework problems of students with learning-disabilities and non-handicapped students. *Learning Disabilities: Research and Practice, 7*, 203–209.

Pooler, V., Pooler, D., & Farney, S. (2004). *Global purchasing and supply management: fulfill the vision.* Boston: Kluwer.

Portin, B., Knapp, M., Alejano, C., & Marzolf, E. (2006). Roles, responsibilities, and authority of school leaders: Patterns in current research, theory, and practice [Electronic Version]. Retrieved from http://depts.washington.edu/ctpmail/ PDFs/ Roles

Prigogine, I., & Stengers, I. (1984). *Order out of chaos: Man's new dialogue with nature.* New York: Bantam.

PSK12. (2010). Public school ranking. Retrieved from http://www.psk12.com/rating/info/aboutus.php

Public Agenda. (1995). *Assignment incomplete: The unfinished business of education reform.* New York: Public Agenda Foundation.

Public Agenda. (1999). *Public schools: Are they making the grade?* New York: Public Agenda Foundation.

Public Agenda. (2003). *Where we are now: 12 things you need to know about public opinion and public schools: Complete survey findings.* New York: Public Agenda Foundation.

Putnam, R. (2000). *Bowling alone: The collapse and revival of American community.* New York: Simon & Schuster.

Rapoport, A. (1986). *General system theory: essential concepts & applications.* Cambridge, MA: Abacus.

Rathbun, A., & West, J. (2003). Young children's access to computers in the home and at school in 1999 and 2000. *Education Statistics Quarterly, 5*(1), 25–30.

Raum, E. (2008). *The history of the computer.* Chicago, IL: Heinemann Library.

Ravitch, D. (1983). *The troubled crusade: American education 1945–1980.* New York: Basic.

Ravitch, D. (2000). *Left back: A century of failed school reforms.* New York: Simon & Schuster.

Ravitch, D. (2010). *The death and life of the great American school system: How testing and choice are undermining education.* New York: Basic Books.

Reese, S., Gandy, O., & Grant, A. (2001). *Framing public life: Perspectives on media and our understanding of the social world.* Mahwah, NJ: Erlbaum.

Reina, D., & Reina, M. (2006). *Trust and betrayal in the workplace: building effective relationships in your organizations.* San Francisco: Berrett-Koehler.

Reiter, B. (2009). *Negotiating democracy in Brazil: The politics of exclusion.* Boulder: First Forum.

Rhodes, L. (1997). Building leadership technology: The missing links between a superintendent's vision and the school district's actions. *School Administrator, 4*, 12–16.

Rivero, V. (2009). Tightening the purchasing process: superintendents get more involved in buying policies. *District Administration, 45*(10), 78–84.

Rockman, S., Walker, L., Cross, S., Campbell, K., Dunn, E., & Hughes, H. (1997). *Report of a laptop program pilot.* San Francisco: MicrosoftRothman, R. (2005). *Inequality and stratification: Race, class, and gender* (5th ed.). Upper Saddle River, NJ: Pearson Prentice Hall.

Rovin, S. (2001). *Medicine and business: bridging the gap.* Gaithersburg, MD: Aspen.

Rowe, K. (2003, October 19–21). *The importance of teacher quality as a key determinant of students' experiences and the outcomes of schooling.* Paper presented at the ACER Building Teacher Quality: What Does the Research Tell Us Conference Melbourne. Retrieved from http://research.acer.edu.au/research_conference_2003/3/

Roy, D. (2004). 10x: Human-machine symbiosis. *BT Technology Journal, 22*(4), 121–124.

Rus, D. (2009). *The dark side of leadership: Exploring the psychology of leader self-serving behavior.* Rotterdam: Erasmus University.

Sarason, S. B. (1990). *The predictable failure of educational reform: Can we change course before it's too late?* San Francisco: Jossey-Bass.

Sarason, S. B. (1998). *Political leadership and educational failure.* San Francisco: Jossey-Bass.

Sarason, S. B. (1996). *Revisiting "The culture of the school and the problem of change."* New York: Teachers College.

Scheeler, M., Ruhl, K., & McAfee, J. (2004). Providing performance feedback to teachers: a review. *Teacher Education and Special Education, 2*(7), 396–407.

Scheerens, J., & Creemers, B. (1989). Conceptualizing school effectiveness. *International Journal of Educational Research, 13*(7), 691–706.

Schermerhorn, J., Hunt, J., & Osborn, R. (2004). *Core concepts of organizational behavior.* Hoboken, NJ: Wiley.

Schermerhorn, J., Hunt, J., & Osborn, R. (2004). *Core concepts of organizational behavior.* Hoboken, NJ: Wiley.

Schmoker, M. (2004). Tipping point: From feckless reform to substantive instructional improvement. *Phi Delta Kappan, 85*(6), 424–423.

Schott, R. (2006). *Agents of change: A study of nonprofit advocacy organizations.* Austin, TX: Lyndon B. Johnson School of Public Affairs.

Scruggs, T. E., & Mastropieri, M. A. (1996). Teacher perceptions of mainstreaming/inclusion 1958–1995: A research synthesis. *Exceptional Children, 63*(1), 59–74.

Seel, R. (2000). Culture and complexity: New insights into organisational change. *Organisations & People, 7*(2), 2–9.

Shapley, K., Sheehan, D., Sturges, K., Caranikas-Walker, F., Huntsberger, B., & Maloney, C. (2009). *Evaluation of the Texas Technology Immersion pilot: Final Outcomes for a four-year study (2004–05 to 2007–08).* Austin, TX: Texas Center for Educational Research.

Sharp, W., & Walter, J. (2004). *The school superintendent: The profession and the person.* Lanham, MD: Scarecrow.

Shaw, D. (1998). Report to the President on the use of technology to strengthen K–12 education in the United States: Findings related to research and evaluation. *Journal of Science Education and Technology, 7*(2), 115–126.

Sheehan, P. J. (1995). *Australia and the knowledge economy: An assessment of enhanced economic growth through science and technology.* Melbourne, AUS: Victoria University of Technology, Centre for Strategic Economic Studies.

Sheridan, V., Stephens, D., Cimini, M., Watson, R., & Talbot, C. (Eds.). (2007). *National trade and professional associations of the United States* (42nd ed.). Washington, DC: Columbia.

Shuldman, M. (2004). Superintendent conceptions of institutional conditions that impact teacher technology integration. *Journal of Research on Technology in Education, 36*(4), 319–343.

Shulman, L. (1986). Those who understand: Knowledge growth in teaching. *Educational Researcher, 15*(2), 4–14.

Shurville, S., Browne, T., & Whitaker, M. (2008, November 30 – December 3). *Employing the new educational technologists: A call for evidenced change.* Paper presented at the Australasian Society for Computers in Learning in Tertiary Education Conference Melbourne.

Silvernail, D. (2007). The impact of the Maine Learning Technology Initiative on teachers, students, and learning. Retrieved from http://usm.maine.edu/cepare/mlti.htm

Slavin, R. (1991). Synthesis of research of cooperative learning. *Educational Leadership, 48,* 71–82.

Slywotzky, A., Morrison, D., & Andelman, B. (1997). *The profit zone: How strategic business design will lead you to tomorrow's profits.* New York: Times Business.

Smith, A. (1976). *The Inquiry into the nature and causes of the wealth of nations.* Oxford: Clarendon.

Smith, R., Clark, T., & Blomeyer, R. (2005). A synthesis of new research on K–12 on-line learning [Electronic Version]. Retrieved from www.ncrel.org/tech/synthesis/synthesis.pdf

Snider, J. (2006). The superintedent as scapegoat. *Education Week, 25*(18), 31.

Spalding, E., Garcia, J., & Braun, J. (2010). *An introduction to standards-based reflective practice for middle and high school teaching.* New York: Teachers College.

Spillane, J. P. (2006). *Distributed leadership.* San Francisco: Jossey-Bass.

Squire, P., & Moncrief, G. (2009). *State legislatures today: politics under the domes.* Boston: Longman.

State Educational Technology Directors Association. (2010a). About us. Retrieved from http://www.setda.org/web/guest/aboutus

State Educational Technology Directors Association. (2010b). By-laws. Retrieved from http://www.setda.org/web/guest/bylaws

Stradling, R., Newton, S., Bates, D., & Hearder, H. (1997). *Conflict and coexistence: nationalism and democracy in modern Europe: essays in honour of Harry Hearder.* Cardiff: University of Wales.

Sweller, J. (1988). Cognitive load during problem solving: Effects on learning. *Cognitive Science, 12,* 257–285.

Tait, K., & Purdie, N. (2000). Attitudes toward disability: Teacher education for inclusive environments in an Australian university. *International Journal of Disability, Development and Education, 47*(1), 25–38.

Talbot, R. (1990). *Meeting management: Practical advice for both new and experienced managers based on an expert's twenty years in the "wonderful wacky world" of meeting planning.* McLean, VA: EPM Publications.

Tapscott, D. (1998). *Growing up digital: The rise of the net generation.* New York: McGraw-Hill.

Thornburg, D. (1995). Welcome to the communication age. *Internet Research, 5*(1), 64–70.

Till, B., & Heckler, D. (2009). *The truth about creating brands people love.* Upper Saddle River, NJ: FT.

Toch, T. (1991). *In the name of excellence: The struggle to reform the nation's schools, why it's failing, and what should be done.* New York: Oxford University.

Toch, T. (2010). In an era of online learning, does school still matter. *Phi Delta Kappan, 91*(7), 72–73.

Tolliday, S. (Ed.). (1998). *The rise and fall of mass production.* Northampton, MA: Elgar.

Tomlinson, C. (2001). *How to differentiate instruction in mixed-ability classrooms.* Alexandria, VA: Association for Supervision and Curriculum Development.

Tuomi, I. (2002). *Networks of innovation: Change and meaning in the age of the Internet.* New York: Oxford University.

Turner, F. (2006). *From counterculture to cyberculture: Stewart Brand, the Whole Earth Network, and the rise of digital utopianism.* Chicago: University of Chicago.

Tyack, D. (2003). *Seeking common ground: public schools in a diverse society.* Cambridge, MA: Harvard University.

Tyack, D., & Cuban, L. (1995). *Tinkering toward utopia: A century of public school reform.* Cambridge, MA: Harvard University.

UNESCO. (2007). *Education for all by 2015: Will we make it?* New York: Oxford.

UNESCO. (2008). *Global education digest: Comparing education statistics across the world.* Montreal: United Nations Educational Scientific and Cultural Organization.

United States Congress. House Committee on the Judiciary. Subcommittee on the Constitution. (1998). *The First Amendment and restrictions on issue advocacy: hearing before the Subcommittee on the Constitution of the Committee on the Judiciary, House of Representatives, One Hundred Fifth Congress, first session, September 18, 1997.* Washington: Government Printing Office.

United States Department of Education. (2002). *No child left behind: A desktop reference.* Washington, DC: U.S. Department of Education.

United States Department of Education. (2010a). Enhancing education through technology state program. Retrieved from http://www2.ed.gov/programs/edtech/index.html

United States Department of Education. (2010b). NCLB: Adequate yearly progress. Retrieved from http://www2.ed.gov/nclb/accountability/ayp/edpicks.jhtml

United States Department of Education. (2010c). Race to the Top Fund. Retrieved from http://www2.ed.gov/programs/racetothetop/index.html

Urban Indicator. (2008/2009). Urban school superintendents: Characteristics, tenure and salary: Sixth survey report [Electronic Version]. Retrieved from http://www.cgcs.org/research/research_pub.aspx

Van Dyke, N., & McCammon, H. (2010). *Strategic alliances: Coalition building and social movements*. Minneapolis: University of Minnesota.

Varma, K., Husic, F., & Linn, M. C. (2008). Targeted support for using technology-enhanced science inquiry modules. *Journal of Science Education and Technology, 17*(4), 341–356.

VeneKlasen, L., & Miller, V. (2007). *A new weave of power, people, and politics: The action guide for advocacy and citizen participation*. Herndon, VA: Stylus.

Vernez, G., Krop, R., & Rydell, C. (1999). *Closing the education gap: benefits and costs*. Santa Monica, CA: RAND.

Wainer, J., Dwyer, T., Dutra, R., Covic, A., Magalhaes, V., Ferreira, L., et al. (2008). Too much computer and Internet use is bad for your grades, especially if you are young and poor: Results from the 2001 Brazilian SAEB. *Computers & Education, 51*(4), 1417–1429.

Wakker, P. (2010). *Prospect theory for risk and ambiguity*. New York: Cambridge University.

Waldrop, M. (1992). *Complexity: The emerging science at the edge of order and chaos*. New York: Simon & Schuster.

Warrington, M., & Younger, M. (1999). Perspectives on the gender gap in English secondary schools. *Research Papers in Education, 14*(1), 51–57.

Waters, J. (2009). Maine ingredients. *T H E Journal (Technological Horizons in Education), 36*(8), 35–39.

Waters, J., & Marzano, R. (2007). School district leadership that works: The effect of superintendent leadership on student achievement. *ERS Spectrum, 25*(2), 1–12.

Wedel, M., & Kamakura, W. (1998). *Market segmentation: conceptual and methodological foundations*. Boston: Kluwer.

Wedel, M., & Pieters, R. (2008). *Visual marketing: From attention to action*. New York: Lawrence Erlbaum.

Weick, K. (1976). Educational organizations as loosely coupled systems. *Administrative Science Quarterly, 21*, 1–19.

Wenglinsky, H. (1998). *Does it compute? The relationship between educational technology and student achievement in mathematics*. Princeton, NJ: Educational Testing Service.

Weston, M. E. (1987). *Directory of legislative studies in education policy*. Denver, CO: National Conference of State Legislatures.

Weston, M. E., & Bain, A. (2009). Engaging with change: A model for adopting and evaluating school-based change. *Journal of Educational Administration, 47*(2), 156–175.

Weston, M. E., & Bain, A. (2010). The end of techno-critique: The naked truth about 1:1 laptop initiatives and educational change. *Journal of Technology, Learning, and Assessment, 9*(6), 5–26.

Weston, M. E., & Brooks, D. (2008). Critical constructs as indicators of a shifting paradigm in education: A case study of four technology-rich schools. *Journal of Ethnographic and Qualitative Research in Education, 2*(4), 281–291.

Weston, M. E., & Walker, K. (1987). Emerging issues: A survey of education committee chairs. *State Legislative Report, 13*(3), 1–19.

Whitaker, S. (2007). *Advocacy for School Leaders: Becoming a Strong Voice for Education*. Lanham, MD: Rowman & Littlefield.

Williams, G. (2000). Blue Hill man inspired King's laptop proposal. *The Ellsworth American*. Retrieved from http://www.papert.org/articles/laptops/blue_hill_man.html

Willingham, D. (2009). *Why students don't like school*. Thousand Oaks, CA: Jossey-Bass.

Wilson, L., & Peterson, E. (2006). *Measuring the value of one-to-one computing: A case study perspective*. Alexandria, VA: Consortium for School Networking.

Winslow, C., & Bramer, W. (1994). *FutureWork: Putting knowledge to work in the knowledge economy*. New York: Free Press.

Wong, K. (1999). *Funding public schools: Politics and policies*. Lawrence: University of Kansas.

Young, B., & Hoffman, L. (2002). *Public high school dropouts and completers from the Common Core of Data: School years 1991–92 through 1997–98*. Washington, DC: U.S. Department of Education.

Zerbe, R., & Bellas, A. (2006). *A primer for benefit-cost analysis*. Northampton, MA: Elgar.

Zucker, A. (2009). The role of nonprofits in educational technology innovation. *Journal of Science Education and Technology, 18*(1), 37–47.

Zucker, A., & Hug, S. (2007). *A study of the 1:1 laptop program at the Denver School of Science & Technology*. Denver, CO: DSST.

Index

About the Authors

Alan Bain is an associate professor in the School of Teacher Education at Charles Sturt University and the author of *The Self-organizing School: Next Generation School Reforms* (2007).

Mark E. Weston is a global education strategist at Dell Inc. and an adjoint assistant professor in the Graduate School of Education and Human Development at the University of Colorado Denver.